4-14-02

To Klazina

Best Wishes

There Will Your Heart Be Also

THERE WILL YOUR HEART BE ALSO

Edgar Cayce's Readings About Home and Marriage

by WILLIAM McGAREY, M.D.
and GLADYS McGAREY, M.D.

Introduction by Hugh Lynn Cayce

PRENTICE-HALL, INC., ENGLEWOOD CLIFFS, N.J.

There Will Your Heart Be Also by William McGarey, M.D., and Gladys McGarey, M.D.
Copyright © 1975 by William McGarey, M.D., and Gladys McGarey, M.D.

Edgar Cayce readings copyright 1971 by the Edgar Cayce Foundation.
Reprinted by permission.

Printed in the United States of America
Prentice-Hall International, Inc., London
Prentice-Hall of Australia, Pty. Ltd., Sydney
Prentice-Hall of Canada, Ltd., Toronto
Prentice-Hall of India Private Ltd., New Delhi
Prentice-Hall of Japan, Inc., Tokyo

10 9 8 7 6 5 4 3 2 1

Library of Congress Cataloging in Publication Data
McGarey, William A.
There will your heart be also.
Includes bibliographical references and index.
1. Marriage. 2. Sex. 3. Family
4. Cayce, Edgar, 1877-1945. I. McGarey, Gladys,
joint author. II. Title
HQ734.M18486   1975   301.42   74-22412
ISBN 0-13-914788-8

Dedicated
to all those
who would find
their home to be
where their heart is also

CONTENTS

For, the home represents—
or is a shadow of—
that eternal dwelling place
with the Creative Forces
(2271-1)

INTRODUCTION

Edgar Cayce became best known as a medical clairvoyant. The accuracy and helpfulness of data which came through his "psychic readings"* continue to be established as hundreds of physicians check and test the suggestions for both cause and treatment of disease. It does not follow that information on other subjects is necessarily correct. However, there is a certain constraint placed on open-minded persons to at least examine other areas covered by the material. The authors of this book, Gladys and William McGarey, both medical doctors, are doing more than anyone else to bring the physical data to the attention of the medical profession and laymen.

Their large general practice as physicians as well as their personal experiences have led them into another exciting and, I believe, very important area of the Edgar Cayce psychic data. This is the material on marriage and the home.

There are 36 books dealing with Edgar Cayce's forty-three years of involvement with the psychic readings which he gave. I have read the manuscripts of all of these books before they were published. Two of them I have written myself and I have worked very hard with the authors on others. Some of the books are on special areas like diet, dreams, or the life story; all seem to have an appeal for certain audiences.

As I finished reading this manuscript, I asked myself, "Why has it affected me so? Why do I feel so strongly that this book should be published and read by every single person who has found any type of information in the Edgar Cayce readings

---

*These were stenographically-recorded discourses given in a sleep-trance state over a forty-three year period, 1901 to 1944.

helpful?" It is the answer to this question which I would like to share in this introduction.

Years ago when Gladys and Bill McGarey first became interested in the Association's work of preserving, studying, testing, and experimenting with the data from the Edgar Cayce psychic readings, their first concerns were with the philosophy. They were later to use and get others to try medical data from a psychic.

Today, the market is flooded with books by doctors on home and marriage. Many deal with explanations of the human body's functions in relationship to birth, sex, marriage, pregnancy, childbearing, and child rearing. What more could possibly be said about these subjects? What could be said that would appeal to a modern generation? Many of the ideas in the Edgar Cayce readings might, on first glance, represent straightlaced policies from almost Victorian points of view. What else could possibly be new, helpful, and exciting about home and marriage?

At first I thought that it might be the nostalgia of recalling hours of conversation my wife Sally and I have had with Gladys and Bill McGarey, as we have talked about their home and their children and our home and our children. Some of these conversations have occurred in interesting faraway places, like the deck of a steamer going up the Nile in Egypt or at a homecoming dinner in a village in India where Gladys was born.

Or, I thought to myself, is it that I have watched the excitement which has been expressed by individuals, young and old, as Gladys and Bill talked on home and marriage?

But these memories do not completely answer and explain the joy and excitement which I felt as I finished each chapter of this book. I began thinking of people—young people, parents of growing children, and adults—to whom I wanted to give this book. First, I thought about my own sons and the importance of putting this material in their hands. How would they react? Would they pick up what I sense in this manuscript?

Secondly, there is the matter of the wonderful combination of Edgar Cayce readings and personal experiences. Most of the people who quote readings (and this applies to me on occasion) use the readings to support ideas. The readings here are quoted (there is a wealth of extracts) in the context in which the authors have tried to put them to use in their own lives or have helped others incorporate the concepts in their experience. The result is a beautiful blending of personal experience and concepts from the Edgar Cayce readings.

There is a breadth in the coverage of the whole area of home and marriage. The book opens up with something on sexual energy, then moves to one of the major concepts in the Edgar Cayce readings, "the oneness of all force," and then goes immediately into the law of karma—cause and effect from one life to another. Whether or not the reader wants to accept the possibility of rebirth, it is taken for granted that at least some consideration will be given to the idea. The third chapter deals with a basic question of pre-marital sex which, for the younger generation, is a natural concern. There is no attempt here to compromise either the point of view of the authors or what they conceive as the point of view of the readings. Chapter headings include: "Choosing a Partner"; "The Marriage Vows"; "Establishing a Home"; and a beautiful short chapter, "The Lighted Way", presenting the importance of setting ideals and purposes. Birth control, abortion, preparing for parenthood, pregnancy, and creating a home are discussed in additional chapters. The ideal home is the concluding section. There is a casual rambling style, a gathering together of stories and experiences intermingled with the quotes from the readings, that draw not only on the readings themselves, but on the tremendous range of counseling that has been the experience of both doctors.

Perhaps I found the book intriguing too, because it contains some of the very best humorous stories from the experiences of both of these friends. Some of them are my favorite stories about karma and some are excellent doctors' stories, at which we have laughed together many times.

There is also another breadth of view, in that they not only draw on a broad medical and counseling practice, but also speak through their children, who address all ages. They have six children and you get to know a great deal about each one of them as you read the book. Also, Gladys and Bill are obviously on good terms with the Bible; there are numerous illustrations and quotes from this source. This material is in sharp contrast to the obvious technical knowledge of the human body and its functions as well as information on modern medical practices involving, for example, childbirth or contraceptive devices. There is a wholesome, broad-minded attitude towards a range of ideas and concepts that, for me, shines through chapter after chapter and page after page of this manuscript.

The McGareys have faced up to many of the questions which are raised by young people thinking about marriage and the question of having children and establishing a home, and by adults who have grown weary in living and working with each other. These are not just physicians with a large family practice. They are not just doctors who are good counselors; not just individuals who have presented lectures, workshops, and classes on home and marriage over a period of years, based on Edgar Cayce's readings. They are human beings who love each other, their children, and their patients. As I have often said to people when recommending them, they give you both pills and prayer, with emphasis on prayer. For me, that spells a capacity for love that I admire and which I think shines through this book.

—Hugh Lynn Cayce

PROLOGUE: ON CREATING A HOME

> But making an artistic home, making a home that is the expression of beauty in *all* its phases, is the greater career of *any* individual soul. This is the closer expression of that which has been manifested in the experiences of man's advent into materiality.
>
> (2571-1)

At least symbolically, the story of the Garden of Eden pre-dates all other accounts of man and woman and their attempt to live together. Adam and Eve didn't have too much trouble in the beginning—perhaps because Adam had been created first, and Eve knew it. But then trouble arose in the Garden. Eve found an apple in a tree. She knew that she was not allowed to eat the apple, but her tempter friend—the serpent, the symbol of worldly wisdom since the beginning of the earth—suggested to her that this would not really be a bad deal and that it might actually be beneficial. So Eve ate the apple.

Perhaps the situation would not have been so bad if it had ended right there. But Eve had to have an accomplice in her activities—which may have been the origin of the observation that "misery loves company." She offered the apple to Adam, figuring that at least she would not be alone. And Adam, poor fellow, took the apple.

That's when things really began to happen—and they have been happening ever since. And when one looks at what is going on today, he is certain that Eve should not have taken that apple in the first place—nor should Adam have accepted it, even

1

to take one bite. But she did, and he did. The apple, of course, represents sex. The garden is the home, and the bond uniting Adam and Eve is what we call marriage.

In January 1946, I graduated from Women's Medical College in Philadelphia and received my M.D. degree. World War II was just over. Bill and I had been married two years before, and he was to graduate from medical school in Cincinnati the following year. The nation was looking forward to a peace won with much suffering and loss. Life was full of promise and hope, and Bill and I did not give much thought to the home as a world-wide institution. Like most people, we were involved in the emotional turmoil of trying to get each other to "see things my way."

As I looked at it then, I felt I had a real mission in life: to serve first as a physician, next as a wife, and—possibly—as a mother. If I had been forced to choose between my two careers at that time, I would have chosen to be a physician. Since I was two years old I had said that I was going to be a doctor, and now this dream had come true. I don't think I could have given up the practice of medicine for a career in the home, but in the years that followed, my husband understood me and never put me to that test of deciding between the two.

After we had finished our internship and established a practice in Wellsville, Ohio, Bill was recalled to two years in the Air Force as a flight surgeon. It was after that, during the mid-Fifties, that Bill and I and our four children moved to Phoenix, where once again we established a practice and where we saw the birth of our last two children. We moved into an old adobe "mud hut"—as our nine-year-old Annie called it—and our home became a real and permanent thing, growing with our practice of medicine.

When we moved to Phoenix, we became interested in clair-voyants, metaphysics, parapsychology—the whole field of the unusual nature of man. And it was during those days of investigation that we came across the story of Edgar Cayce. Fascinated at once, we became rather quickly involved in the activities of the Association for Research and Enlightenment (A.R.E.) at Virginia Beach, Virginia.

Here was a man who could do things that I had not even thought about before. Even though he had been dead for ten years when we discovered him, his impact upon our lives was not diminished. Until his death in 1945, Edgar Cayce had lived a life of highly unusual service. A specific movement of inward energy allowed this man to enter repeatedly an altered state of consciousness. From this state, he gave discourses on a variety of subjects—even on the very energy which allowed him to do it. Cayce continued his work for more than forty years, and in the process produced more than 14,250 psychic readings, as they came to be called.

On the average of once every single day he went through a simple ritual and then probed the reaches of man's consciousness that most of us tap only in a dream or in a flash of intuition. As those about him waited, Cayce simply loosened his tie a bit, unbuttoned his shirt at the top, took off his shoes, lay down on a couch or bed, and closed his eyes. Then he placed his hands over his forehead. When he moved his hands down and crossed them over his solar plexus, he had already experienced "the light," and his conscious mind had moved aside. He was now ready to give a reading. If not spoken to at this point, he would lapse into a deep sleep and could not be roused for a while.

Given the proper suggestion, however, Cayce would begin a discourse on health or sickness, psychology or religion, philosophy or the stock market, dreams or the upbringing of a child—depending upon what was desired for the individual for whom the reading was being given. And the person did not need to be present—he could be five thousand miles away, just so long as he was where he was supposed to be when the reading was being given.

As we studied the fascinating information that came out of this sleeping man, a whole new world of possibilities opened to us. If this material were true, then our minds, our beings, our

3

true realities extended beyond the limits of our apparent spatial frames, beyond the barriers of time, beyond what we call birth or death. In other words, man is much more limitless than we have been led to believe—except in the Bible, where we are told these same things, only to believe with faint faith.

In particular, these possibilities gave us a different insight into our practice of medicine. If one mind can reach out as Cayce's did, then anyone's mind is truly infinite in its capacity to learn and to develop. We came to believe that our patients' potential was much greater than we had been taught in medical school. We began looking at them as if they had the ability to know what was going on inside their own bodies. Indeed, if Cayce's information and activities were factual, our total understanding of things also had to undergo a complete revision.

These ideas made lasting impressions on our lives as a family, as each of us in turn considered his role as father, mother, husband, wife, son, daughter, brother, or sister.

One of Cayce's statements about the home and its importance has stayed with us through the years:

> For in the home is the music of what? As indicated, it is an emblem of the heavenly home. And as these [experiences] are made into the harmonious experiences that may come in the associations, they may bring indeed the music of the spheres in the activities as one with another, and those that must be contacted in the highest of man's achievements in the earth—the *home*!
>
> (480-20)

Now, after more than a quarter of a century of practicing medicine (and even more years as a wife), I know that I would choose the home over my career as a physician. I say this after spending untold hours in the office counseling confused and undecided women about what their role should be—as a career-woman or in the home. I feel now that the career of wife and mother is the most important in the world, and perhaps in this book we may bring this awareness more into focus.

Bill and I try to see the problems that face us and our

4

patients as lessons in living a spiritually-oriented life; lessons that are "learned" if we deal with them in the right manner. The rightness, we assume, is the message that has been handed down to us throughout history by prophets who all seem to tell essentially the same story—that man draws closer to God and his own destiny not by strength, but by living simply, and by being kind and patient and understanding to his brother—who happens to be any other human being on the face of the earth. It is natural for a man and a woman to be drawn together by some unnamed and mysterious magnetic attraction. And it is most natural for the two to want to live together and have children, again for reasons we cannot quite pin down. In the eyes of man, marriage has become the ceremony which signifies God's acceptance of this joint desire to establish something of creative potential—and it is usually indicated that God actually joined these two people together in a mystical union.

As Bill and I began to watch destiny and its activity in our lives, Mr. Cayce's ideas made living together a high adventure and a lot of fun. When we began to make our home more of what we realized it should be, it seemed like second nature for us to adopt, for instance, a concept such as the following:

> In the establishing of the home, make it as that which may be the pattern of a heavenly home. Not as that set aside for only a place to sleep or to rest, but where not only self but all who enter there may feel, may experience, by the very vibrations that are set up by each in the sacredness of the home, a helpfulness, a *hopefulness* in the air *about* the home. . . . Make thine home, thine abode, where an angel would *desire* to visit, where an angel would seek to be a guest.
>
> (480-20)

Every home should manifest each couple's own individualized joint experience of God in the earth. It becomes a place of living and experiencing, where two people learn first to live with each other, and then in turn show those children whom they invite into their home how to live too. The home can become a warm, living experience in the lives of everyone who visits there.

Ever since the tribulation in Eden, man and woman have attempted to live together harmoniously in the home, utilizing marriage as the ideal state in which such harmony might be achieved. But opposites attract each other everywhere, and the home is no exception.

More frequently than not, two people who live together as man and wife create a home torn with argument, strife, and discord. This is hardly in accord with what we understand as a creative experience. But Cayce had much to say about this also:

> If ye have builded such that hate, envy, malice, jealousy are the fruits of the same, these can only bring dissension and strife and hardships. But if the seeds of truth and life are sown, then the fruition—as life goes on together—will be in harmony. And He, the Father, being thy guide in all, will bless thee, even as He has promised from the beginning. For in the fruit of thy bodies may many be blessed, if ye will but seek that *through* the union of thy purposes, of thy desires, with their import in things spiritual, such may come to pass.
>
> (480-20)

Most homes are part harmony, part strife and dissension. Because they never end up being completely one or the other, problems become part of the process of finding one's ideal home. That's part of the game.

Cayce's readings have consistently stressed the importance of seeing marriage and the home as institutions created in accord with God's plan for mankind. They see the home as a unique opportunity where individuals seeking life's meaning can grow spiritually toward an understanding of their life purpose and destiny. To one person (#2072), Cayce said, "For, as in the relationships ye have born in the earth as husband and wife, that which is the ideal as set by the Maker Himself is in those means in which there would be two manifesting as one in their hopes, in their fears, in their desires, in their aspirations." To another who was thinking about creating a home, Cayce had

6

this to say: "For the home is the foundation of the ideals and purposes of the nation. And these should be; these are sacred in the experiences of those who would serve Him wholly and surely" (3241-1).

It was out of the multitude of events that followed our research into the concepts of life found in the Cayce material that the material for this book emerged. My understanding of my place in the family as wife and mother has been completely overhauled in the process. I find myself a wife first, a mother second, and a physician last (but not least)—and such a scheme fits my ideas, my ideals, and my inner feelings.

As my husband and I have discovered, step by step, the delicious mysteries and wonders of marriage in our own lives, we have not only found it compatible with the practice of medicine, but we have seen Cayce's readings as valuable and meaningful in all of life's situations. They have helped us find the *joie de vivre* that everyone needs, the silver lining in every dark cloud, the joke that pulls one out of despondency, and the pun at the dinner table that teaches children that life is not really that serious.

Two people rarely write a book, although many books are coauthored. In this book, the mother becomes the first person singular while the father becomes "he" or "him" as the story moves along. Both of us have contributed to the writing; both of us have taken liberally from lectures and classes we have given on the subject of the home and its meaning. Perhaps "I" have done more of the inspirational work while "he" did more of the putting together of ideas and the shaping of the manuscript. But all of the ideas, stories, and concepts express what we think a home and marriage should be.

In this book, then, we will look at such widely divergent topics as pre-marital chastity and pregnancy; birth control and interesting children; homosexuality and the ideal home; and we will explore the many facets of home and marriage in the manner that we have found helpful and creative.

We bring to this book over a quarter of a century of living together, with the joys of a home filled with fun and laughter.

We bring tears to such a book because without sorrows no honest marriage can exist—nor can it deepen into richness and worth. We write such a book in full knowledge that its real validity can be substantiated only by what happens during the next twenty-five (or fifty) years of our marriage and by the lives our children forge from the tools of their upbringing.

So join with us, as Gladys brings you the story of home and marriage as we see it.

Gladys T. McGarey, M.D.
William A. McGarey, M.D.

1

SEXUAL ENERGY AND CHOICE

I have set before you life and death,
blessing and cursing: Therefore
choose life, that both thou and thy
seed may live.

(Deuteronomy 30:19)

The major factor that separates male from female might
be encapsulated in one word: sex. And it is that force, that
factor, which for some has spelled happiness, creative genius,
fulfillment, and joy; and for others it has meant misery, sorrow,
and sometimes total destruction.

Every person in this world finds himself in some sort of
relationship with sex. In early years, he might simply be a pro-
duct of a sexual union, finding the world opening up to him. Or
he may be coming into the age of puberty and the teens, when
the boy-girl relationship becomes real in all its aspects. He may
be married, divorced, or widowed. He may remain unmarried by
choice or circumstance. Is there really a common ground of
understanding that makes all these possible relationships a single
related field? Among the multitude of questions that arise
about sex, is there a basic understanding that can lead one into
a successful life?

It seems so simple, as Edgar Cayce explained it in his readings.
As we go from one incarnation into another, we are born into a
family situation that meets our inner needs and an environment
that will draw out qualities that need development. And we are

9

constantly given the opportunity to face ourselves or to run in the other direction.

Choice, then, seems to be a vital point in Cayce's whole philosophy of living. Perhaps we realize gradually that we are where we are because we *chose* to be there—and we can correct our course if we choose to do so. That sounds all too simple, but it is logical if we take Cayce's information to be valid, or if we look to the Bible for an answer.

The Bible states simply that we reap what we have sown—that our decisions and thoughts bear fruit, so to speak, and that we find the results in our experiences and our position in life. In Moses' concluding charge to the children of Israel before they entered the land of their promise, he said, "Today . . . I offer you the choice of life or death, blessing or curse. Choose. . . ." (Deuteronomy 30:19). This was part of the covenant made at that time, implying that we always have the right—and the necessity—to choose in which directions we will turn, what thoughts we will create, what actions we will originate.

It becomes more complex than that, of course, but the principle is the same. Most of us choose whether we wish to get married, and whether, in fact, we *do* get married. We choose whether to have pre-marital sexual experiences, indulge in adultery, or remain a virgin. If Cayce and a host of other sources of information are correct, we even choose whether to be born male or female, whether to take the active role in life as a male or to be receptive, as a female, to inspiration and inner direction. Some get goofed up, of course, but confusion is a human predilection that occurs more often than we suspect. So we find those who are somewhere between the male and the female in disposition, as well as those who should be male but find themselves in female bodies, and vice versa.

But if Cayce is correct, these conditions are rarely if ever mistakes, but rather challenges to be met by the souls involved. For sex is not only the capacity to reproduce one's kind in this three-dimensional world we live in, it is also an energy that throughout the ages has been described as a creative spark

10

which, when magnified through a desire to serve, can uplift mankind in a multitude of ways.

Sexual capacity makes courtship enjoyable, love a reality, marriage a rational dual arrangement, the home a place of joy, and children a feasible possibility; without sex, none of these could be. When one considers sex a source of creativity as well as a means of reproduction and mutual heterosexual relationship, then all the world's genius hinges on this one quality. Without that energy in man's makeup, we would not have music, art, or even the ability to build music halls or art museums; we would not have homes to live in, families to live with, science as a means of material improvement, factories to work in, even money to fight over, or war machines to kill with.

It is perhaps this creative energy which saints and sages have described as the movement of the spirit within that motivates certain chosen individuals at critical times in the history of mankind. It is the movement of this energy within a person— often in meditation or high spiritual upliftment which has produced the experience of enlightenment that Bucke so aptly described in his book, *Cosmic Consciousness.*[1]

The apple that Adam accepted from his beloved has indeed had a monumental career throughout the ages. So the *energy* of sex becomes a meaningful concept as we explore some of the intricacies of living together as man and wife. The idea that a home can be a building stone for a nation; the concept that sexual intercourse can be a portion of a person's relationship to a Divine Creator; the possibility that the home can be a woman's greatest career—all these become challenges in understanding who we are and what we are doing here.

Out of choice, sexual energy, and the spiritual nature of man, we must fashion a basically sound and understandable foundation. This is essential if we are to start from where we are now and go ahead into the future with intelligence and a sense of adventure.

---

[1]Bucke, Richard Maurice. *Cosmic Consciousness.* New York: E. P. Dutton & Co., 1969.

Any foundation meaningful to one's spiritual nature must speak the language of the spirit, and the language that God has used to communicate with man has always been symbolic. Bill and I have discovered that symbolic events are perhaps more real than this three-dimensional world we live in. The stories from the Bible are highly symbolic, highly meaningful, and often set the pace and direction for the descendents of Abraham: Abraham's faith in God at the time he was told to sacrifice his son Isaac; Jacob's twelve sons; Moses' experience with the burning bush and later on with the column of fire by night and smoke by day which guided him and the children of Israel out of Egypt. All of these and a legion of other accounts suggest the importance of symbolic events.

It is the *function* of a symbol, rather than its shape or size, that tells a story. More symbology can be found in the Book of Revelation, for instance, than in any fairy tale. As Bill pointed out to me several years ago, symbols such as those in John's vision appear in our daily lives.

One Saturday afternoon Bill was trimming our palm trees, which by then had reached several feet in height, and he saw me coming out the front door. "Gladys," he asked, "how many palms do you think we planted?"

The study we had been making of the Revelation of John—and the understanding we had developed about the meaning of numbers in our lives—made me hesitate for just a second. Then I said, "Well, I have never bothered to count them, but the way you ask the question would make me think we had seven." There *were* seven, of course—four on the right-hand side of the driveway and three on the left. They looked almost like the seven candlesticks which John described in this last book of the Bible.

We had read Cayce's suggestion to the effect that any physician would understand the body's endocrine system and how the body functions much more clearly if he studied the symbolism of Revelation. So we worked at it—for nearly seven years!—and we marveled at the story the symbols seemed to be telling us. It is a story that brings us into direct contact with the creative energy of God and that, in a way, opens up a new

12

vision of what the glandular centers are, how we symbolize our desires and our thoughts in our bodies, and even how illnesses and abnormalities tell a story that the conscious mind is often unable to put into words.

Cayce suggested that the Book of Revelation is a discussion of the various stages of consciousness that one goes through in coming to an awareness of himself as a true spiritual individual created in the image of God.

The repeated sevens found throughout the Book of Revelation—the seven churches, the seven candlesticks, the seven angels, the seven seals—are symbolic of energy centers where man's spiritual being makes contact with the human flesh. These seven points of consciousness or awareness are recognized in the physical body as glandular centers; the adrenal, the pineal, the pituitary, the thyroid, the thymus, and the reproductive centers (the gonads which manufacture the sperm or the ovum, and the cells of Leydig which create the sex hormone); and the energy that brings about the expression of what we call life, which moves uniquely through these seven centers.

Like the palm trees in our front yard, the seven glandular areas of activity in the Revelation are divided into four lower centers—as symbolized by the four beasts in the vision described in the fourth chapter (also seen in Ezekiel's vision, Ezekiel 1:1—3:15)—and the three higher centers, seen in the symbology of the Christian Church of today as the trinity of the Godhead. These are the points of spiritual energy described in the religious literature of the Far East as *chakras,* and the lower five have been related to the five senses of the body in a particular manner.

The seven together have been symbolized as the pyramid of ancient lands, which has four sides on the earth and the three in the form of a triangle. The shepherd's crook is the same symbol. When man stands upright, a line drawn through these seven centers makes an upward line that curves over to form a crook as it passes through the thyroid, pineal, and pituitary glands.

Cayce points out that the book with the seven seals represents the body with the seven centers of spiritual energy, seven endocrine glands, pouring out minute amounts of hormones that control and alter the size, shape, activity, and health of the individual human being. The opening of the seals is a process of change and clarification which is necessary for every human being to undergo in order to realize his full potential. There is movement of energy through these centers, sometimes when we are aware of it and sometimes when we are not. The energy—according to mystical understanding from centuries back—arises in the gonad center (the lowest of the seven) and moves upward as one prays or meditates. This also happens when we relate to others according to spiritual laws that have been in existence since the creation of man.

The movement of this energy becomes creative in a person's life as it is lifted in an upward direction—part of the activity that produces what has been called enlightenment. The filling of the cup comes about (symbolically), and the energy spills over. At that point the energy is used. It becomes pure creativity. It cleanses; it heals; it produces changes in other people's lives and in the life of the one who has had the experience. At this point in time, genius quietly comes into being. All expressions of human creative ability come in this manner.

Cayce implied (in reading 2475-1) that there is a spiritual center in the body where the soul is expressive and creative in its nature. This is the so-called Leydig center—the activity brought about by the cells of Leydig. As the life-force is expanded, it moves in an upward trend from this center through the adrenals to the centers in control of the emotions and to the pineal gland.

The Leydig cells are the interstitial cells deep within the structure of the testes in the male. In the female they are known as hilar cells. In both male and female, these cells secrete hormones which bring about the secondary sexual characteristics—a stubbly beard in the male and rounded curves in the female. It has always been interesting to me that all sexual structures are present in both male and female, being predominant in one and vestigial in the other, depending on whether estrogen or testosterone is in a higher proportion in the body.

14

There are other factors of course, but to simplify, the hormone is the determining agent.

As a spiritual center, the Leydig is highly important for it becomes the center of choice at a very basic level. It apparently has to do with direction, with use of the basic energy which comes out of the gonads. Differentiation of direction then comes about when one seeks either an upward movement of creative energy, which results in expansion of consciousness, or the contrary direction (as Moses explained), which becomes gratification of one's desires. These desires encompass not only the simple gratification of the sexual urge, but also the desire for money, power, fame, food—any urge that becomes in its expression a means of self-gratification. Some symbolize this secondary, self-directed choice as a circular motion through the four lower centers of the body, best seen as the wheel of karma.

Certainly, choice is a matter of individual will, but because it also involves desire it is not always a simple thing. Desire is the power that motivated me to finish medical school, and it often actually controls my choices. Desire is not simply a longing or a craving for something or someone, but it is also an attribute of the human soul that helps direct his ways.

In the relationship between man and woman, desire is sometimes confused with love. But it should be understood, rather, as part of the whole business of making one's way through life—of choosing, of taking direction. Desire, Cayce maintains, can have different motivating forces, which are themselves well-known and as old as mankind.

> Let the *spirit* be the motivating force in thy desire, rather than the exaltation of the flesh in any individual experience. For God giveth the increase, whether in the flesh or in the mental forces, as thou hast purposed or desired from within. For thou *art* gods in the making. What wilt thou be to thy fellow man if the desire is for exaltation of self? For thus sin entered in the flesh.
>
> (262-67)

Within the context of these concepts found in the Revelation,

15

my understanding of sexual intercourse leads me to believe that choice upwards or downwards operates here also. One can use his sexual expression only to satisfy his wishes and his desires, which is simple self-oriented self-gratification and leads to magnification of the ego structure. This brings to one's experience the "curses" which Moses talked about. As experienced within the structure of laws which have been with us for centuries, however, sexual intercourse is a creative activity, and one must have consideration for his partner as his prime motive. Here the life energy moves upwards and expands. Cayce had something to say on this point:

> The purpose of life, then, is not the gratifying of appetites nor of any selfish desires, but it is that the entity, the soul, may make the earth, where the entity finds its consciousness, a better place in which to live. . . . You have a greater opportunity at the present time than you will have at any other period of this particular sojourn. So you'd better be up and doing, keeping self in accord with God's laws.
>
> (4047-2)

All of the glands, Cayce said, could be illuminated and turned toward a higher awareness, or they could remain tuned to nothing greater than self-satisfaction. Illumination, the goal sought by mystics, comes into being whenever the life force is lifted up. As the life force passes through the glands—in meditation—Cayce implies that it illuminates them.

As this energy moves upwards, there comes about in the physical body a degree of health and vitality which was not there before. Over the ages this undoubtedly has occasioned man to picture this energy (which moves much like a serpent) as a symbol of healing.

The serpent has been described as representing temptation (as in the Garden of Eden). It may also be called desire or the activity of life itself expressed in the material world apart from the Source of life. When that life is then lifted to the realization that it *is* spirit, it becomes healing to the body.

One of the fascinating stories of the Bible is found in Numbers

16

21:5-9, where some of the children of Israel have been bitten by snakes. Moses is told by the Lord to fashion a snake of bronze and lift it up on a standard—and those victims of the snakes who look upon it will be healed. That story is emphasized by the gospel of John where Jesus says (John 3:14, 15), "This Son of Man must be lifted up as the serpent was lifted up by Moses in the wilderness, so that everyone who has faith in him may in him possess eternal life." The snake here becomes an agent of danger and destruction and at the same time a symbol and bringer of healing.

Over the ages the symbol of the snake has occasioned different responses in the unconscious mind of man. In Egypt, for instance, he was seen as a hooded cobra, representing power and wisdom. When shown over the head of the Pharaoh, he portrayed the rising of creative energy to its highest point, thus endowing the Pharaoh with the right and the ability to rule over others. The oriental symbol of eternal life is the serpent with his tail in his mouth, perhaps symbolizing the wheel of karma in another sense. In Hatha Yoga, the snake uncoils and stretches up through the *chakras* of the body until it reaches the third eye of Shiva. At that point, according to the Hindu belief, man recovers his sense of the eternal. And medicine today uses as its symbol the staff with the serpent circling it—which replaced the older caduceus with the two intertwined serpents.

Carl Jung sees in the serpent a well-documented archetype, and in Freudian symbology the snake becomes a phallic symbol. The coiled serpent certainly symbolizes danger and also potential expression of energy. In the Revelation, the serpent is the dragon which appears with seven heads, ten horns, and ten crowns. The five pair of horns and crowns probably are placed on five of the seven heads of the serpent and could well symbolize the manner in which this energy, as used in the material world, brings one toward the worship of what one contacts through the medium of the five senses. Thus "sense consciousness" may be truly a comprehensive meaning for the serpent as we try to understand him today.

Cayce's information, on the other hand, goes directly into

17

the experiences of individuals. He related their experiences in lifetime after lifetime, pointing out how the choices of one life create the circumstances of the next; how the "good or evil" of Deuteronomy 30:15 brings blessings or curses. But we always determine—probably at a strictly unconscious level—conditions where we can fulfill the choices that we have set into motion.

It would seem then that we are all just where we ought to be, in just the right place to start fashioning a future course filled with a bit more of the blessing and somewhat less of the curse. Such a course would be filled with a continuing stream of possible decisions, and, symbolically, the choices would always be toward life or death. Such a view suggests that choice must always be exercised in the use of sexual energy too, for certainly the opportunity is always before us.

What our senses give us may—as the serpent—be leading us down the trail of Adam and Eve or may be a means of upliftment, of healing, as it is transformed in its movement through the body. The choice that we make is the key. As Cayce put it:

> Decide in self which you will choose, for there is here set before thee good and evil, life and death, choose thou and know ever within self: If ye are one in and with the Lord in His purpose, naught can be against thee.
>
> (5056-1)

OTHER RELEVANT READINGS

> The purpose in life, then, is not the gratifying of appetites nor of any selfish desire, but it is that the entity, the soul, may make the earth where the entity finds its consciousness a better place in which to live. You have a greater opportunity at the present time than you will have at any other period of this particular sojourn. So you'd better be up and doing, keeping self in accord with God's laws.
>
> (4047-2)

> . . . as should be from every individual, there should be agreement between those individuals in such [sex] relationships and only when there is such should there be the relationships. For the lack of such agreement brings more discordant notes between individuals than any portion of relationships

18

with the opposite sex. The disagreements may be very slight at times, but they grow. For these relationships are the channels for the activity of creative forces and not by mere chance.

The abilities then are for the entity to build that within self to make this experience in the earth harmonious, bringing peace, happiness, and joy, cultivating those things deep within self that are the fruits of the spirit.

Man may not live by bread alone. Man may not live the gratifying of appetites in the material world. For man is not made for this world alone. There is a longing for those experiences which the soul, as an entity, has experienced. And without spirituality the earth is indeed a hell, an individual soul do what it will or may. Such longing may not be gratified from without or in the consciousness of, and the experiences that pertain to, the forces and influences about self. For the body is indeed the temple of the living God. Act like it! Keep it clean. Don't desecrate it ever, but keep it such that it may be the place where you would meet thine own better self, thine own God-self. As ye do this, there may be brought harmony, peace, joy.

(4082-1)

... thy body is the Temple of the Living God. Use it as such, and not as a place for the lowest of earth and low thinking. Rather, treat it as the altar of God. Sacrifice therein thine own appetites and offering to Him those praises. ...

(3492-1)

Q. 15: Why is my husband so unmasculine and abnormal sexually?

A. 15: This is from physical conditions that exist in the physical make-up of the body.

Q. 17: Please explain our sex incompatibility.

A. 17: As those conditions that make for those relationships in this connection are accentuated in the various manners through those conditions existent in the physical body of each, these bring about those abhorrences and those changes that make for this portion of the life to become a thing that is to be feared, rather than as nature has made to be enjoyed or in the manner that finds the expression through the activities of the body in every force; for as is seen, this may be found to be that which would be well for all to consider:

As sex is that channel through which creation in the

19

material world brings forth that which is of creating itself, so are the organs of same—the centers through which all creative energies—whether mental or spiritual—find their inception in a material world for an expression. As has been given, when this force in sex is raised, or rated, in its inception through the mental forces of the body, this finds expression in that of giving the love influence in the life or lives of the individual, as well as that which may be brought into being as a gratification of a physical desire.

Hence this portion, this incompatibility that is between the two individuals as given here, is that which makes for the inability for any *creative* forces to become compatible between the individuals; for there is no soul but what the sex life becomes the greater influence in the life. Not as always in gratification in the physical act, but rather that that finds expression in the creative forces and creative abilities of the body itself.

(911-2)

First, we would begin then at the beginnings: man's advent into materiality or into a material world and becoming as individual bodies of the world, who became observing of this fact in the material world from that he (man and woman) saw in the earth. Hence it is given in thy writing of Scripture (although in a hidden manner, ye may observe if ye will look) how Adam named those who were brought before him in creation. Their *name* ndicates to the carnal mind their relationships in the sex condition or question. Hence the question ye seek is as old as, or older than, man.

This has been the problem throughout man's experience or man's sojourn in the earth; since taking bodily form, with the attributes of the animal in which he had *projected* himself as a portion of, that he might through the self gain that activity which was visualized to him in those relationships in the earth.

(5747-3)

In the body there is that center in which the soul is expressive, creative in its nature—the Leydig center. . . . As this life force is expanded, it moves first from the Leydig center through the adrenals, in what may be termed an upward trend, to the pineal and to the centers in control of the emotions . . . when the self-consciousness has been released and the real ego

20

allowed to rise to expression, is to be in that state of the universal consciousness—which is indicated in this body here, Edgar Cayce, through which there is given this interpretation.

(2475-1)

Desires are good, are desires controlled by the best *interests* for the body mentally and physically. Not merely those as satisfy the desires of the body physical . . . *preferring* another . . . before self . . . those of the home are *nearer* akin to the sincere innate desire in *every* individual.

(3795-1)

For will and desire are spiritual as well as carnal, as well as mental. These are attributes both of the spiritual influences and of the carnal forces in every entity's activity.

(315-3)

. . . *mind* is the builder. If the thought is directed in those lines that consider most the material things, then carnal must be the outlook. . . . The spirit *gives* understanding and freedom. *Carnal* thought (and self) brings contention and discord. The way is before thee.

(2126-1)

Is [the] desire of that that builds in the proper sense, in the proper order with spirit, soul or mind *and* body? For the spirit is life; the mind is the builder, the physical is the result. . . .

(349-4)

He will overcome it, if he will only set himself. Hard, to be sure—for builded as desire. Desire is of a threefold nature and must be controlled only by the mental and the spiritual held as an ideal. This may be overcome.

(5-2)

Let not thy longings too oft become desires that are contrary to thy ideals.

(2428-1)

Desire may be godly or ungodly, dependent upon the purpose, the aim, the emotions aroused.

Does it bring, then, self-abstinence? or does it bring self-desire?

Does it bring love? Does it bring longsuffering? Is it gentle? Is it kind?

(1947-3)

21

Where there has been the application in the past or in the present experience of those laws—and loves—that pertain to that which is constructive or in keeping with that set as the ideal in the spiritual expressions in material manifestations, there has been growth. Where there has been desire or the application of self in those things or conditions whereunto the developments were for the satisfying or gratifying of self's own interest alone, or for the aggrandizement of self, this has made rather for retardments—or meeting in the varied manners and experiences, as has been seen in the present. . . .

(524-2)

Q. 1: How can I maintain a physical and mental balance without so much physical exercise, and produce a normal balance in my sex urges?

A. 1: As has been indicated, the glandular system has been disturbed. Now: By the creating of a normal balance within the body for its physical and mental and spiritual well-being, we not only create a normal physical balance but then give—in the expressions of what has been indicated for the physical and mental body—an *outlet* for the beauty of sex.

Do not look upon sex as merely a *physical* expression! There is a physical expression that is beauty within itself, if it is considered from that angle; but when the mental and the spiritual are guiding, then the outlet for beauty becomes a *normal* expression of a *normal* healthy body.

Q. 2: When did this condition begin?

A. 2: About a year and a half ago, it began—when there were excesses as to leaving off of energies that found expression in the minds of others rather than in the expression of doing for others.

Q. 6: I am particularly disturbed at times with conditions of the female organs. Please explain.

A. 6: As has been indicated in the activity of the glandular system, these are a portion of the mental and physical and spiritual being. Those channels through which procreation in the activity of the material forces becomes active, the central organizations through which the vibrations may be consciously raised within the body *for* activities in the deeper meditations—these have *overcharged* by lack of applying the conditions or supplying the physical emergencies or physical conditions and the using of the energies by the activities of the body in deeper meditations, the breathings and other activities which have been a portion of the body-physical's resources.

Q. 8: Have I been wrong not to have sexual contact? Would it do me any good?

A. 8: The body has not been wrong! The body would *not* be physically benefited as such—until there are the activities within the physical, the mental, the spiritual self for the proper balance in activities in the Creative Forces, as well as the mental and material things for the better coordination in all.

Do the first things first, as has been indicated for the body; following same with the mental attitudes, putting self within the care, the keeping of the Infinite Love that is thine, that ye may show forth the love of the Father, the beauty of a life lived that the glory of the Son may be manifested in the lives of thy fellow men.

Not unto thyself but in Him is all might, all power, all glory.

(1436-1)

. . . *nothing* may separate the soul of man from its Maker but desire and lusts!

(1293-1)

. . . service to others is the greatest service to the Creator. . . .

(2725-1)

2

KARMA

Q. Have I known [ex-husband] in previous lives; was the marriage a karmic debt and is it now finished?

A. It is now finished. There was much to be worked out. It is complete in itself, but will be met again in another experience.

(2185-1)

Lunch is a great time for us, because we share food with so many interesting people during those hours. Some people come through Phoenix from Japan, some from Europe—and all have the most fascinating stories to tell us. One day an old friend from Cincinnati stopped in to say hello, and while we ate lunch he told us a story that needs to be repeated here.

You remember that little optometrist's office right near Vine and McMillan? Well, just about two weeks ago I stopped in to pick up a pair of glasses for my wife. I had never been in the office before, but had talked to Johnson on the phone several times.

He was talking to someone at the back of the office as I walked in and introduced myself. As we started to talk about the glasses, the other man came toward me, reached out to shake hands and said, "Joe, I'll bet you don't even remember."

Obviously he knew me, but I drew a complete blank. He turned to Johnson and said, "You didn't know this, but this guy saved my life about forty years ago, and I've never been able really to repay him." As he talked, my mind started clicking, and the years rolled back a long, long way. I did remember.

I was twelve years old, and one day stopped by Mark's house—I wanted him to go swimming with me in the Missouri River near where we lived. His mother claimed he could not swim well enough, but he sneaked off with me anyway.

I always went swimming just off the end of the bar that extended out from the shore near my home. There was a rock about twenty feet out from the shore where we would often swim and stand, submerged in the water up to our chest, while the waters of the river flowed past. It was great fun. It took a bit of courage for Mark to follow me out to the rock. The current was strong that day, but he managed to make it. I helped him get his balance on the rock, and after a bit I started in toward shore again. I could always swim pretty good.

Halfway in, I heard Mark cry out, and I looked back to see him going under downstream from the rock. He must have lost his balance. The water was over our heads at that point, and I knew he was in trouble. I swam out quickly and caught him under the arms just as he was going under the second time, and I pulled him to shore with not too much trouble. He claimed that I had saved his life, but you know, when you are kids, you never think anything about such an incident after it's over. Part of the game is taking chances, and you do it all the time. But we didn't tell his Mom—that's for sure!

Apparently, Mark never forgot the incident though—and here he was standing there, nearly

25

forty years later, and the memories of that time
rolling over me like a wave. I hadn't recognized
him until he pushed a button. It could have been
another incarnation—you know?

I couldn't help but think—wasn't Joe's experience like what
one would feel if he were quite sensitive and met someone with
whom he had had such an experience in a past life? Feelings,
memory patterns, and sensations that could not be pinned
down previously would come rushing back. A good friend of
ours told us that the first time he ever saw Bill and me was at a
meeting. When we walked into the room, he felt an electric
shock go through his body. It was only later that his dreams
revealed that he had actually known us in past lives. The con-
necting link in both instances was memory, which was clouded
by time.

As I see it, many factors influence us as we live in whatever
context life offers us. India is the land of my birth, but the
Indian concepts of living were not dominant in my life since I was
the daughter of Presbyterian missionaries trying to bring Christianity to the people of that nation. Thirty to fifty years ago,
the teachings of the Presbyterian church contained nothing, for
instance, about reincarnation, which most of India believes is
the natural course of events.

My environment as one of the Taylor "mish-kids" did much,
however, to orient my thinking in a way that made the concepts
in the Cayce readings tenable as I studied them later. I even
found the ideas of reincarnation reasonable within the Presbyterian church framework.

But my development in my parents' home preceded both the
church teachings and the ideas which I gathered from the Cayce
material. Dad was a strict disciplinarian. If I were to sneak out
of the house and stuff myself with the fruit of the tamarind tree
in my backyard when I had been told to stay inside, I knew
what would happen if I got caught—which I usually did, and I
wouldn't be able to sit down for the rest of the day. But this
did not keep me from loving my father, who I knew loved me

26

very much. And when times of punishment came about, Mother's humor always made things a little easier. She could always make us laugh, even when I thought my sister, Margaret, was getting off easier than I, or when my three brothers seemed to be taking advantage of us.

As we grew up, however, John, Carl, Gordon, Margaret, and I all felt most sensitively our parents' attitude of love and security. We lived in a Christ-centered home, and this constancy in attitude seemed to give us a knowledge of what to expect. I'm sure stability, constancy, and consistency are all part of love as we know it, and I think it is safe to say that I was surrounded by love as I grew up. I am certain this was the most important single factor to me in later years, as my life took form and direction.

It would be misleading if I were to indicate that we think the home environment, schools, universities, churches, books, news media, and people of all descriptions become the only influencing factors in shaping an individual's life. As we studied Gina Cerminara's book, *Many Mansions,*[2] about karma, the law of cause and effect, and the present emotional impacts that stem from past life experiences, we began to see reasons why I was born in India of missionary parents; why I was rebellious enough to sneak away and stuff myself with those delicious tamarinds; why it was easy for Bill and me to understand the concepts of reincarnation; and why we have been so interested in discovering ways to bring healing to mankind. These reasons all emerge, at least in part, from the character-building lessons and experiences of past lives that made us what we tend to be. Bill and I have since read material from Leslie Weatherhead[3], the renowned Episcopalian theologian; from Dr. Ian Stevenson's Twenty Cases Suggestive of Reincarnation[4]; and from the Bible,

---

[2]Cerminara, Gina. *Many Mansions.* New York: William Morrow & Co., 1968; paperback: New York: New American Library, Inc. 1967.

[3]Weatherhead, Leslie. *The Case for Reincarnation.* Surrey, England: MC Peto Publishing Company, 1966.

[4]Stevenson, Ian. *Twenty Cases Suggestive of Reincarnation.* New York: American Society of Psychical Research, 1967.

in which Jesus tells the story about Elijah reincarnating as John the Baptist (Matthew 17:10-13). Understanding the full continuity of life, extending from one lifetime to another with purpose as God has set it forth, added more depth to our lives and to our concept of what life was all about. The pieces of an otherwise impossible jigsaw puzzle begin to fit together suddenly, and life makes more sense. If two people have an unfulfilled marriage relationship in one lifetime, they may indeed be drawn together again in another lifetime to bring the relationship to fruition. Or perhaps a marriage that is creative and joyful and productive in all respects in one lifetime will naturally draw those same entities together again in another lifetime for a greater purpose.

Why would any young man and woman be strongly attracted to each other and end up fighting bitterly after only a few years? It isn't reasonable to think that this is just coincidence. But two individuals who fought and hated each other in one lifetime could certainly be drawn together by what we loosely call love—the attraction of one sex to another—for the purpose of uncovering those past animosities long enough—and thoroughly enough—to make peace with each other and with themselves.

Perhaps that same time factor is a kindly effect that helps us see ourselves in different contexts with some of the sharpness rubbed off. Because of the karmic force that brings us face to face with ourselves, we are probably better off having forgotten some of the causes which have brought the present effects into being.

Stories about reincarnation, however, do not have nearly the same impact as honest-to-goodness personal experiences which sometimes bring stark reality to a hypothetical question. Many years ago I was speaking to a church group when my attention was drawn time and again to a mother and her four-year-old daughter who were sitting near the center of the room. I couldn't keep my eyes off them. Later on that evening I was introduced to the mother, who was tall and slender, fair-skinned, with large, dark blue eyes. Her straight black hair was cut in bangs, and hung down to her shoulders. She had a regal bearing and looked for all the world like an Egyptian princess, and her daughter was the spitting image of her mother. I was fascinated.

Less than a year later the two of them appeared in our office as patients. The daughter had a problem, and her mother thought perhaps I would be able to help. Each night for perhaps a month this beautiful little "Egyptian princess" had been waking up screaming with the same nightmare. All her mother could get from her was that the poor little girl kept trying to escape from millions of flies and frogs. Shades of Moses! Could it be that these two beautiful individuals had been Egyptians when the Pharaoh "hardened his heart" and would not let the children of Israel go? That's when the plague of the flies and frogs—among many other things—afflicted the Egyptians. If reincarnation is a fact, *some* of those Egyptians must still be around, carrying in their deepest memories the experiences of that lifetime with its joys and its sorrows, its triumphs and its terrors.

The mother loved her child and wanted to help her, so she took rather easily to my recommendation that she talk gently to her daughter before she went to sleep. She was to tell the little girl that she was loved, that she was safe in her own home, and that the flies and the frogs need not bother her any more. Her mother did this for a week, and the child's nightmare never recurred.

I'll never forget one instance in our own family where Beth and David—who now, in their teens, are great friends—tangled in a tremendous argument when they were nine and six respectively. It seemed that Beth had picked on David since he was little. Bill and I pulled them apart. I took David to one side to quiet him down, and Bill took Beth into the next room. The eldest always gets the most lectures, of course, so Bill was telling Beth, "You shouldn't pick on David like that—you need to make peace with him. Remember, before you were born, you *chose* to come into this family.

Quick as a flash, Beth came back with, "Yes, but that was

before I knew David was coming!" It was a reasonable answer, anyway, in her eyes.

But karma doesn't always have bad connotations.

Annie, now married to a physician and mother of a beautiful little child, has always loved to cook. We always wondered why, of course, because not all girls take to this art as naturally as she has. We have understood she was an excellent cook in a past incarnation and loved it, so it was retained in her natural aptitudes as a specific ability. One of Cayce's readings refers to this type of situation:

> The ability to be a good cook arises from those activities, under whatever may be the environ, and you have recipes all your own. Keep them. And give them away if you would keep them. For, remember, you can never lose anything that really belongs to you, and you can't keep that which belongs to someone else. No matter if this is spiritual, mental or material, the law is the same.
>
> (3654-1)

Of course, the concept of reincarnation need not be wrestled with emotionally. It's either a law, or it isn't. If it is, it operates whether we believe it or not. If it isn't, we still have to choose, don't we? But Bill and I have seen evidences tending to substantiate it, and we have not yet seen any good evidence to the contrary. And so we approach the many opportunities of home and marriage believing that we are spiritual beings, created by God in the beginning, in His image. Taking on a material life time and again, we gradually work off the rebellion that has separated us from the closeness to God that is our true heritage.

In our home we have let all our children come to the understanding that such an equalizer is active in their lives as well. One day our twelve-year-old Johnny came running through the kitchen where Annie was baking some cookies. Her ponytail was quite in evidence, and he answered the natural temptation to give it a yank, and then beat a hasty retreat to the back door. Bill, sitting at the dining-room table reading the paper, had seen the whole thing out of the corner of his eye, and as Johnny came rushing past, Bill reached out and gave him a swat on the seat of the pants. Without missing a stride, Johnny said, "Quick karma!" and disappeared out the door. So the message gets across to the children bit by bit, in strange and exciting ways.

Karma may act over the span of many lifetimes, or it may be a quick acting reflex, but it is always there to teach and aid, to give the individual a better mirror with which to see himself. It always deals with the unregenerate self, in a true sense, bringing the searchlight to bear on the emotions and glandular activity of a person—never on the ability of the mind to correct things, because that is ever present.

Some have said that karma is simply memory. Others think it has to do with what other people have done for and against us, and that we must pay off a karmic debt with these individuals in whatever life we might find them. Cayce was asked about a karmic debt in many readings. This one gives a good example of the attitude prevalent in these readings on this subject:

Q. 6: Is there some karmic debt to be worked out with either or both and should I stay with them until I have made them feel more kindly toward me?

A. 6: These—What is karmic debt? This ye have made a bugaboo! This ye have overbalanced within thyself! What is thy life but the gift of thy Maker that ye may be wholly one with Him?

Thy relationships to thy fellows through the various experiences in the earth come to be then in the light of what Creative Forces would be in thy relationships to the act itself! And whether it be as individual activities to those who have individualized as thy father, thy mother, thy brother or the like, or others, it is merely self being met, in relationships to that they themselves are working out and not a karmic debt between but a *karmic* debt of self that may be worked out between the associations that exist in the present!

And this is true for every soul.

If ye will but take that as was given thee: "Neither do I condemn thee—neither do I condemn thee."

(1436-3)

So, in Cayce's viewpoint, one is never condemned to meet

31

himself, even in a so-called karmic debt. He is forgiven, as in "Neither do I condemn thee." Karma is simply a force which brings us toward the moment when we must correct what we have been creating in exchange for a more constructive attitude and subsequent action. But somehow we rebel a bit at the idea that we must pay for what we have created. We have a distinct abhorrence of seeing the cause of our present situation lying on our own doorstep. We'd rather point the finger at someone else. So most of the time we insist on meeting that karmic debt to ourselves through our associations with others. The problem is that we continue to think it is a karmic debt *with* someone else.

A woman whose father is an alcoholic may blame her childhood experiences for leading her to marry three alcoholic husbands when she herself loathes drinking. She doesn't read her Bible where she is told that whatever she fears, whatever she hates, will come about in her life. Karma, for her, is the process of meeting herself long enough to realize that she must not judge others. Until she learns, of course, she will continue to face that which she has judged in the person of those who meet this situation for their own particular needs.

Cayce spoke interestingly on this subject to one who thought that his early life experiences caused his trouble:

> Q.: To what extent have childhood home influences incapacitated the entity for a normal, happy marriage?
> A.: Just as much as the individual entity lets it have. For when ye were a child, ye thought as a child, but when ye became a man, ye should have put away childish things and not blamed others for same. For each soul is an entity, body, mind, soul. If it will use its will in applying the fruits of the spirit to those conditions about it, the entity may attune itself to the Infinite. If it attempts to abuse such, the entity pays the price. ... It has those complexes, but it also has its own individuality . . . ye are the son of the Almighty, the Creative Forces, even as Satan. Whose side are you on? Ye alone can determine.
>
> (4083-1)

Vera's story deals with some of these karmic forces, but it

has an unusual ending—much better than most. As a very young girl, Vera was married to her first husband. After twenty years of apparently good relations, her husband filed for a divorce—it seems he had found a more exciting partner. The divorce went through without being contested, and Vera lost touch with him.

She worked in a new career she created for herself, and only after fifteen years did she meet another man with whom she could feel real companionship. This marriage was a happy one—Vera found fulfillment that she had not experienced before. But in six years, her husband became chronically ill, and he died three years later. Now, at the age of sixty-five, just months after the death of her second husband, Vera went back to Maine where she was born and where she lived with her first husband for twenty years.

And there, sure enough, was her first husband, and unattached. Both of these time-worn individuals fell in love all over again. The old emotions which she thought long-since finished and put aside were reawakened. As they traveled through the same country roads they had walked as young people, it was like turning back the pages of time. They realized where they had made their mistakes in their first attempt. Now they are going to go at it again, and chances are that they will face themselves in a more realistic manner. It's like another life experienced all over again; reincarnation within one lifetime. Only this time, the veil of forgetfulness had not fallen so completely as it does between lives. Vera was given an opportunity to find fulfillment which otherwise might have been put off until a later incarnation.

Cayce suggested that this need for fulfillment of one sort or another was the real reason why two people were drawn together.

> To be sure, those activities and relationships which have brought the influences which one has upon the other in this experience, arise from those associations as indicated—in which there were those opportunities, those desires that were ungratified.

Yet, as we have given, those possibilities, those opportunities which have arisen through the associations in the present—especially the opportunity for those activities and relationships as to the offspring—become the *great* opportunity, and yet the great problem in the experiences of the entities in the present sojourn.

But *find* self not in the gratifying for the moment, nor in appetites. Not that anyone is to become goody-goody, but good *for* something! That all may see, may know, that there *is* the purpose, there *is* that in which God has not chosen unwisely in giving this entity and its companion such a soul for development in this experience.

(934-7)

Vera doesn't have a child as part of her opportunity in her remarriage, but she faces perhaps similar challenges—an unfulfilled life has certain inner forces which allow unfulfilled desires to be met, either for good or for evil.

We wonder how hate or distrust could really bring us back like a magnet into association with the same person who engendered those feelings. A file at Virginia Beach, for instance, tells the story of the Crusades and some of the inhuman activities that went on during those times.

Q. 1: I have a very gentle, patient, and understanding husband. Yet after almost eight years of marriage, I continue to have terrific fear of the sexual relationship. What causes this? How can this be overcome?

A. 1: Knowing as to why and when, this must be overcome in the mind itself. As has been indicated, there are manners, there are means in which there may be aroused the desire for association, for companionship, for affection, for love. Choose such with thy companion.

... There the entity was associated with, and the companion of, the present companion. Because of those manners in which there were the doubts, the fears as manifested by the companion, and the manner in which there were those precautions to prevent the relationships of the sexual nature with others, when the companion went to the Crusade activities, there are those doubts and fears arising from latent hate—created in that experience for the entity during that material sojourn. ...

> For if ye would be forgiven, ye must forgive. . . . These
> must be met in self.
>
> (2762-1)

A chastity belt and hate for the husband in one incarnation produces in another experience a loving husband but problems with sex. A similar instance from the Cayce readings tells its own story, and one can just imagine the interesting complications that such a past relationship might introduce into a present marriage:

> Q. 5: Have I ever contacted my husband [2493] in any other
> experience; if so, in what way?
> A. 5: He bought you! Doesn't he act like it at times? . . . The
> entity was traded once for two thousand pounds of
> tobacco.
>
> (1222-1)

We apparently need to be taught under diverse circumstances in order to learn what is right for us to do. If we hold on to those emotions that are not constructive, perhaps we don't really leave our past behind us. A friend of mine is learning that lesson right now. She was a businesswoman in her early thirties, when I first came to know her. She had planned on a career and wasn't thinking of marriage at all when she met a man in her business contacts who fascinated her, even though it wasn't love at first sight. After a year of dating, they decided to get married. Fran did not really know why—she didn't think she actually loved him, she told me, but she just had to marry him.

But they were married, and the troubles started—other women, scrapes, finally real antagonism, separation, and divorce. In the meantime a son was born to them, and he stayed with his mother. Fran moved out of town and started up in business again, but the divorce did not end the turmoil. Her ex-husband bought a business right next to hers and continued to give her troubles and worries. Life was miserable for years, but it finally wore him down before it did her, and it looks like a karmic debt might have been met—perhaps for both of them. Yet, who can

35

look inside another person's heart and see how the problems were solved at a soul level?

Many problems of this nature undoubtedly originate in some past life and surface when one can best learn his lesson. Hate doesn't always show up when two people first meet—as in Fran's case. But life partners need to recognize that the nature of the vows they took in the wedding ceremony hold precedence over the influences of relationships that may have existed in past incarnations. If they wish to continue in a spiritual direction upwards, they have a charge they must keep. Even when miserable experiences have brought about the present relationship, we need, as Mr. Cayce put it, to forgive, if we would be forgiven. This, of course, is the essence of what Jesus gave as the ideal prayer.

The memory of another person that persists from one incarnation to another can do a great deal of damage—if one allows it. We have seen the occasion where two members of a study group, for instance, come to understand that they knew each other as lovers in a past incarnation and must renew that relationship. Some think they are soul mates. The problem that faces the two comes in the persons of her husband and his wife—for both are married. Sometimes such a situation is resolved in a spiritual awareness that they have already accepted a life partner this time and that they have an opportunity to find greater love through adversity. In other cases, double divorce crystallizes the situation, and one wonders when the cycle will end.

One individual, seeking help in a situation like this, asked Mr. Cayce for information.

Q. 1: Where and how was I associated in past incarnations with N-?

A. 1: He broke thy home in the experience before this. Will ye break his, or thine own, in the present?

Q. 3: How should I go about breaking off my relationship with him and re-establish myself so that I would be happy and forget him?

A. 3: In doing something for someone else! Not in gratifying

36

of self's own desires, nor in answering to the desires of the body. Make those relationships with one with whom ye have *almost* broken off. *There* ye will find help and strength *if* ye *will* but take hold! Trust in the strength and the might of Him who hath given, "I do not condemn thee, but sin no more!" His power alone may now take you away from the unholy desire that consumes thee, in thy relationships just now.

(2960-1)

Of course, some couples meet in ideal situations, their purposes in life set even prior to birth. They are sensitive enough to the guidance God gives them in various ways to fulfill their life purpose together. The inner urgings of souls are not often bared to the sight of those outside the immediate home, so we don't know how many ideally fitted couples there are around us. The story of Edgar and Gertrude Cayce is certainly one of those purposeful journeys together through life that was brought forward with resolution, strength, and insight from the distant past.

Cayce saw this happening with other people, of course. A reading was given for such a couple, who had productive and spiritually oriented past lives and who were in the process of fulfilling their soul purpose this time, too. They won't have much in the way of deep problems between themselves—only opportunities concerning how they might better serve their fellow man.

These, as we find, as has been indicated, spiritually, individually, as to their activities in the earth and their associations in the present, are as near ideally fitted as a complement one for the other as may be expected to be found in a land like America that differs so much in the vibrations of its group study. . . . There have been many periods when those activities in the earth have fitted each for that in the present which may make of them an individual group that may give to others examples . . . .

As is oft indicated through these channels, individuals should, as this couple, work towards a oneness of purpose. This is indeed a couple where in purpose, in ideal, they are

37

one. Hold to this above everything, grow together, unfold in
the study of spirituality, of spiritual things, of God, of God's
relationship to man through the example of the pattern given
in Jesus the Christ. . . .

(2072-15)

Karma, then, is perhaps neither good nor bad. It is simply
that which one has created and is now experiencing as a result
of what he has put into motion. It is a meeting of oneself so
that one may grow spiritually. It becomes a recognition of self,
as when one places a mirror in front of himself and sees what he
is for the first time. Karma is neither mean nor kind—rather it
is.

We need to remind ourselves that it is never a relationship
with another person that brings about karma—rather it is an
attitude, an emotion from within our own being toward
another. We may sow a relationship with another person, but
we reap the results of what we have sown within ourselves. The
problems and the darkness, the knowledge of the difference
between life and death, between good and evil, lie within ourselves, and there they must be met.

A family situation is a great workshop where love can be the
great solution, where living together will give much opportunity
to work things out together. When members of a home do not
utilize the fruits of the spirit in association with others, they are
failing to see the spring of water in the midst of the desert.

Our relationship with God is perhaps best understood
through our relationship with other people. When we learn how
to love another, we may know more about how we are loving
God. So the person to whom we are attracted karmically—
whether he is husband or wife, child or parent—becomes a point
in time and space allowing us to see better how we are doing.
Our oneness with that other person can be made real, no matter
what his response is. His like or dislike of us should make no
difference. We don't need to pay him back in kind. When we
love him despite his hate, we are free of the relationship.

This type of solution brings God into the picture, because we
have allowed the spirit of God to work through us in solving the

problem in a creative way, in utilizing the fruits of the spirit. We have not risen above karma in one sense, or met it face to face in another sense, but we have *allowed* it to be set at rest. This is the nature of forgiveness—letting go of all those things with which we have been contending and arguing. It means changing ourselves completely inside. Then the sickness which has afflicted us melts away, and we see new horizons through new eyes, with a new body that measures up to its spiritual counterpart that has grown closer to its Creator.

OTHER RELEVANT READINGS

Q. 1: In what way was I associated with my husband in previous incarnations?

A. 1: He was your husband in the one before this, but when you got rid of him, you got along much better; you may do the same today.

Q. 2: Why is there so little harmony in our relationship now?

A. 2: It is still just the meeting of your own selves.

(3379-2)

In the experience before this—you ran him ragged for a while, and then settled down to bring about those influences that aid many individuals. In the present the experience is almost reversed, but ye will keep the faith together. Ye have much to work out together.

(3407-1)

But judgments of morality, judgments of activity through those periods would not be in the same class as in the present. Though truth and morality is ever the same, the outward application of same has changed as man's application of ideals as related to same has changed.

(2772-5)

Q. 4: How can I explain the relationship between my husband and myself? What were the associations in the past, and what are the urges from same?

A. 4: Ye were enemies in the past, in the sojourn in the lower part of what is now the German land; later became friends. Ye are reversing the conditions in the present. But

39

hold fast to that which is the helpfulness needed between you.

For ye have much to work out, and much good may be accomplished from same.

Q. 5: What is meant by the conditions being reversed in the present?

A. 5: In the present they began as close friends and are growing to be enemies.

(2073-2)

If such emotions are kept pure, they are as blossoms in the garden of God. If they are destroyed, they become stepping-stones to hell.

(413-11)

Act toward the wife, or thine own activities, as ye would like her or others to act towards thee. *Ask* no more than ye give. Demand no more than ye allowed, or allow, to be demanded of thee. Marriage, such an association, is a oneness of purpose. Unless there is the oneness of purpose, there can be no harmony. This can be accomplished, not of self alone—for remember, you made a mighty mess in the experience before this—ye suffered for it! Better make it up now, or it'll be ten times worse the next time!

(5001-1)

Q.: Is there anything in particular I can do now to accomplish the reason for present incarnation?

A.: If there hadn't been, you wouldn't be allowed to be in the earth in the present! These become self-evident facts in themselves, or should, to those who apply themselves: Belief in God, belief in self, belief in the divinity of man's relationship to God, accomplished for, by, and through Jesus, the Christ. The belief, the faith, the doing of that thy hands find to do which is in accord with, in compliance with His desires, gives reason, gives purpose, accomplishes that. For what were His words? "Father, I come to thee. I have finished." Hast thou finished the work He gave thee to do; hast thou sought to know the work? Hast thou walked and talked with Him oft? It is thy privilege. Will ye?

(3051-7)

3

PRE-MARITAL CHASTITY

... as indicated in thy abilities to
attract the opposite sex—for what
purpose is it? That ye may aid them
or that they may contribute to
your vanity? Think well on these
things ... the Giver of all good and
perfect gifts has not endowed thee
with attractiveness to be misused.
(3640-1)

As a child I remember being told a very ancient fairy
tale. In the garden of a maharajah in far-off India there was a
very beautiful and wonderful rosebush. This rosebush had blossoms so fair that royal visitors came from many countries to
view the blooms. The roses themselves knew they were beautiful, and whenever a young prince would come, they would nod
and bow very coyly and attract his attention. So colorful and
fascinating were these roses that the princes could seldom keep
from actually touching them. The princes would reach out to
fondle the roses, and sometimes even pluck one, often even
before they were in full bloom.

Toward the back of this magnificent bush, however, there
was one rosebud who did not try to seek the attention of the
visiting princes. The other roses laughed at her and chided her
for her lack of response, but she remained true to her chosen
position.

One day, the true prince of the land, who was to be married to a
beautiful princess, came to the garden to choose a rose for his
bride. Almost every rose on the famous bush was bowing and
nodding, but the prince saw that each one was now imperfect.

Some were bruised, some were pinched or missed a petal—none satisfied him. Finally he came to the rosebud that had held aloof from the rest. She now had blossomed into a perfect rose of incomparable beauty. The prince exclaimed for joy, and with love and gentleness he plucked the rose without blemish and took it to his bride.

When we choose to talk about pre-marital chastity, some may think the days of fairy tales are past. But in man's unconscious mind there will always be a prince, often riding a white charger; there will always be a Snow White, and, of course, the Seven Dwarfs, for these characters represent something real inside us and touch on the true aspirations each of us feels. They are like dreams, like the stories in religious literature, like the writings of mystics throughout the ages. They put us in touch with our Source, the Creative Energy of the universe, which we in the Western world call God.

Like an ideal that we choose to follow, a fairy tale gives us in a different manner the course that we might take, uncluttered by the desires, emotions, and prejudices of the world we live in. It has a clarity, a purity, a symbolism that brings meaning to any soul seeking its way in life.

Every age has had its variety of problems with sexual desire. Indulgence in sexual intercourse prior to marriage has been sanctioned only by a very few cultures in the world. Where there has been belief in One God, the unity inherent within this belief always filters down to a unity of home and family. The sexual act, then, is reserved for one person, like the rose in the fairy tale.

The Cayce readings back up the injunctions in the Bible and often clarify them for us. So we look also at what Mr. Cayce had to say. One of the questions put to him was:

> Q. 4: Is it desirable for this body to have sex relationships other than that attainable through a marriage, if it has its inception in the spiritual mind?
>
> A. 4: The relationships that come from that which is of the highest vibrations that are experienced in the material world are those that may be found in such relations and

42

are the basis of that which is termed the original sin; and hence may be easily misunderstood, misconstrued, misinterpreted in the experience of *every* individual; but these should be known—that the control of such, rather than being controlled *by* such gives that which makes for the awareness of *spiritual* intent and purpose. To overstep those conditions created by those environs and social relations and atmospheres that are brought about by such, however, is to take those leaves with self that may not be *easily* retained. Take not, give not, that that cannot be taken and given in the spirit of "*His* will, not mine, be done!" Each must judge such for themselves, in the light of *their* understanding. Each has the right to say I will, I will not.

(911-5)

But unfortunately, a great number of people in every age, whether they understand the message or not, choose to establish sexual freedom. Our age, of course, is marked by the advent of birth control pills and intra-uterine devices which make sexual license without fear of pregnancy possible. If the sexual urge is natural, shouldn't we respond to it?

By way of analogy, I remember a one-year-old patient who was brought to our office many years ago. This little girl had such a tremendous appetite that she would sit up at the table and feed herself until she actually regurgitated. The parents thought this was cute and encouarged her. Today she is obese—severely so—and shows the result of her over-indulgence in an appetite of the body.

We hardly condone this type of self-indulgence. Food is really meant to sustain the body and keep it healthy. Sexual desire is an appetite of the body in much the same manner. And if it is over-indulged in, often before marriage, there are consequences, many of which we do not yet know or understand. Sex and food are very real examples of how man, with his God-given creativity, abuses and over-indulges himself in his animal instincts—which even the animals use properly. (A male dog has intercourse with the female only when she is in heat—and then she gets pregnant.)

43

Sexual freedom is often equated with sexual revolution, a manner of establishing Freedom, a rebelling against old rules that went before. This type of activity is understood in the Cayce material as ultimately a rebellion against God, since it is always a movement to establish and reinforce one's own way of doing things. Anything which gratifies one's own self-oriented desires thus moves one away from his destiny, which is oneness with God. In such a concept, there are only two directions—toward God or toward self—with lots of activity in between. Since you can't go both ways at once, you are moving constantly toward one eventual goal or the other. And to simplify our definitions, Cayce has labeled the movement toward self-orientation and self-gratification as sin. Each person must decide in which direction he is moving.

Using our God-given creativity to indulge ourselves in food, clothes, laziness, money, or *anything* is rebellion, is self-centered, is sin, is harmful to the one who does it. And like the rubber ball that is bounced against the house, it returns to the originator of the action in a way that becomes an instruction, a teaching mechanism. The teaching, however, is not always to the person's liking.

Sex education has become commonplace, as if accumulation of facts alone would provide the answer. Understanding, on the other hand, is more desirable—it might be defined as the mental comprehension of these facts. Wisdom, which is often sought after but seldom achieved, is the ability to use those facts in a creative and growth-producing manner. So, lacking understanding and wisdom, can the unmarried person use the story of the rosebush in the maharajah's garden?

If Cayce is correct in his implication that the sexual relationship is the highest vibrational relationship that can be achieved in the material world, we should choose the one we share it with very carefully. It should not be a casual contact or an experience where we think only of our own satisfaction. It is of deepest importance.

How do these ideas fit into our dealing with our patients?

When he was giving his readings, Cayce, was a strict adherent

44

to the Mosaic Law, but he did not forget the law of forgiveness. And he saw how important it was to allow people to view things from their own point of view and understanding. This is perhaps the problem most of us have in counseling others. Each person on the face of the earth has his own level of awareness. He has to answer eventually to that which brought him into creation. Thus we can neither judge him, nor can we judge for him.

Young men and women have many questions, of course, about sex prior to marriage. Certainly no one sitting on the sidelines of life can be a judge for them. There is the true Creative Life Energy within them which does judge, however, according to what they are striving to do through their actions. For what would be constructive for one person might be destructive for another. That which is constructive comes only from God, so it is reasonable to assume that God sees that which is constructive to be right in His eyes. But when any of us chooses to act contrary to that which we know to be right, just, and correct in the total scheme of things as we understand it, we pay a price. And, I suspect, God grieves a bit, as do His loved ones.

In our office we are frequently asked, "Is it all right for us to have sex before marriage?" Though we let these young people choose—for it is their right to do so—we try to give them some idea of how to choose according to certain yardsticks. Sometimes, of course, a patient may not be looking for anything more than something to get him past a momentary physical crisis. But even after getting into a difficult situation, others are searching for the right answer.

Joan was fifteen and unmarried when she delivered her first baby. She had to give the baby up for adoption, and, as these things were being taken care of, her mother came to me, still quite upset, and said, "When Joan comes back into the office, please give her some birth control pills, because I don't think this is finished between her and her boyfriend. I think they still have a relationship going."

What did I suggest to Joan? She was open to reason, so I pointed out that if she did not want to have further sexual

45

relationships with her boyfriend, she should *not* take the pill—then she could tell him that she knew the outcome of this type of activity and that she wanted no more of it until she got married. This made her course of action easier, because she really did want to get her young life straightened out. So she avoided the problems of involvement with the same boy again, and at the same time, she avoided the possible drug complications of the pill.

Perhaps Joan will fail in her attempt at "going straight," but, on the other hand, she may find that sexual expression with a man should be an outgrowth of their relationship together rather than the single purpose of their relationship. This concept in itself would place her closer to what her soul is probably trying to tell her. Cayce was talking to a very similar questioner when he gave the following reading:

> Hence, in their very basic forces, the relations in sexual life should be the outcome—not the purpose of, but the outcome of—the answering of soul to soul in their associations and relations. And the act, or the associations in this nature, should be the result.
>
> ... And that there having been set laws, by associations and relations in the material life (which are again shadows of the associations for which man in a material form was brought into being to become a companion of the Father), and that morality, virtue, understanding, truth, love, are those influences that make for judgments of those that view the activities of individuals in the material life and judge according to those rules that govern such relationships, then it behooves—and becomes necessary—that there be the adherence to such regulations, that thy good be not evil-spoken of.
>
> For in the understandings, know that Love and God are One; that relations in the sexual life are the manifestations in the mental attributes of each as to an expression of that that becomes manifested in the experience of each so concerned.
>
> (272-7)

One of the concepts that we learned from the Cayce readings, but which is incorporated into every body of knowledge dealing with health and disease in the human being, is the premise that

46

each part of the body, even each cell, has a type of conscious-ness which is sufficient to guide that part or that cell in doing its job properly if all other body conditions are stable and basi-cally normal.

This idea has been instrumental in utilizing the power of suggestion in hypnosis, subliminal suggestion, autogenic train-ing, and biofeedback training. In these methods of training the "unconscious" parts of the human body, an idea is conveyed through the nervous system to a group of cells, an organ, or a system of the body. The cells that constitute the target of each suggestion are able to change their activity through the power of thought directed toward them. This implies that they have consciousness of a sort and are amenable to suggestion.

It is probably reasonable to suggest that wherever there is consciousness, there is also memory. I don't intend to explore these ideas in depth, but Cayce went scientists one better when he stated—on numerous occasions—that there is consciousness even in the atom.

Perhaps the consciousness—or memory—in the different parts of the body adds understanding to the stories of two other teen-age girls who, using the creative power of sexual desire in a way contrary to their deepest urgings, found themselves preg-nant outside of marriage.

Linda had had an almost continuous menstrual flow since Sep-tember, and it was now July. She had been taken to surgery for the problem, and the doctor did a dilatation and curretage; she had subsequently been put on birth control pills and had been given hormonal therapy—all to no avail. She still continued to bleed.

As I questioned her further, the real story began to shape up. A year before she started her continuous bleeding, she had delivered a baby out of wedlock. She adopted the baby out, felt that she had accepted the situation, and was bothered with no particular regrets. Then, during the following year, she was married to a man who had full knowledge about her baby. They both felt this was past history, and there were no emotional entanglements from it. One year after the baby had been born, however, the bleeding started and had not ceased.

47

As we talked about it, Linda realized how deeply giving up her baby had affected her. She had covered it up pretty well on the surface, but her uterus had not forgotten, and she was afflicted with what has been called the "weeping womb."

Someone asked Cayce a question that Linda would have saved herself much grief by asking prior to her own experience:

> Q.: Is sexual intercourse outside of marriage injurious morally and spiritually?
>
> A.: This must ever be answered from one's own inner self. Those attributes of procreation, of the pro-activity in individuals, are from the God-Force itself. The promptings of the inner man must ever be the guide; not from *any* source may there be given other than, "Study to show thyself approved unto the God that thou would worship." As ye would have men do to you, do ye even so to them. In the light of thine own understanding, keep thy body pure, as thou would have others keep their bodies pure. For thy body is the temple of the living God. Do not desecrate same in thine own consciousness.
>
> (826-2)

The other girl's story is more traumatic, but similar in many respects. Diane's mother disliked her daughter, thought she ran around with boys too much, and called her a prostitute. Diane rebelled, of course. Inevitably, she got pregnant and was furious that she had accepted her mother's label and had made it a part of herself. Her pregnancy was miserable—she hated every minute of it, repeating over and over again that she would never become pregnant again. The delivery was traumatic also, and when the baby was delivered, she put it out for adoption.

Diane, like Linda, said she had no regrets—not consciously. But her pelvic organs have never forgotten the experience. She is now married and wants very much to have a child. Because of the pelvic congestion and, probably, other factors, she has not been able to conceive a child since her marriage. Her whole system is still responding to her vow that she would never again become pregnant.

Parents are often unaware of what they are saying, doing, and teaching to their children. I had just finished doing a college physical exam on an eighteen-year-old girl and started to record the findings when I saw the note that her mother had clipped to her form: "Please give Sue some birth control pills."

I asked Sue if this was what she wanted, and she said she didn't know. I asked her if she felt that it was right to use the pill and have intercourse while at college. Again, she said she didn't know. As we talked on, I came to understand that this sensitive, morally aware, responsible young woman was representative of many young people asking questions of us adults.

She really did *not* know whether it was right or wrong. She certainly didn't want to get involved in that kind of responsibility and deep personal commitment. All she really wanted at this point was to go to college, get an education, have some dates, and have a good time, but she wasn't interested in going to bed with any young man.

Sue's mother had missed the boat. By her action, she told her daughter that she thought it was all right for her to go to bed with anyone she wanted to—or she may have thought Sue was too immature to have self-control or self-respect in regard to her potential sexual relations. So the mother was taking the safe way out, rather than facing the problem and having a sufficiently deep conversation to help her daughter with her decisions. Basic rules, basic understanding, basic commitments are the needed ingredients for such a situation.

Sue did not get the pill because she didn't want it. She has grown inside herself by making a decision. Her soul is undoubtedly happier.

With Carl, as with all our other children, we have emphasized that dreams give accurate guidance if they are interpreted honestly and with balanced insight. Cayce gave dreams high importance:

> The dreams which come to the body give the lessons that,
> were same applied correctly in the life of the individual, there

will come the more perfect understanding, and those pleasures and joys which would be derived in living that life.

(538-13)

The dreams, as we see, are the correlation of the physical with the cosmic forces and the subconscious weighing or giving that experience to the body-mind for the development of same.

(341-13)

In our family, it was always Carl showing the way—even in a dream he had once about swimming out from a sheltered place into the wide expanse of the ocean, with his brothers and sisters following him. So one day, when he was seventeen years old, it wasn't too unexpected when he came to me and said, "Mom, what does it mean if you dream of spiders?"

I was in the midst of fixing school lunches. "Spiders," I told Carl, "usually imply a warning of one sort or another. What was your dream?"

"I dreamed that I was watching TV somewhere, and the program was about a boy and a girl about my age who were sitting on the front porch of a house. Then I was in the picture myself, and I was on the front porch with the girl. We were talking for a while, and then she started off the porch and motioned for me to follow her. I looked out in the yard, and it was teeming with big, black spiders.

"I warned her that there were spiders out there, but she didn't seem to hear me and went on out into the yard. The spiders started climbing up on her feet and legs and started biting her, and she started screaming. I ran down into the yard to try and help her, but the spiders got on my feet and legs too and started biting me. I woke up real scared."

Carl obviously thought the dream was important—since his dreams always had provided him with clear, dependable guidance at important and critical times in his life. I was busy working with the lunches, but off the top of my head I said to Carl, "What have your thoughts been about girls lately?"

50

He looked at me a moment, murmured "Oh" to himself, and walked away. I finished the job at hand and promptly forgot about Carl's dream until late that night when he came home from his part-time job as a waiter in a restaurant.

While he was eating a late snack before going to bed, the subject of the morning occurred to me, and I asked Carl about his dream.

"Don't worry about things, Mom. That's taken care of." And he went off to bed, still munching on a piece of toast. That didn't put me any more in the light, but I let it go at that, thinking I'd talk to him more about it later on. And the occasion did arise again. A couple of days later, Carl told Bill and me the dream again along with the background information I knew was so important.

It seemed that there was a girl working at the restaurant who, according to Carl, had been making advances to him at odd moments. Carl enjoyed this—what male wouldn't? Things had progressed to the point where he was about to ask her for a date. Then he had the dream.

His higher self was in effect giving him the word that the relationship was fraught with danger. If he were to continue, both he and the girl would be hurt. In most dreams, the black spider symbolizes danger and intrigue, and usually sex. Carl told us that he had let the girl know that he was not interested, and that was the end of the incident.

Of course, this kind of choice, derived from an internal source, is is what all of us would prefer to experience. That internal source is composed of all that might be called past-life experiences, genetic tendencies, astrological urges, periods of learning in this present life, and the guidance available from spiritual sources or from what we might call the Higher Self— that portion of ourselves that is one with the Creator.

So in making his decision, Carl utilized what he had at hand, and in the process, he grew. It was only four years later that he met Dee-Dee, the girl toward whom he was always being guided, and they were married just before he started his medical-school career. This was part of the destiny for each of them.

If sexual energy is the most powerful force within our physical bodies, we must give it deep respect and keep it as a trust. As we use that creative energy properly we will begin to understand how we relate to the world around us in its ultimate sense, and how we relate to that Force that brought us into being.

Many years ago Thomas à Kempis, in his own particular style, commented on the fruits of what he would have called a spiritual existence, compared with the life of the carnal man:

> When a man desires a thing too much, he at once becomes ill at ease. A proud and avaricious man never rests, whereas he who is poor and humble of heart lives in a world of peace. An unmortified man is quickly tempted and overcome in small, trifling evils; his spirit is weak, in a measure carnal and inclined to essential things; he can hardly abstain from earthly desires. Hence it makes him sad to forego them; he is quick to anger if reproved. Yet if he satisfies his desires, remorse of conscience overwhelms him because he followed his passions and they did not lead to the peace he sought.
>
> True peace of heart, then, is found in resisting passions, not in satisfying them. There is no peace in the carnal man, in the man given to vain attractions, but there is peace in the fervent and spiritual man.[5]

Today, we don't talk about carnal appetites, and the language of Thomas à Kempis is strange to us. But the idea is still there. If we are to find our way in life, we must evaluate our actions before we embark on them, according to the rules and values which we hold most dear—and which all have a quality of eternity in them.

---

[5]Kempis, Thomas à. *The Imitation of Christ.* Milwaukee: Bruce Publishing Company, 1940.

OTHER RELEVANT READINGS

Q. 6: How should love and the sexual life properly function?

A. 6: This, to give even a summary dissertation, would require a great deal of time and space.

In a few words, as we have indicated, the material things (or those in a three-dimensional world) are the shadow or the reflection of those in the spiritual life. Then, as God or the Creative Influence is the source of all things, the second law in spiritual life, in mental life, in material life, is preservation of self and the continuation of likes, or propagation, in sexual intercourse or life.

... in thy abilities to attract the opposite sex—for what purpose is it? To be sure, molasses draws flies but it makes an awful mess if they get mixed up.

(3460-1)

Q. 7: There seems to be a standard of nature and one of man. Just how should they harmonize?

A. 7: Not with man's but rather with God's laws. One the outcome of the other. One the impulse of the other. Not the aggrandizing of the impulses that may be fired by material things, but that which is the outgrowth of the soul's expression in a material world, with the necessity of conforming to that which has been set by man as his judgment of his brother.

(272-7)

Q. 7: Am I sexually normal?

A. 7: It has been indicated for the body that the very conditions which have been necessary, for the requiring of stimuli to the various organs of the body, tend to *make* the body *over*-sexed. This must be met in the same way and manner as every other condition that brings *for* the body those *harmful* conditions, or conditions that tend to make it *harder* for the ills to be passed. Not that these desires are not to be gratified to the extent that makes for the developments in a normal manner, but to gratify *any* desire in the carnal forces *of* the body—rather than in the satisfying of the spiritual life that comes of creation itself in such emotions—is to become such an one as to make for the pricks that are to be kicked against time and time again. Self well

53

understands that such gratification has been and is conducive and inducive to those periods of torments that arise at times; which with the applications in foods, in activities, with the outlets of self mentally and physically, these associations may be brought to mean much. Cultivate the *spiritual,* the mental and physical desire, rather than those carnal desires that are gratified only for the moment.

(911-7)

The abstinence of or from relationships with the opposite sex is well when the creative force is put to creative activity in the mental, but when these are at variance with other conditions these may become just as harmful to the imaginative system or to the central nervous system, from breaking of activities with the sympathetic and the cerebrospinal, and thus become harmful.

(5162-1)

Q. 7a: Is masturbation or self-abuse injurious?
A. 7a: Ever injurious, unless it is the activity that comes with the natural raising of the vibrations in system to meet the needs or the excess of those impulses in a body.

(268-2)

It [the kundalini] has risen at *times* but has not remained; else there would *not* be those periods of confusion. For, when this has arisen and is disseminated properly through the seven centers of the body, it has purified the body from all desire of sex relationships. For *this is* an outlet through which one may attain to celibacy—through this activity. That it has *not remained* indicates changes.

(2329-1)

... that even that (desire) of the flesh may be—with the proper concept, proper desire in all its purity—consecrated to the *living* forces as manifest by the ability in that body [Jesus] so brought into being, as to make a way of escape for the *erring* man.

(364-6)

For, while the mind is of the creative forces, it is also that of which it partakes or dwells upon; thus shaping itself into that very activity which is so oft visioned in the *experience* of the entity in the aura or the vibrations of those the entity may contact.

54

It is not then in closing self away from the great mass of conglomerate influences that brings development, but in self keeping an eye single to *service!* and in honor, in glory of the Creative Forces that may manifest through thy every wish, even!

(1580-1)

4

CHOOSING YOUR PARTNER

Be rather in that position that when
the complement of self in the opposite sex appears, thy heart, thy
mind, thy body will recognize
same. For without that complement the self will be as naught and
become nil.

(5002-1)

From the time I was two years old I had said that I was
going to be a doctor, and all my friends' comments to the
contrary fell on deaf ears. It was June 1941, and I had been
accepted into medical school for the fall term in Philadelphia.
After finishing my medical education I had planned to enter the
mission field, much like my parents had done, and so now I
found myself at a Presbytery meeting at the Immanuel Presbyterian Church in Cincinnati. I needed to go under their official
care so that they might sponsor me during my further education
and so I might be eligible for a scholarship.

Bruce McGuire was minister of the College Hills Church
where my three maiden aunts were members, and he brought
me to the Presbytery meeting. When we sat down in one of the
pews of the church, I noticed a young man near me. His eyes
were of such a bright blue that I had trouble not staring. During
the meeting, he and I were introduced and discovered we both
were students to come under care of Presbytery. His uncle,
Albert Hjerpe, the minister at Immanuel Church, had been a
source of inspiration to him and one of the major reasons why
he had decided to study for the ministry. As he spoke, I could

hardly believe the emotions and feelings that surged up inside of me—it was almost as if a long-forgotten dream had come true. After he sat down, I found myself turning around in my seat to make contact with those blue eyes.

Then, after the meeting, he introduced himself as Bill Mc-Garey and asked me if I knew Bill Hatch, a classmate of his at college who had been born in India. "No, I don't know Bill Hatch," I found myself responding, "but I'll bet one of my brothers would know him." He asked if he could write and find out if we had Bill Hatch in common. I agreed—perhaps too rapidly—and a few days later a six-page letter arrived from the man who later became my husband. There was a postscript to his letter: "Does one of your brothers know Bill Hatch?" To this day, Bill Hatch is a stranger to my family.

But the beginning of a relationship such as this, with a type of instantaneous recognition—and Bill had the same sort of an experience—now tells me that I have had my eyes on him for many lifetimes; and that this has been a bringing together of the hopes and dreams and loves of all these times, with renewed opportunities to forgive, to understand, to be patient, and to control our emotions. When we saw each other in that church many years ago, we were not really strangers—we really knew each other quite well. But there were reasons why we should come together once more. And I think it was highly important, symbolically, that we met just as we were both dedicating our lives to serving God, that we found our paths crossing for the first time in a church which is dedicated also to that purpose.

There is no more important choice we have to make in life than that of our helpmeet, for many a bright future has been marred by problems and strife with the very one who should be helping to meet the challenge of life. From the time a child reaches adolescence, he is looking for, and (whether he knows it or not) is choosing, his marriage partner. That choice is the result of years of planning, dreaming, and working, but, unfortunately, most of this activity is on an unconscious level. We dream and plan without putting our conscious minds and ideals to work.

All of our thoughts, attitudes, and actions, the very books we read, the shows we see, the games we play, the friends we keep, even the food we eat—all are preparing us for this choice. If a man is interested in good food and eating well, will he choose a good cook? If he is interested in sports, will he choose an athlete? If he is interested in making money, will he choose someone who is interested in spending it? Then suddenly one day, there she is—they fall in love. Most people have not prayed or even thought about it. They have just allowed it to happen, and they are in love.

Such a choice is influenced by unconscious desires, forgotten memories, relationships and influences which can only be described as karmic in nature. And as we have seen, karma is like bouncing a ball against a wall: What you throw, you get back. The emotional storms that we aim at other people will eventually come back to us, as Jesus described in the Bible: "As ye sow, so shall ye reap." Since karma always has to do, not with other people, but with one's own self, the good created by one's actions in life also returns, sometimes in the guise of a husband or a wife that is a helpmeet for a lifetime. However, since we see ourselves only reflected in a mirror or in other people, we assume that the law of cause and effect deals with those others too. It probably does, in the sense that the changes in attitudes that bring about the release of karma are always in relationship to other people. In the total concept of reincarnation, we may be dealing again and again with the same entity, or just with the same patterns expressed in dealing with different people, different situations, and different times. So, again, karma becomes a personal problem for each of us to deal with. We are not *forced* to marry any specific person, not even by the weight of many lifetimes.

If we consider ourselves as spiritual beings experiencing an adventure here in the physical world, we need to understand our situation as we set about to choose a mate. If one abides by the promises of the marriage ceremony, there is little doubt that one makes that choice for a lifetime— so it is an important decision.

One of the commonest ideas of the Edgar Cayce readings is that "the spirit is the life, the mind is the builder, and the physical is the result." Mind, in Cayce's concept, stands between the spirit and the physical (or material) world. This is where the ability to

58

choose finds its domain. Thus, the mind builds a physical body and a material life by every thought, and we find the results of our thinking in our physical being. The mind partakes of the spiritual reality, and at the same time it often builds emotional patterns which create havoc. The mind can choose to lead one to pray for his fellow man, or to kill and destroy. Thus, of all things inherent in the human being, the mind is the most powerful.

If the mind can lead one into a karmic choice, it can also lead one into the state of grace: an undeserved blessing, it might be called, or forgiveness. Others have described grace as a condition where God's love flows freely and things happen that are so wonderful that it is hard to believe. How can one bring about such a situation when we cannot direct God's action?

Bill and I worked out a little diagram which helps explain this idea. Taking a spiritual path in choosing your life partner leads you into the experience of grace, rather than karma.

```
                          ( Eros                )
                          (                     )
BODY (Material)---( Self-Gratification )  ═══ KARMA
                          (                     )
                          ( "Carnal Nature"     )



                              ( Material Mind  )
                MIND (Mental)---(                )
                              ( Spiritual Mind )



                          ( Agape                )
                          (                      )
SPIRIT (Spiritual)---( Self-denial          ) ═══ GRACE
                          (                      )
                          ( Fruits of the Spirit )
```

59

Much has been written about the difference between *eros* and *agape*. Both mean love, but the English language fails in its attempt to differentiate between them. The word *eros* is found in the more familiar word *eroticism*, or *erotic*, which relates to the arousal of sexual instincts. In more ancient times, there were temples of Eros, the god of love, which glorified the sexual act and personified it in a deity.

Eros is understood in theological circles as being the kind of love with which man reaches up to God. He sees the mountains and the stars, the skies and the sun, the beauties of nature—and he loves them because they are beautiful. In the same manner, man sees the beauty of a woman and loves her for her beauty. Eros is brought into action because the self is being gratified.

Agape, on the other hand, is a different type of energy, the kind of love that flows from God. It has been likened to the love that by its very action, transforms the unlovely into something beautiful simply because it is loved. It is selfless because it does not consider self, but that which is outside self.

In the act of meditation, eros can be likened to the energy aroused within the human body which may be lifted up to the sixth center of the body—the pineal center—at which point the mystical marriage, the creation of light, illumination, comes about. This happens only because an energy descends to that center from the Creator, an energy which can be likened to agape, the love which is at all times present and available from God.

In this instance of two energies coming together, one can see the symbolism of the star of David. The trinity of Creative Energy comes down to meet the uplifted trinity of man. When they meet and superimpose, they become the famous star of David, and King David becomes in a very real sense the Old Testament symbol of love.

60

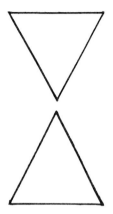
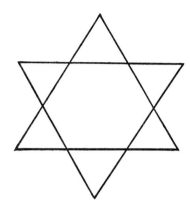

Choosing a partner out of a karmic influence is what happens most of the time, simply because we don't understand ourselves or know which of our habits are destructive—or even constructive, for that matter. As we have seen from the discussion of the snake, however, one can always choose in an upward direction if he wishes. It takes a bit of doing, but the information is there to guide us. An upward direction meets one's *needs* rather than simply one's *wants*. To put it another way, when we eat too much or indulge in too much sex, this is what many have called a carnal expression of life. To satisfy the *needs,* however, is to utilize our mind and spiritual nature in a way that will make us more of a whole being in the physical world. Cayce had something to say about this particular subject:

> ... to gratify *any* desire in the carnal forces *of* the body— rather than in the satisfying of the spiritual life that comes of creation itself in such emotions—is to become such an one as to make for the pricks that are to be kicked against time and time again. Self well understands that such gratification has been and is conducive and inducive to those periods of torments that arise at times. ... Cultivate the *spiritual,* the mental and physical desires, rather than those carnal desires that are gratified only for the moment.
>
> (911-7)

61

So, when one is seeking a lifetime marital partner, how does the mind bring about a desirable choice? The mind, being active, chooses the path of self-denial, seeks to show to another the fruits of the spirit (Galatians, Chapter 5), and, by so doing, becomes a channel for agape. When this happens, the law of like attracting like leads one into having a mate who will be a blessing rather than a hindrance, a creative rather than a destructive influence, this is that critical time when karma ends and grace begins.

To be lovable, one needs to know how to love. The kind of love we are talking about here is the kind Paul discussed in Chapter 13 of his first letter to the Corinthians. Love of this nature is patient, kind, generous, never selfish, boastful, conceited or rude, but always delighting in the truth. This love can face anything, and there is no limit to its endurance, its hope, or its faith. It never holds a grudge and never gloats over others when they fall short of their mark.

I suspect that one who attempts such a course of action with his whole heart while choosing a mate will always find his life reflecting what we have called grace.

When the process of courtship has advanced to the point where two people start to think in terms of a life together, ideals and purposes begin to play a part in the relationship. If ideals are not identical, problems of a serious nature will probably arise.

Two young people—friends of ours—met in college and got married. She finished her nurse's training, and he was starting in medical school. She supported him during those years, which often happens, but they were both happy, both working hard, and both moving closer to their goal of his obtaining his medical degree. Finally he got his M.D. and finished his internship and residency. It was at this point—when he started his practice and they established a home—that things started to go to pieces. In spite of their two children and ten years of marriage, they got a divorce. Why?

We think it's because they had reached their goal—they really had no *ultimate* ideal set for themselves, and suddenly they found themselves with nothing in common except two children. Everything they had planned on had been completed, and suddenly here they were, strangers.

Ideals are like stars in the sky for a ship navigator. They are always there, they never vary, and they guide one through the voyage he is taking. If two marriage partners have the same ideal, they will continue to draw closer together, no matter what their temporary goals may be. But they have to know what an ideal is, and they must be convinced that it is worthwhile.

Cayce had several things to say about how ideals and purposes relate to choosing a marriage partner. To one person (2072-1) who was asking about marriage, he said:

> For what is marriage? A man and a woman laboring toward an ideal set by God Himself—two souls manifesting as one in hope, in fear, in desire, in aspiration.

Cayce always saw a growth into oneness as being a desirable thing. The building of a unity, the peace and love that go into it, and the nature of oneness as it comes from diversity—these were stressed, as in the following extracts:

> These as individuals chose one another as companions. For what? Because they fitted into such companionship, becoming more and more daily as one and as a complement as one, finding in the other that which would answer their needs.
> ... Let each be the complement, the mortise and pestle, or the dew upon the flower, or the rainbow in the cloud, or as the voices in the night.
> (2072-15)

> ... Friendships and loves that are builded on peace *grow*, while those things that partake of earth become weatherworn, and with age unfit, unuseful; yet those that partake of those things that bespeak of the abilities that come with love *in* its higher sense *build*, grow more beautiful as time, age, comes on.
> (2364-1)

> In seeking then to find union, as we have just indicated and given in that just said, if ye seek the beauties in each and unite

in the efforts of each, they become as a stay one for another. See?

For, as a crude illustration:

Two brooks in all of their beauty, in all of their freshness, seek to wend their ways upon the bosom of the earth; each enjoying the beauties that they are given. Yet as they unite, they give then strength and the power and the majesty of His beings in the abilities to give to those forces and powers of many. In a way, they intermingle as one and yet each enjoys those beauties, those abilities, those effacements of self in this union for the glory of the power and the might that may be manifested of that they *as* individuals worship as the one God. . . .

In making the application, do so in a union of purpose for the glory of God and not for self!

(688-4)

Perhaps self-indulgence and self-gratification cause most of the troubles that arise in a marriage and mark most of the instances where two people are ill-suited for each other. In the little diagram which we drew up, this self-action brings about karma, which is in reality one meeting oneself and the problems which he has created. As one begins to lose sight of himself and focuses on an ideal outside himself, a spiritual force is put into action which can guide his life from that point onward.

A host of comments in the Cayce readings deal with this very problem, for it was troubled people who sought out his advice. Here are three interesting extracts:

But ye each have an ideal—not ideas alone, but an ideal.

Study, then, to show thyself approved unto that ideal. Not merely because of what others may think, or because it is law, or because of that as may be said or thought, but because *self* desires to meet the problems—here—now!

And these will bring harmony, these will bring understanding; if there is the determination on the part of each to give and take.

(263-18)

Selfishness is the greater fault in *most* individuals. There should be set before self an ideal, a *spiritual* ideal. Not such an ideal that "I would like to have a house like John Smith's, and

64

a wife that dresses like Mrs. Smith, and a car like John Smith's boy runs, or a dog or a horse such as those." That's material! Rather set an ideal in the *spiritual* sense, and know that he that would be greatest among men will be the servant of all. The servant *cannot* be selfish, either in nature, in person, in fact, but prefers the other in preference to self.

(912-1)

All entities—as these two entities—meet for a purpose. As to whether their ideals are the same, in the meeting, does not depend upon the attraction they may have one for the other; rather upon what they have done about their ideal in their associations one with the other in varied experiences, or in some definite period of activity. Whether these have been for weal or woe does not prevent the attraction.

Thus, whether that attraction is to be for the advancement or the undoing of something in themselves depends, again, upon what is the ideal of each.

(2533-7)

Two people with great differences in temperament may find themselves in love and wanting to get married. One may be reserved and the other highly expressive; one may be active in outdoor sports and the other a home-loving individual with not much desire to be outside. What is the answer to such a dilemma? Should they really plan to marry? Again no matter how far apart two people may be at the beginning, the movement toward a common ideal is a solution *if* love and understanding are merged into the picture. Such a couple posed that question for Mr. Cayce.

These of course come as innate urges. One as of the philosophical nature; the other rather as of a passive nature. These we find then become as sudden conditions arising, extremes. And these are as dashing fire and water together. For they represent the elements in the earth and those differences. Yet doth not water temper the steel? Doth not the steel supply the manner or means for the preserving of the influence of the water forces?

Hence these understand; and as has been indicated, seek not the differences but seek rather the oneness. See the beauty in each, and these influences that stand as conditions that appear

to be natured in each become as *welding* each into a oneness
of purpose in Him that is mercy, love, peace, and justice to all.

(688-4)

So Cayce sees even a Scorpio and a Leo as compatible if each
seeks the qualities in the other that are attractive, that produce
a unity between them. He urged those who were planning on
marriage to work toward a common spiritual ideal, no matter
where they started. And at times, he waxed poetic as he described how one would know whether he really had chosen his
mate well:

> ... are the thoughts, the activities, the desires, a comple-
> ment one to another? ... when these become as the mortise is
> to the tenon, as the copper is to the nickel, as the morning
> rays are to the dewdrop, *then* ye may know that such associ-
> ations are chosen well.
>
> (440-20)

I suppose one may find as many problems arising in the
choice of a mate as there are people in this world. One of these
people presented herself to me as a patient. She was fourteen
years old and in love with a man who was nearly twenty-six.
She was mature for her age, but the two of them were not
planning marriage for a few years—or such was the present plan.
The question was: What was their best course of action? They
were already having sexual intercourse—could she have contraceptive protection?

They felt there was a strong karmic relationship, and, of
course, I agreed. This did not mean, however, that they were
building a constructive, *creative* relationship. A girl of fourteen
needs to go through her adolescence and her young adulthood
before she gets married, or she may find dissatisfaction with her
marital partner. Then divorce becomes inevitable. On the other
hand, were she to continue her sexual relationship with the man
she said she loved, it was highly improbable that they would
later decide to get married—or even stay together.

Any advice given here, I knew, would probably fall on deaf

ears since sexual desire was dominant, blocking out the time-honored steps which would fall in chronological order to produce a sound and lasting marriage. But since we have learned that one of the best courses to follow in counseling people is to give them a choice to make, I pointed out that she could either choose to abstain from sexual intercourse until she was old enough to get married, or that she should go ahead with her present course of action.

She chose the latter, I think, for I never saw her again. Perhaps it might be thought pointless to expect a girl who had already experienced sexual relations to hold back until marriage. But for a girl of fourteen, such a choice has all the earmarks of a karmic relationship that just won't stop until real trouble arises and both parties meet the products of their own activities.

In our own family, we made it a practice to instruct our children in how to choose a mate *before* they began meeting possible husbands and wives. We told them, in effect, "You choose the person that you want to be associated with, and we will love anyone you choose. But we want you to think about ideals when you meet other young people. Choose someone that fits as far as your ideals are concerned, because there are lots of people whom you can love physically." When our daughter, Annie, finally chose a husband, we knew he was the right person for her to marry. Not only did we see this at a conscious level, but before the wedding Annie had a dream which she shared with us.

In the dream, she and Rich were both on a sailing vessel with great, high masts and beautiful billowing sails. They were both climbing up on the masts, swinging out over the water and back again, having the time of their lives. The ship entered rough seas, but it was sturdy and sailed on majestically through the bad weather and storms. Through it all Annie and Rich were enjoying everything. Finally the ship came through the bad weather and entered peaceful waters, and Annie awoke with a tremendous feeling of joy, peace, and contentment.

The ship, of course, was their ship of matrimony, and the

67

ocean was the sea of life itself. The dream was telling the story of what their marriage was going to be like—as indeed it has been.

Sometimes, of course, children are not encouraged to make a spiritual choice of a life partner—the home environment has not made him aware that he is in reality a spiritual being. This, of course, becomes the responsibility of parents. As consciousness grows in the world, such a concept—if it is a true concept—will be adopted by many young people as they become parents. Perhaps this will be one manner in which homes will produce citizens that make for peace.

What about a highly impatient woman who chooses a man who is the essence of patience in his daily life. Isn't this a complementary selection? Instinctively, I think, we all strive to be whole. It doesn't always happen, but frequently we choose a life partner who complements us and fills in where we have a gaping lack. Every human being has his rough edges, and often they get rougher as time goes by. As both strive for a common ideal, it is the complementary action by a life partner that allows these rough edges to wear down.

One of the most remarkable stories I know was sent to me in a letter by my Aunt Belle. It is a story of a woman of forty-nine, who had already made a career of being a missionary in India, and how she found a husband.

8/9/39

Dear Nieces and Nephews,

Wonder where you are? What are you doing? . . . You know I told you God was showing me Edward. Before He took me to the camp meeting, He gave Gen. 2:22 ("And the rib, which the Lord God had taken from man, made he a woman, and brought her unto the man"). But I came back feeling that I had made a mistake. But the Wednesday after you left, I got a letter from a preacher I had met there. God said to me for two days, "Go with him, nothing doubting." On Friday I got in my devotions—II

Kings 1:15 ("And the angel of the Lord said unto Elijah, Go down with him: be not afraid of him. And he arose, and went down with him unto the king")—and then Friday another letter from him. On Saturday God gave Acts 10:20 ("Arise therefore, and get thee down, and go with them, doubting nothing: for I have sent them") and another letter came. Then Monday he came down to see me and told how just before he went to camp meeting he was praying, "O Lord, if you want me to marry, bring her to me if you have to bring her from the ends of the earth." And then when he met me, such love came into his heart as he knew it was from God.

Well, what could I say? God had made it so clear. When the letter came Friday, I took it to the Lord and said, "Lord, is this the one you have been speaking to me about?" And I wept a bit, for I hadn't been attracted to him at all except to know he was a good man. So God gave me Isaiah 53:2 ("For he shall grow up before him as a tender plant, and as a root out of a dry ground: he hath no form nor comeliness; and when we shall see him, there is no beauty that we should desire him"), and said he was a fine man and I would care for him.

His wife died only in April, so he thought he should wait a year. I said that was all right with me, and I would go to India and get things all in order there. He turned pale and said that if I went, I'd have a funeral on my hands, for he couldn't stand to have me so far away. Well, Tuesday night I got to thinking about it and realized I didn't love him at all—I was only obeying God. So Wednesday I told him that. We agreed we couldn't marry unless I did love him. That night, he said he was crucified, but by 5 in the morning he had the victory and could say, "Thy will be done." Then Wednesday night God gave me "We love Him because He first loved

69

us" and made it clear to me that I would love him and not to worry. Thursday morning when he came about 9:30, he surely looked like death. Well, Thursday night he drove me out to a village where I was to speak (in his Chrysler eight) and by the time we got back, I knew I was beginning to love him and was ready to accept the wristwatch he had been wanting to get as an engagement present, for he didn't believe in diamonds. We are not sure what the next step is and are letting God make that clear, as He has every other step yet.

Mr. Edward Fredrich Michael Staudt was born in Germany and came to America when 10. He is a Pentecostal preacher in Baltimore, 63 years old, not very handsome, 5 feet 10½ inches tall, has a bay window, had an accident and has a very slight limp. But he is a gentleman, uses better English than I, and has refinement. He is very thoughtful and devoted, and I love him.

I know my work in India is not finished, and some day I shall go back. Perhaps we'll both go for a year. God has the plan, we just need to take a step at a time.

His wife left him some money and a Chrysler car. He has a nice home with everything in it.

With much love,
Aunt Belle

P. S. It's better to wait and let God make your arrangements than to rush into marriage. Hallelujah!

Aunt Belle did marry Uncle Ed, of course, and they had an eventful life together. He was fourteen years her senior and passed away several years ago. Now Aunt Belle is back in India again, as she predicted she would be, caring for untainted children of leper parents. She's been there now since 1950, and she wouldn't change a word in her letter. That's the way she lives her life.

Cayce suggested several prayers for those who wished to find the proper mate. I've put together one from our background which seems to me to do the same thing:

Lord, guide me that I may find that one to whom I can be of the most service as he seeks to find his path back to Thee. And the one who can best help me to do the same.

OTHER RELEVANT READINGS

Is there really the desire to know love, or to know the experience of someone having an emotion over self? Is it a desire to be itself expended in doing that which may be helpful or constructive? This *can* be done, but it will require the *losing* of self, as has been indicated, *in* service for others. . . . For only that ye give away do ye possess.

(1786-2)

Be rather "done" by all—than ever taking advantage of *any* individual!

(1792-2)

. . . Do not confuse affection with love. Do not confuse passion with love. Love is of God, it is Creative, it is all-giving. What should be the result if God manifested forces in thee and not the expression of patience, not the expression alone of beauty that is gratification but a fulfilling of a longing, a hope that is latent and deep within each soul?

(3545-1)

Love, in its greatest aspect, does not *possess!* It *is.* It is not then possessive to be real.

(1821-1)

Love is universal, as God. Crystallized, it is beautiful, but minimized in selfishness or spread abroad in the aggrandizement of self becomes those stumbling blocks over which many tumble into restlessness for gratification, for activities to satisfy self.

(3573-1)

First, as in making then the application of same, we see that in their development they have ideas individually; yet basically, centrally, their *ideals* are one. As they each make their individual application of that which motivates their influences in giving

71

expression of these, patience, persistence, consistency must be the basic influence, the basic truth, the basic force that would make for that which would make or bring into the experience of each, not what is ordinarily termed as development "down the road of life together" but rather *up* the road, back to those influences and imports towards the light. . . .

And each then becomes as a stay one for the other; becoming as a prop, as a brace, as a helpmeet. . . .

Not that turmoils, not that strifes oft, not that disappointment in the activities of men and of individuals here and there will not make for hardships. But *even then,* if their purposes are only that they may—as one, effacing self—show forth the glory of *God,* they may become—through such experiences—a strengthening influence one to another.

(688-4)

Then in the choice of a companion it is seen that it becomes necessary to choose one whose purpose in such would become or be as one with the entity's; and not such a one that would tear down such a place. Choose one who also seeks for a home; not rest, not convenience alone, not that which is an excuse for the activities of satisfying the bodily needs, the bodily ambitions for fame, fortune, position, or the exploitations of its worldly knowledge, but that at such a fireside, at such a place, in such a home, there might be peace and harmony and an understanding of those influences that make for the creating of that which becomes as the material or earthly representation of that called a haven, a heaven, a place of rest; a place where the turmoils of the world, the cares of the days may be for the moment laid aside and there be visioned rather that hope, that promise which has been ever in the hearts of men since it has been given: "Be ye fruitful, multiply, establish thyself in the earth; for thou art lord of the earth and not lord of one another." Never has been the command to man to lord over his brother. For indeed he is his brother's keeper.

(1238-1)

All things are possible with God. Though it may bring some heartaches [to attempt to straighten out thy tangled affairs] though there are already many regrets, begin with the *spiritual* activity. . . . Indiscretions, and the sentiments that are based wholly upon material satisfactions must bring the tares and the weeds in the experience of the body. . . . Remember, God is not mocked; remember, that thou sowest must ye reap.

(971-1)

In these manners, in these ways, studying one another; not as to finding differences but as to union of purposes, as to the *glorifying* of that Savior of men, that makes for love that binds the hearts of the children of men as in oneness of ways and manners, that brings peace and happiness and joy, that maketh not afraid, that brings to those that seek those things that make for peace and joy and harmony. And as such they are the children of God.

... Children, live the life—in *oneness* of purpose to those measures that through thy hands, through thy associations, through thy love as one for another in Him, ye may be the means, the channel, through which others may know the living God. Living each *your* life, to be sure, but in Him, in His ways.

As then each saw the best, the beauty of each as from afar, in the present each seek *that*—not the difference! The shortcomings of each are understood, but cover them up with the *beauties* of each; in such ways and manners that those things that were seen then in their activities may be experienced—in the beauty of nature, in the *healings* as from the herb, in the beauties of the plumage of the bird, in the beauties and the songs of nature. So see the song, see the beauty, see the abilities of each in their own sphere, and *aid ye one another* in these directions!

Thus ye bind together the best in each and ye overcome in the other and in each those differences, and not magnify them!

(688-4)

Q. 4: We desire to undertake a healing work together. Explain why we are drawn together and yet repelled at times.

A. 4: Just as has been indicated; one is an activative force, the other becomes not a negative but as an impelling force from within self by a *subjugation* of the influences about an individual. *These* become the repellent forces one in another, as has been given.

(688-4)

Love the Lord, eschew evil. Do not find faults nor look for faults in either. Not that they do not exist and that thou art not conscious of same; but more and more become conscious of the beauty in each. And we will find happiness, joy.

Sorrow, hardships—yes; but glory rather than these make for a *new day*, a new opportunity for each to be the stay as for the other in *their* seeking as one to be a channel of blessings to others.

(688-4)

73

5

THE MARRIAGE VOWS

... Study and know that this union of activity has been and is chosen by self. Then remain true to the promises, to the obligations, and be not in self overcome with those things which if embraced will cause continual stumblings in thy experience through the earth at this time.

(1449-2)

When two people plan to live together as man and wife, they usually make adequate preparations, choose the place and the officiating clergyman, get a blood test and a marriage license—and then, with all the rest of the trimmings, they have the marriage ceremony performed, rush away to a honeymoon spot, and enter the community as newlyweds. They are now legally married, and it has been officially sanctioned by their religious order.

This is not the case with all couples, however. Many young people of marrying age are asking questions. Why do we need to get married? Why take the marriage vows? What good is a marriage certificate anyway? It's just a piece of paper. You can tear it up, and it's gone. Is there really anything valid to these ideas that have emerged over the ages? Why should we do these things?

These questions, I think, are prefectly proper and deserve solid input so that the questioner becomes satisfied with his answer. We should certainly keep in mind that concept we discussed earlier—"The spirit is the life, the mind is the builder, and the physical is the result." If we do not resolve our problems so that all three aspects of ourselves are satisfied, we have not been honest with ourselves or with others.

This means, of course, that actions in the material world are manifestations of mind-spirit realities that in a very real sense precede what we see with our physical eyes. Thus, a law in the physical world is a shadow of a spiritual law. A pact made by two people in a marriage ceremony is the manifestation of a vow already consummated at a higher level of one's being and symbolically performed in the presence of God.

We cannot conceive of man as a spiritual being and yet dismiss a physical act, a signed agreement, or a law as being simply physical and no more. It has more ramifications than that. It concerns the whole being of the persons involved, their relationship to each other, to others, and to God. So the signing of a marriage license has deep significance. When a couple decides to live together without an outer manifestation of marriage, they miss something inside themselves.

It was several years ago that Bill and I were at the airport waiting for our plane, and I overheard the following conversation behind me. A girl, who was also leaving on the same plane, was saying to her companion, "But you told me that your cousin was more in love now that they are married than he was before, when they were just living together." Obviously in disagreement and trying to convince her, the boy answered, "Well, as I understand it, it wasn't that piece of paper that made the difference. It was the living together." Apparently this couple was living together also—and she wanted to get married, but he didn't. When his cousin made his marriage legal by obtaining a license and going through the ceremony, he had found things quite different. Something inside both of them had been satisfied.

One young couple we know quite well lived together for six years without "taking the plunge." She finally tired of the idea—perhaps because she felt the insecurity of knowing that there was no legal reason why her "husband" needed to stay with her; perhaps she sensed that an action in the material world had not been fully completed. Whatever the reason, she

75

insisted that they be married. Their wedding was a simple thing, but they had a minister, a best man, a matron of honor, and a marriage license.

It was just several weeks later that the two of them sat down across from us in our living room and said, "You just can't believe what this simple piece of paper means. We can't believe the difference it makes. We are really husband and wife!" Now that they had made their relationship legal, they realized that they belonged together. Perhaps it is just as simple as that.

When two people stand at an altar, looking in each other's eyes, forgetting for that eternal moment that life exists elsewhere, and answer the minister's question with the time-honored "I do," the moment of truth arrives in the lives of each. At the same time they have established a foundation for their lives together, taken a mutual direction, and chosen an ideal by which to live. And whether they know it or not, their brief ceremony has created a pattern that will largely fashion the kind of marriage they experience in years to come. Not only the things that have been said—the promises, prayers, and songs—but the thoughts, aspirations, hopes, and desires of the two also bring about the life that they will share. These realities are being recognized more and more as we move into a new age.

Bill and I have seen marriage ceremonies in great cathedrals, modest little chapels, impressive church settings; in homes, and beside a murmuring brook. All were impressive in their own way. Each carried the touches of the people involved, making the weddings occasions to remember.

We saw the beauty of a ceremony where seven lighted candles told the story of a spiritual journey in store for the newly married couple. We saw two young people each carry a lighted candle up to a larger unlighted one. Together they ignited the larger candle and then extinguished their own—another journey in life started with a singleness of purpose.

We watched while two bright and shining young people stood in the afternoon sunshine, making their vows together after three days of prayer, meditation, and fasting. A great beautiful monarch butterfly hovered around the bride as the ceremony was completed.

And then, when we came to the twenty-fifth anniversary of our own wedding, Bill and I went through the entire ceremony again under the guidance of Bill's uncle, Albert Hjerpe, who married us in 1943, and Herb Landes, our minister in the Valley Presbyterian Church in Scottsdale, Arizona. And I wore the same gown that I wore at our first ceremony.

So, is there any question in our minds about the importance of the marriage vows? We find necessity in their performance, beauty in their meaning, and guidance in their symbolism. When Edgar Cayce was asked, "Is marriage as we have it necessary and advisable?," we would answer in the same manner as he did—"It is!" (826-6).

Cayce elaborated on that affirmation in another reading:

> Know that each enters the experience into materialization for a purpose. That purpose is that each soul may be aware of its relationship to the Creative Forces, or God. Know that each enters with those activities in which each has lived and manifested, as a part of its natures, as a part of its *mental* environs.
>
> Also know that the meeting, the association, the activity in the material experience in the present is *not* of chance, but a purposeful experience for each: and that each may be a help-meet one to the other in attaining and gaining such an understanding of the purposes of that meeting, that assocation, as to *attain* the correct concept of the *purpose* of their incoming or entrance into this material experience.
>
> Know that this has not been completed in the present, and thus is to be *met in each!* Then, why not now? It is a practical, it is a purposeful experience for each.
>
> (1523-6)

The Edgar Cayce readings saw that life together without the marriage bond was neither helpful, nor proper.

> Q.: Is marriage an aid or a detriment to . . . man?
> A.: Ever an advantage, ever a help. . . .
>
> (257-15)

77

... "Until death do us part!" This is not idle; these were brought together because there are those conditions wherein each can be a complement to the other. Are these to be denied?

(2811-3)

The law in our country concerning marriages is really based on the laws that Moses brought down to the children of Israel. But like any law, it is one we can obey or disobey. There are many laws, perhaps, which we don't like, but there is advantage in obeying them. Change them properly, if you will, but obey them while they exist. Those who are obedient to the law come into the understanding of the meaning of love. This is seen in the story of the Bible, where the Chosen People were first given the law. Then, as they strived—often unsuccessfully—to obey that law, they saw the coming of the Messiah, who was the reality of love as it was manifested in the earth. Moses and the law first; the Christ and love next.

As one obeys the law, many things happen that are important to his spiritual growth and the attainment of an illuminated consciousness. Other things happen as the reality of love grows within him, but love cannot grow to fulfillment until obedience to the law is accepted and lived. Perhaps this is a factor in the unconscious desire of some people to legalize their relationship.

Law, love, truth, and God are deeply related here. Cayce's comments about it are cryptic, perhaps, but certainly clear:

Truth is the unalterable, unchangeable law, ever. What is truth? Law! What is law? Love! What is love? God! What is God? Law and love! These are as the cycle of truth itself. And wherever ye are, in whatever clime, it's ever the same. For, as it is said of Him, He is the same yesterday, today, and forever —unalterable!

(3574-2)

And Cayce had even more to say about these strange relationships:

Through that love, as man makes it manifest in his own

78

heart and life, does it reach that law, and in compliance of A Law, the law becomes a part of the individual. *That is the law of love.* Giving in action, without the force felt . . . but makes *the law of recompense, the law of faith, the law of divine, with the law of earth forces. . . .*

So we have *Love is Law, Law is Love. God is Love. Love is God. . . .* Now, if we, as individuals upon the earth plane, have all of the other elementary forces that make to the bettering of life, and have not love we are as nothing—nothing. . . . In many, many ways may the manifestations of the law of love be shown, but without the greater love, even as the Father giveth, even as the soul giveth, there is no understanding, and no compliance of the forces that make our later laws to this, of effect.

(3744-4)

The marriage vows, then, perhaps have a relationship to the basic laws of life itself, and certainly with love as we can understand it. These spiritual laws—I suppose this is what one should call them—have to do with the nature of man himself, and they argue strongly in support of those who would in this manner become husband and wife.

The marriage ceremony itself is often formulated by the participants. In this way, the couple has a part in what happens and what is said, and this, to an extent, acts as a guide for their lives together.

Not too long ago, two young people were married who had been active in the "Search for God Study Group" program sponsored by the Association for Research and Enlightenment. They were not only in love, but they were also dedicated to serving God. Steeped in the readings that Cayce gave, they wanted a ceremony that would fit their lives as they saw them shaping up for the future. Perhaps their marriage vows would illustrate the ideas that we have explored.

FOR WHAT IS LOVE?

Love is looking outward together in the same
direction; linking our strength to pull a common

79

load; pushing together toward the far horizons, hand in hand.

Love is knowing that when our strength falters, we can borrow the strength of someone who cares.

Love is a strange awareness that our sorrows will be shared and made lighter by sharing; that joys will be enriched and multiplied by the joy of another.

Love is the Sphinx of Creation in which all secrets dwell; the sparkling Essence of Divinity.

Love is of God, for God is Love. When we love, we touch the hem of the robe of the Lord.

Love, the Climax of Being—the First Cause of all that is and evermore shall be.

When a man's hand touches the hand of a woman, they both touch the heart of Eternity. But love that does not renew itself every day becomes a habit and in turn a slavery. If you give Love instead of asking for it, if you love openly, defenselessly, discarding the proposition, "I'll love you if you'll love me," then you will discover a wonderful serenity in your life. Give Love, tenderness, affection, warmth, interest, be unafraid to share your fears and worries, show the other that you need him too, and you will have Love in abundance.

Let Love be without dissimulation—that is, without possession, that as in that manner that He gave, "Love one another, even as I have loved you," willing to give life, the self, for the purpose, for an ideal. Love is giving; it is a growth. It may be cultivated or it may be scarred. Selflessness on the part of each is necessary. Remember, the union of body, mind, and spirit in such as marriage should ever be not for the desire of self, but as one. Love grows; Love endures; Love forgives; Love understands; Love keeps those things as opportunities that to others would become hardships.

FOR WHAT IS MARRIAGE?

A man and a woman laboring toward an ideal set by God Himself—two souls manifesting as one in hope, in fear, in desire, in aspiration.

In marriage Love begins to render the prose of life into hymns and canticles of praise. Here Love's longing draws back the veil, and illumines the recesses of the heart, creating a happiness that no other happiness can surpass but that of the Soul when she embraces God.

Marriage is the union of two divinities that a third might be born on earth. It is that higher unity which fuses the separate unities within the two spirits. It is the golden ring in a chain whose beginning is a glance, and whose ending is Eternity. It is the pure rain that falls from an unblemished sky to fructify and bless the fields of divine Life. As the first glance from the eyes of the beloved is like a seed sown in the human heart, and the first kiss of her lips like a flower sown on the branch of the tree of life, so the union of two lovers in Marriage is like the first fruit of the first flower of that sowing.

"I knew at our first meeting that I had known you for ages. My first glimpse of you was not in truth the first. The hour in which our hearts met confirmed in me the belief in Eternity and in the immortality of the Soul. For I know it is within you to bring forth the power that God has bestowed upon me, to be embodied in great words and deeds, even as the sun brings to life the fragrant flowers of the field. And thus, my love for you shall endure forever."

Then make thy home as a shadow of the heavenly home; for the home is the nearest pattern in the earth to man's relationship with his Maker. The home should be that which is the material and mental expression of an at-one-ment with the Father. Never leave the home without offering a prayer together: "Thy will, O God, be done in me this day." Make the home a place where each one looks out for the other to make that day and that hour a little more sacred, a little more peaceful, little more beautiful; so that thanks may be given to Him on high who will, who does, prepare the home.

How beautiful is the face of those whom the Lord, the Christ, smiles upon. In his presence abide. Let His Love be the impelling influence in thine associations one with the other. Count it joy, then, that ye are called by Him in a service—in a loving service—to thy fellow man. He would bless this house, will ye keep Him near at hand. He is alive within thee, wilt thou but love one another even as He has loved you.

And now, one moment at one altar, before one God, to become one flesh.

And so they were married. Could they help but live happily ever after?

OTHER RELEVANT READINGS:

Q. 1: Is monogamy the best form of home relationship?

A. 1: Let the teachings be rather toward the spiritual intent. Whether it's monogamy, pologamy, or what not, let it be the answering of the spiritual *within* the individual!

But monogamy is the best, of course, as indicated from the Scripture itself—*One—ONE!* For the union of one should ever be *One.*

Q. 2: Is marriage as we have it necessary and advisable?

A. 2: It is!

(826-6)

Q. 14: Should the entity marry, and if so, when would be the best period for this to take place, in the entity's development?

A. 14: When there is found the individual or the other portion of self, as it were, that may be as a unison. He that marrieth doeth well; he that marrieth not—that has gone into service—doeth better!

(1249-1)

For all knowledge of all power is of Creative Forces—or God. And it is a law that is love if man will but embrace and live and manifest same in the daily experience.

(1432-1)

And while the entity will find that all love is lawful, of every nature, not *all* is *expedient* unto good works.

(1632-3)

While the activity in the Armed Services would be galling at times, and offer opportunities for many forms of indulgence, we find that if ye will take it seriously, ye will have the opportunity in thy experience that will bring to thee by the third day of January 1945, the happiest day of thy experience in this life. Don't lose that opportunity, for it will be as a cycle of time, as in commemoration, as it were, of the blessings of the hand of the Master upon thee, if ye choose that day to give thy body, thy promises to a companion who may become a part of thy life on that day. Keep that body then, as it were, for that day ... and when the opportunity is presented as for January 3, 1945, set that as thy wedding date.

(5049-1)

6

ESTABLISHING THE HOME

> ... the home is the greater develop-
> ment for any soul. For, in the ma-
> terial world it is the nearest akin to
> that expression, "I prepare a place,
> that where I am there ye may be
> also."
>
> (349-17)

It was Christmas vacation. I had a full week away from my medical school studies in Philadelphia, Bill had only Saturday and Sunday off, and we were married on the Monday, December 20. That week we moved into a third-floor room with a bath on the second floor, but we loved it. After all, it only takes two people who have made their lives one to create the most magnificent home out of a 10 foot x 12 foot bedroom.

When does a house—or an apartment or even a room—become a home? What ingredients are necessary?

The first step in the making of a home is the act of giving, for that is the evidence of selflessness. And unless both think first of the other marriage partner, something is lost. Perhaps our home really had its inception when Bill took my coat after we entered that little room and hung it up in the closet; it only takes something as simple as that. But had we not continued to give, even though imperfectly most of the time, our home would not have flourished and grown.

To give, to be kind, to be patient with another—these are part of what the Bible identifies as the manifestation of love. Love in its highest sense is identical with God. One way of putting it is that a house may be built by man, but a home can be constructed only by God. The spirit that inhabits the home identifies it.

> ... the highest of man's achievements in the earth—the *home* ... but let each give and take, knowing that this is to be a fifty-fifty proposition. ... When necessities require waiting and patience even in those things that may at the time appear to be negligence on the part of one or the other, do not rail at such times or allow those things to become stumbling blocks, but always reason well together. ... In *every* association, whether one with another or with your own friends, or with strangers that enter, let your activities be such that there may come more and more of that which is *directed* by the spirit of *hopefulness*, helpfulness, in your attitudes one to another. And as these grow to the harvest in life, the *Lord* may give the increase.
>
> (480-20)

Perhaps every young married couple finds their first home to be the greatest, whether it is a mansion or a rented room. The afterglow from the marriage should bring that into being. But the manner in which a home endures indicates its value, its integrity, and its effect upon the world around it. No matter how many houses the home has moved into, a home remains what those who created it have built over the years.

Vibrations are a reality, as keen observers have known throughout history. A physician friend of ours spent some months traveling in Europe. Being a Jungian psychiatrist, she had watched her dreams and interpreted them for many years. While she was traveling, she camped out a great deal and often slept on the ground.

For several days, she had slept in one particular place. Throughout the night, every single night, she woke up startled by dreams of war, fighting, and blood. Very disturbed, she tried to analyze what this meant in her own personal life, thinking in terms of conflicts and inner patterns of behavior. But she could find nothing which made sense. Then, as she was sightseeing and touring the area, she found that the place where she slept

85

had been the site of many fierce battles in World Wars I and II.

She remembered the story of Cain and Abel in the Bible, and knowing the laws of psychometry, she realized that she had been picking up in her dreams from that very ground the hates and fears, the bloodshed and the pain of the people who had fought and died there. When she realized the source of her dreams, she prayed about it, found a release, and was able to continue sleeping there peacefully until the end of her visit.

The Bible is replete with stories of blessings and curses; of holy ground where Moses saw the burning bush and the Sodom and Gomorrah destined for destruction. If a battlefield retains the fears of those who died there, then certainly a blessing on a home creates its lasting vibrations. And the thoughts, the actions, the cares, the problems—and their solutions—all will aid in shaping the vibratory nature of every home. From one of Cayce's readings comes the same story:

> ... think indeed what is meant by that spoken to Moses: "Take off thy shoes, for the ground on which thou standest is holy." Why? Did you ever try to analyze why that ye enter some places, some homes which are indeed homes and others, from the very feel, if ye are sensitive at all, there is confusion; there is anger, there is abuse, of all those natures present in that house, not a home? Try this by entering a church and go from there to a jail and then go from the jail into the church—you will find it.
>
> (2072-15)

When the spirit of hopefulness and helpfulness exists, when giving is a basic part of every activity, a vibration is built up in the home that changes even its material structure. Some people begin their homes with a housewarming—a delightful custom. And some have a home-blessing, where friends gather to invoke a blessing on both the home and those who will be part of it in years to come. If Jacob and the other patriarchs could bless their children and their inheritance, it is only reasonable to bless a home. Such an event lends its particular vibration to the home and becomes a part of it.

Is there importance to blessing a home? David and Susan think so. David is Jewish in religion and upbringing, and it was difficult for his parents and grandparents when he married out of the faith. Susan was Catholic, and the only saving grace in their marriage, apparently, was that they loved each other. But David's family decided that since the Lord had blessed Ruth when she married Boaz, they could find it in their hearts to bless Susan and David's home. When the first grandchild came, it made things better, and now there is much peace and happiness in the home. Problems, they found, were opportunities.

Whatever a home is to become is determined at least partially by what a couple visualizes when they are in the midst of establishing it. In the same manner that Abraham set the course for the people of Israel through his faith in God, a just-married couple can make their new adventure a thing of high importance and a light to the world. It depends on what they take as their ideals as a married couple, and what qualities of living they inject into their lives together. Nothing will replace faith in God as a primary guiding quality. But then, if they choose to aim their marriage to be a light to the world, they may find themselves in the midst of decisions which guide nations and people. Cayce commented on such a concept:

> In the activities the entity builded for the home, which is in the experience of every soul that nearest akin to a spiritual understanding. And the highest to which a soul may attain in material activities in building, creating a *home* that makes for the molding of character, the molding of ideas, the molding of that which the *rulings* of the state, the nations, depend for their very existence in material forces.
>
> (1222-1)

In current evaluation only two out of ten marriages prove to be compatible, actually lasting on a sound love basis over the years. Four of the remaining eight marriages result in divorce, and the other four see a sort of mutual truce arrangement. The battleground is well marked, but those last four couples chose the cold war technique while remaining together. Not a very happy solution, certainly. More light is needed, to be sure, if only two out of ten are part of the solution to world affairs, while the other eight are helping to create part of the problem itself.

Even if they are stumbling around in the dark, newlyweds still need certain things in order to begin a marriage in a constructive way. Time is an essential element in giving these two beginners an opportunity to establish the integrity of their home.

One couple we know moved into a three-bedroom house after they were married. Several of their friends were still in the service, and they thought it would be helpful if these men had some place to come to when they were discharged. Being adult, ex-servicemen would not want to go back to their homes. Our friends took the position that most newlyweds are too selfish right after they are married and remove themselves from others too much. They wanted to be broad-minded and helpful—to utilize an extended consciousness to be of aid to their friends.

We suggested to this couple that it takes time to make a real home with the vibrations in it that the two of them wanted. They needed time to discuss things; time to get their unconscious minds oriented with each other, to take positions, make decisions, and create something that is uniquely their own. Each moment in living together produces a possibility of choices in even the most minor matters, and these choices make for proper or improper vibrations in the home. If we are attempting to bring healing to the world, to sow peace instead of discord, we need to be healing to each other, we need to experience peace inside ourselves and with our life partner. A structure in one's life is built line upon line, precept upon precept, even as a building may be constructed by placing one brick upon another—gradually the shape comes into being. Cayce talked about these very things in many ways. This is one of his comments:

> ... There are in the body, as is indicated, a body, a mind, a soul—or the physical body, the mind body, the soul body.

88

> Physical manifestations are the result of the activity of the mind and the soul upon relationships that exist between individuals' conditions or circumstance. Choices individuals make in the relationship bring good or bad. Or as given, there is each day set before thee life and death, good and evil—choose thou. The constant thinking, the constant thought ... of hate, malice, jealousy, brings physical conditions as a result in the physical body as it does in a state or a nation. It is such results that produce warring conditions of nations, disputations in state, physical disturbances in a body.
>
> (3246-2)

In other places, of course, Cayce went on to say that when two people constantly think in terms of accord and peace, making decisions considerate of the other person, they are producing health in the body and peace in the home. This is the basis upon which states and nations, and even couples, can build greatness. The vibrations that are created are real, and they continue to build, whether we are aware of them or not. This becomes one of the important reasons why man and wife need time together, without other people around, in order to establish their own unique contribution to society. Like a little baby, the couple cannot be exposed to the rather harsh world too soon without detriment.

The newlyweds who wanted to have the servicemen stay in their home were motivated in the right direction. Their wishes were constructive and helpful. They needed to learn only one thing: Time is a factor in all aspects of this three-dimensional world. Cayce described the three dimensions of the mind as time, space, and patience. Jesus spoke of these things in relationship to a person's ultimate destiny when he said, "In patience possess ye your souls" (Luke 21:19).

In our home we try always to make the dinner table a happy place of joy and peace, not one of bickering and dissension. One way of trying is to invite those people into our home who will add to it and what it is trying to do, for like does attract like. As we invite others to be guests at our dinner table, we are invoking an eternal law that builds peace and

89

oneness in the world. As the home is being established, it becomes a valuable addition to invite others into it. This sort of
thing was dear to the heart of Mr. Cayce, as can be seen in the
readings that came from this man when he entered an extended
state of consciousness:

> In the establishing of the home, make it as that which may
> be the pattern of a heavenly home. Not as that set aside for
> only a place to sleep or to rest, but where not only self but all
> who enter there may feel, may experience, by the very vibra-
> tions that are set up by each in the sacredness of the home, a
> helpfulness, a *hopefulness* in the air *about* the home. . . . Make
> thine home, thine abode, where an angel would *desire* to visit,
> where an angel would seek to be a guest.
>
> (480-20)

> . . . "I go to prepare a place, that where I am ye may be
> also." Then, in the home, prepare such that all who may enter
> —the stranger, the foe, the friend and the brother—may find it
> a joyous place, one wherein they oft desire to be. For, those
> who have entertained others have oft entertained angels un-
> awares. For, God uses men and women as His emissaries, in
> words; those that are just kind to those who enter their home.
> Woe to those who would make their home, their place of
> abode, as a place where others are afraid to come.
>
> (578-2)

A tradition has grown up in our home (and I think every
home should build its own simple little traditions) and has
taken form around our dinner table. I don't know when it
started—it had its roots in the Bible, but its starting point in our
home is obscured by time and indistinct memory. Every so
often, we are never quite sure how many people are going to be
eating there, so we set an extra plate. If somebody does not
come and fill the spot at the table, we figure it's for Elijah.
Then, if someone does finally arrive and take Elijah's place, we
explain it to the visitor. I'm sure Elijah doesn't mind.

So, we give things an added dimension of patience, allowing
the flower to bloom when it is ready. In time, a home will
become a place where angels will visit and be companions. You
may not see the angels or recognize them as such—and you may

not even believe it happened until much later—but that's as it should be.

When Elijah was taken up in a fiery chariot to heaven, there were literally dozens of the prophets looking on. But none saw the event except Elisha, and Elijah couldn't have predicted before time whether Elisha would see it or not. Our eyes are often blinded for specific purposes of soul growth. So if we look for angels, it is not likely that we will see them. But it is our challenge to have faith that they will come, much like Elisha's prophets trusted him when he said that he had seen Elijah ascend in the chariot of fire. They couldn't quite *fully* believe, however, and they spent three days looking for Elijah. Then when they came back they took up their patient pathway of seeking to be prophets for the One God and followed Elisha.

Another way of building the home was expressed in Cayce readings, dealing with the manner in which we can find God expressed in all things. The great lessons in life are often mirrored for us in the world about us. If we will only look and learn, these things are not easily forgotten:

> ... flowers should be the companionship of those who are lonely. For they may speak to the "shut in." They may bring color again to the cheeks of those who are ill. They may bring to the bride the hope of love, of beauty, of a home. For flowers love the places where there is peace and rest. Sunshine and shadows, yes. There are the varied variety from those open fields to those which grow in the bog, but they grow.
> Why won't people learn the lesson from them and grow, in love and in beauty, in whatever may be their environ? Learn also from the flower that where thou art, ye, too, may make that place more beautiful for your being there, whether it is in this or that or whatever place. Whether in the hovel or in the home of the mighty, make it beautiful as do the flowers.
>
> (5122-1)

Every springtime, one of the most gorgeous sights in Arizona is seen on one of the desert spots near our home. On our way to church we pass beautiful golden flowers, their cheery faces reflecting the beauty of the sunshine. African daisies, even in the heart of Arizona, know how to be beautiful right where they are, and they add to the joy of the world.

Musicians have said that God created the earth and the universe through the music of the spheres. Others who have had transcendental experiences say that color, light, music, and form are the same, and that it is out of these that creation came about. The mathematician claims that God must have been well-grounded in math to bring about such a well-ordered and well-established creation.

No matter how all this came about, math in its simplest form does have a bit to say about the establishment of a home. We are all aware that one plus one equals two. We also know that one *times* one equals one. Therein lies a great truth. If two people join in marriage and maintain their complete individuality, refusing to give up their identity, they remain as two in the state of wedlock, and do not become as one. There are two ideas, two directions, two ideals, perhaps, two thoughts, two personages, two of everything that may end up in diverse directions, divided purposes, and divorce. On the other hand, if they multiply their desires, ideals, and directions, they find that they become as one.

One side of a coin doesn't exist without the other. But, as the two sides join together to form one, they become a valuable commodity. It is out of this kind of unity in a home that children seeing the example set for them, can grow up to create the same kind of a marriage—where they do not feel that they are losing themselves, but rather truly discover meaning and life.

If a husband and wife are still struggling to maintain their own individualities, their home will be torn with strife and lack of unity. However, if the two are mature enough to know who they are and what their life together should mean in the world, all who enter their home will find stability and love. Enhanced, stabilized, and beautified by the other, the true nature of each individual then emerges. By losing ourselves in the love of a marriage situation, we find our real selves. One person should be multiplied by the other to attain *true* oneness.

92

Each soul has its share not only of responsibility one toward the other, but of dependency one upon the other.

Let both ever strive in their relationships, then, to become more and more a complement one to the other. And in this manner may there come to each a life experience more and more worthwhile. Then more and more may the beauties of purposefulness, of righteousness, of patience, of love, grow to be more beauteous, more worthwhile in the experience of each. . . .

Let the ideals ever be set, then, in Him. Then those periods of turmoil, of fears and doubts on the part of each, will become stepping-stones for a greater and greater love, a greater expression of His love.

Let both find their own *interpretations*, but let both apply those interpretations in the light of His love; then they will be found to be *one*.

(849-12)

Perhaps it is wrong to consider the home as a career *only* for the wife, for each partner must share in the responsibilities and the challenges, as well as the rewards. It is probably more realistic to consider the home as a career for both male and female. There are a variety of specifics to be fulfilled. By the very nature of things, children become a greater responsibility for the wife. But other problems are solved in a variety of ways by different couples: housecleaning, the purchasing of groceries, cooking chores, setting the table and dish washing, purchasing and washing of clothing—all these things and more are divided up according to what seems reasonable.

In the context of reincarnation, one must consider the experiences these two people living together have had in past years. Both may have been happily married before, in which event establishing a new home would be familiar, easy, and happy. But what if one or both had stormy, difficult marriages in past lives? Or perhaps one had been a bachelor for many incarnations? These patterns of living are often not even recognized but are always active in one's daily living, posing problems that need to be met.

A former bachelor, for instance, would find it hard to make the home a career. He might end up in marriage only through the persistent corraling of a loving girl friend. And he would probably find it difficult to look at marriage as anything except a reason to beat a hasty retreat. But since every human being comes from the union of two other human beings, it is only reasonable to assume that somewhere along the way each of us is destined to see marriage as an opportunity to find part of his way in life.

Cayce once told a young man (369-16) words to that effect when discoursing on this subject: "Prepare self (for marriage) more and more, by being as a living, helpful force and influence in the lives of all, young and old alike." And to another asking advice about entering the state of marriage, the following information was given:

> Q. 13: Would I be happy married?
> A. 13: If there is the proper coordination of the purposes of others, yes. If there is that in self which is not in coordination, not so well.
> We would advise, though, the home building for everyone.
>
> (1540-1)

And, as if to follow through on his advice—all of which seemed to be based on eternal principles—Cayce told a third party that the home as a career is to be earnestly sought:

> Do make the home the career, for this is the greatest career any soul may make in the earth. To a few it is given to have both a career and a home, but the greater of all careers is the home. . . . For this is the nearer of the emblems of what each soul hopes eventually to attain. . . . Then make thy home as a shadow of a heavenly home.
>
> (5070-1)

If a home is to be sought as a career—if it is to be the creation of two people who work together in a building, constructive manner—the results will be good no matter what comes out of it in a material way. Children may find distant places more desirable, but the times spent in front of the fireplace at night, the puns and discussions at the dinner table, and the way problems are worked out based on love and consideration build the character, peace, and contentment that helps to build and sustain a nation and keep it in its right direction.

As two people fashion their home, as they make it an established structure in the community, what stance should they take? We recognize that it is hard for us to assess ourselves very well, and it is not really wise to assess our partner as we see him. We may say that we invite criticism, but we don't really want to see it coming, especially from the one we love. It builds too many walls of separation and goes in an opposite direction from the helpful wisdom of the ages: Magnify the virtues in another; minimize or forget the faults.

One admission that Bill and I have taken as an admonition is the statement made by Paul to the Philippians: "For I have determined in whatsoever state I find myself, therein to be content" (Phil. 4:11). To us, this means that when we have only a single room as a home, we find joy, peace, and contentment in it, while we work hard at whatever we are doing. We don't feel put upon, we know that all things really do work together for good to those that love God that are called according to His purposes. We realize that the future holds promises for other situations in which we can find a similar amount of satisfaction and happiness. Paul was content when he was in jail, for he knew it was part of what was needed for him. But being in jail didn't keep him from visiting with those that came to him, or from writing his letters which helped shape Christianity as we know it today.

Establishing the home, then, is not like building a house, although that too can be a creative thing. But a home is a place to give, and it needs to be blessed so that it may in reality become a light to the world. It takes time to develop the integrity that will make a home powerful and worthwhile, a place where people want to go, where angels can be entertained. The well-established home requires that those involved in it show their beauty to the world like the lily sought out only in the deep woods, or the little cap of color that the desert saguaro cactus wears on its head.

95

Those who start such a home gain what they have created, with an added bonus which often they don't even know is coming. Cayce said it this way:

> But if the seeds of truth and life are sown, then the fruition —as the life goes on together—will be in harmony. And he, the Father, being they guide in all, will bless thee, even as He has promised from the beginning. For in the fruit of thy bodies may many be blessed, if ye will but seek that *through* the union of thy purposes, of thy desires; with their import in things spiritual, such may come to pass.
>
> (480-20)

OTHER RELEVANT READINGS

Q. 1: Is commercial building or residence building my proper field?

A. 1: The residence building . . . for in the abilities to lay out those that become to individuals not just a place to "hang out"—just a place to stop over—but as *homes*, as a place where there is the crystallizing of ideals, the building of characters, the foundations for those things that must bring into the lives of those that become associated with such surroundings, that which makes for the more *beautiful* things in life. As beauty appeals to the body, so make in those constructions, those laying of plans, those concrete ideas as may be presented by individuals, as in studying their needs, their wants, their desire, so may there be laid out in those of the plans, those of the constructions for such individuals, that which will not *only* bring for *self* more of this world's goods, but that satisfaction also that the body has lent something of self and self's abilities to others, in building that which must tell in the lives of those yet to come!

(322-1)

For the home is the foundation of the ideals and purposes of the nation. And these should be, these are sacred in the experiences of those that would serve Him wholly and surely.

(3241-1)

For the home is the nearest pattern in the earth (where

there is unity of purpose in the companionship) to man's relationship to his Maker. For it is ever creative in purpose from personalities and individualities coordinated for a cause, an ideal.

(3577-1)

Should they either become self-centered or allow selfish motives to make for demands one upon the other; or become at such times so self-centered as to desire the gratifying of self's desires irrespective of what the satisfying of same might bring into the experience of the other, then these would become as those things that would divide the purpose. And a house divided against itself *will not* stand.

(939-1)

. . . *renew* in themselves, their mental beings, that which has been given as to what it must mean in the lives of each to build a home. And, as to how each must give and take—give *and* give, that there may be in this home the moral, mental and material manifestations in the lives of each, for those who are dependent upon each; that the home may be—and *should be*—the material or earthly manifestation of a permanent abiding place—a haven, a home—a heaven, a home!

(903-17)

. . . give of self in the betterment of those about self, ever learning and knowing that the riches of Heaven and Earth consist in the ability to give rather than accept.

(4313-4)

Love is the giving out of that within self.

(262-44)

. . . that law here does not refer to penal law, but rather to that called love; knowing that in love all life is given, in love all things move. In giving one attains. In giving one acquires. In giving love comes as the fulfillment of desire, guided, directed, in the ways that bring the more perfect knowledge of application of self as related to the universal, all powerful, all guiding, all divine influence in life—or it *is* life.

(345-1)

For so long as there is life, there is hope. So long as there is hope, there is possibility. So long as there is possibility, love may better direct rather than hate. And love is God. If God is present, there may be brought opportunities for all, as well as

97

for the entity, in whom such manifestations may be made manifest.

(3647-1)

... there is the greatest opportunity for expression the purposes or desires to be somewhat argumentive upon theological subjects. Keep away from this in the home, however; but do the practicing in the home of that you would argue in this respect with others! The home is the best place to try it out; and that which is not practical, or that may not be applied by self, is not well to be preached to others!

(2385-1)

... hence in either thine own home or in the keeping of the associations of those of the young, in the aid to those that are weak in body, in mind, may the greater *strength* be found, and the greater harmony, the greater peace in self be expressed in the present.

As indicated, in making the home for the homeless; in making for that experience in the lives of the young, or in the lives of those that are weak in body, of that love that is shown in the *Master's* love.

(702-1)

Then there may be the joys of a career as well as a home well established, for the purposes of making it an Eden for those who may dwell therein—and *without* the tempter therein!

(1828-1)

... With this once set, seeking—seeking—applying, applying self—any condition may be builded by one, are they willing to pay the price.

As has been given, there may be chosen the career or there may be chosen the home. Whichever one will make you happier than the other, then choose that! As has been given from the first, know the desire of the heart—know that as is the ideal—then choose and work towards that! Why ask the *rest* of these, if this has been chosen?

(349-8)

7

THE LIGHTED WAY

Know, all the desires of the body
have their place in thy experience.
These are to be used and not
abused. All things are holy unto the
Lord, that He has given to man as
appetites or physical desires, yet
these are to be used to the glory of
God and not in that direction of
selfishness alone.

Let this be rather the tenet of
the mind, of the soul, of the body:
Success must be to the glory of
God rather than to the gratifying of
any appetite, of any desire, of fame
or fortune. Know that fame and
fortune must be the result of thy
seeking in His paths first, and then
all will be lighted along the way.

(3234-1)

This manner of living—the lighted way—has been called
many things throughout the ages. Mystics and saints who have
traveled the lighted way have all known that the upward movement of energy in the human body during meditation is that
same creative power that we call sex, the central point in
creating and solving all our problems here on earth.

As two people begin a marriage intended to last a lifetime,
they begin to see that few, if any, problems facing them are not
in some manner related to the use or abuse of this all-pervasive
creative energy.

Unless one begins to understand this unity of life energies
and starts to direct them toward a creative activity in all

situations, he will experience nothing but confusion in his daily relations with his fellow man. An understanding of the best possible use of sex and the sexual relationship, then, becomes a must in creating an ideal home and marriage.

The story of Adam and Eve symbolizes the beginning of man's experience in the earth, as he made his first choice toward self-gratification. Man was not aware that he was using life energy in that action, but his choice encompassed the very essence of life itself, out of which God actually created man in the beginning.

Thus, it is important that we have a symbolic lighted way to lead us toward our destination and to give us basic understanding of what we are doing with God's gift of life itself.

As we have seen, the creative energy used in sexual intercourse has its inception in the gonads, the lowest of the seven endocrine glands of the body, the seven spiritual centers which act as doorways to the unconscious mind; the seven points of awareness for the soul as it makes its journey through the earth.

Arising in the first center, in meditation, this life energy moves upward through the Leydig center to the adrenal glands, then to the thymus, the thyroid, and the pineal, illuminating the glands as it passes through them. From the pineal, it directs itself to the pituitary, where the symbolic cup overflows. The energy spills over, cleansing and purifying as it moves downward through the body. Thus it has been described from a variety of sources.

This same energy is used to paint a masterpiece, create music, write a book, or compose a poem. It is this same energy that changes a house into a home—that takes a structure where a family lives and makes it into a temple. The same energy takes a burden of sadness and tragedy and transforms it into a stepping-stone toward God. It listens to an infant's wordless jabbering and realizes that a soul, like a flower, is unfolding and sensing the world around it; it sees in a simple act of washing dishes or making a bed an opportunity to make life happier and more joyful for someone else; it sees even in a broken and suffering body the spirit that reflects the Creative Essence of the world.

In answering questions on any subject involving the home, the relationship between sexual energy and the life force itself must be comprehended to some extent or solutions will be hard to come by.

Cayce had much to say on this subject; and only small parts of it can be quoted here:

> ... for there is no soul but what the sex life becomes the greater influence in the life. Not as always in gratification in the physical act, but rather that that finds expression in the creative forces and creative abilities of the body itself.
>
> (911-2)

Therefore, we might understand sexual energy as the manifestation (at a different level) of original creative energy, which may be moved in meditation to bring about the changes that we are talking about. Cayce had something further to say on these relationships:

> But there should be those precautions, understandings, relationships as to how and in what manner there becomes the biological urge; which through the proper training may become a pathological condition in the body of the individual. For it is as from the beginning of puberty the essence of the Creative Forces or Energies within the body of the individual.
>
> And if such forces are turned to those channels for the aggrandizement of selfish motives, or for the satisfying of that within the urge for the gratification of *emotions*, they become destructive; not only in the manner of the offspring but also in the very *physical body* of the offspring, as well as in the energies of the bodies so producing same.
>
> (826-6)

In exploring the nature of the energy potential that lies within each human body and how it relates to pure creativity and the bearing of offspring, Cayce gave the following:

> . . . within the nucleus at conception is the pattern of all that is possible. And remember, man—the soul of man, the body of man, the mind of man—is nearer to limitlessness than anything in creation.
>
> Hence, those who consider the manner of being channels through which souls may enter are taking hold upon God-

101

Force itself; and it is not the same as an animal, insect or any
of the rest of creation—which is limited always.

(281-55)

The creative energy might be used for normal sexual expression, which is as natural for man and woman as for the flowers
to bloom in the spring. Meditation as a consistent discipline in a
marriage also brings about a proper use of the same energy.

When one is simply kind to another person, he is involved in
a creative act that brings an individual into a creative relationship
with his fellow man, utilizing the same life energy. It is a cleansing, purifying process for the body, much in the same manner
that we have described in meditation.

Any creative activity involving imagination or artistic ability—
painting an ocean scene, singing, playing a violin—is another
way in which the Life Force might be used to be of benefit to
others.

Perhaps, then, the solution of life's problems consists of re-
directing that energy that has brought us destructive influences
in the past, using it anew in a constructive, helpful activity that
might bring comfort, aid, and assistance. It doesn't seem reasonable that such important information could be that simple, but
all great truths are simple. God is One. He should give us basic
answers and probably does. Then He watches while we com-
pound them.

How does this apply in specific cases? Within a twenty-four-
hour period I had two women consult me for a problem very
real in many homes—how a wife should respond in sexual
intercourse.

The first woman is a very young mother of four small children. When she climbs into bed at night, she is tired and completely uninterested in sex. Her husband, on the other hand, has
not suffered from his daily work away from home. With this
situation extending over a period of time, her husband feels that
she no longer loves him, since in her words, she "could take it
or leave it."

She feels she does love him, of course, but for reasons she

102

does not understand, she is just not interested in intercourse. Not that she isn't aroused some of the time, but she just doesn't find herself initiating any activity or even responding spontaneously. She thus has feelings of guilt and inadequacy. Her husband has read all the books he can find and has done everything he can to stimulate her interest, but when she climbs into bed, she just wants to go to sleep.

She has had interesting dreams of past lives as a celibate, as a nun, and also as a yogi. She feels a fondness for these disciplines in the waking state. It is likely that there is reality in this pattern.

This young mother could apply some of the principles we have just outlined, if her husband were to join her in the effort. Seeking to satisfy her husband's needs, she would move more toward accepting intercourse in her marital relationship. She is already up to her neck in the creative work of raising a family. Meditation for both would be a great aid. The husband, for his part, could be more sensitive to his wife's needs for rest, perhaps taking on some of the heavier household chores that have been tiring her out, perhaps allowing her to sleep later in the morning while he cares for the children. He may need some creative work himself to balance the energies within his own body.

Cayce gave a very interesting reading on a woman who strove for asceticism in this life:

> ... sex, that very oft become repulsive to the entity, especially in sexual relationships. These are builded urges latent and manifested in the experience of the entity.
>
> For as the entity took those vows of chastity, purity and devotion to celibacy, these have become innately displeasing at times, never satisfying or never gratifying desires for self or for others.
>
> (4082-1)

The second woman who came to our office has some of the same problems. She is a 45-year-old artist who, though married for twenty years, has had no children. For her, sexual intercourse is "mildly pleasurable—sad if I let myself think about it. There are those rare, rare times when we zero in on the same wavelength, when there is nothing between us. But those times are few and far between." She feels that life is passing her by and that she isn't measuring up to her potential. She has a real gift in her painting, and a great deal of her creative energy is directed toward the expression of her art. Yet she wants the fulfillment of a "normal" sex life.

She, too, has recalled past lives as a nun. Her story dwells more on her own problems and leaves her husband out of the picture. Perhaps self is too much involved here. An exploration on her part to find out how to give love to her husband might be a revelation to her as far as her own responses are concerned. Knowing she took vows in a past life should make her more patient with herself as she tries to balance out the energy pattern in her present. Often, time is the only answer in solving a difficult problem. And as she joins with her husband in daily meditation, as she loses her own problems in helping him solve his, she will find the fullness of the Life Force expressed in her life.

A woman in her late thirties was near the breaking point one day when she sought some help and advice. Her husband had just told her that he no longer loved her and that she was leaving. This came on top of her discovery that he had been spending nights with a girl friend while he was supposedly out of town. There were three children in the family, none of them grown. What to do?

Eternal principles point the way for anyone, but specific actions have to come about as a result of the free choice of an individual. So what would be this woman's answer? In living the fruits of the spirit in her life, she would be in a position to forgive her husband and to be patient as she waits for him to return. If she were meditating and praying daily, this would help to clarify a solution. It is simple to give up and divorce the man who has rejected the vows he took when they were married. This may indeed be the best course to take, but it may also be the least desirable. One must choose one way or the other and then be patient, acting in a constructive way while the picture gradually clears as to what needs to be done next. No decision is made easily, and growth comes about only through choice exercised in the middle of a situation.

What does a husband do about a promiscuous wife? One person can really do very little about another, but when anyone wants to do something about *himself* much can be accomplished. A woman once asked me what she could do about this kind of a problem—she found that men would be attracted to her like bees to honey wherever she met them, and now her marriage was about to break up. Once she had even gained a lot of weight in order to discourage them, but to no avail. I suggested practical things, like going places only with her husband, never frequenting bars, and never being alone with another man. But she liked to drink occasionally, while her husband didn't. And secretly, she loved these contacts with other men—which often led to sexual intercourse.

Some problems are part of the soul pattern we have built. They are so deeply ingrained in us that we have great difficulty in seeing them for what they are—there's even more anguish in correcting them for what we know they should be. The solution comes only in the re-directing of the Life Force no matter how long it may take. The soul pattern is not easily changed, so the correction process is sometimes rather frustratingly repetitive.

This young woman must have enough consideration for the one with whom she took the marriage vows to have sexual relations only with him. The power that can be brought into being by living the simple tenets found in the fruits of the spirit—patience, love, kindness, gentleness, consideration for the other—can change not only the marriage state but can renovate a person's life. As Cayce put it,

> Here is an entity who, if it passed through a throng of men without speaking, all of them would follow if they were free to. . . .
> How to turn this into a helpful experience: By nature the entity is a teacher, as will be seen from the experiences in the earth. The entity is a natural magnet for the opposite sex, as well as a great influence among its own sex. Use these, then, as

a means for telling of the love of Jesus. Let it become such an activity in self that everyone may come to know what would be the first words of the entity, and let them be this, though changed in form for the entity's own friends and experiences. Have you prayed to God today? . . . Have you prayed to God today? Men won't follow you; men won't think you are an easy mark. Mean it, for in that manner ye may teach many a man with evil intents to know his place.

(5089-2)

Anyone who has difficulty controlling his sexual urges needs desperately to channel that creative energy through other activities of the physical body. Working in a garden, digging and creating beauty out of the earth would be helpful. Often vigorous physical exercise, or simply walking until one is exhausted, will act to redirect the sexual drive. Often, if one just gets busy enough, this energy is dissipated . . . simple, but very effective. But the soul choice, the movement in another direction, the use of the cleansing power of meditation, the asking in prayer—these are the mechanisms that will correct and re-align one's life.

Cayce gave several readings on this particular problem:

> . . . as indicated in thy abilities to attract the opposite sex— for what purpose is it? That ye may aid them or that they may contribute to your vanity? Think well on these things . . . the Giver of all good and perfect gifts has not endowed thee with attractiveness to be misused.
>
> (3640-1)

> As the entity finds, it is attracted to and attracts many an individual of the opposite sex. This at times, unless the entity has set its own ideal or idea of metes and bounds, may bring disturbing conditions to the entity. These may be used and not abused, such that the entity may become a contributing factor to the betterment of all whom the entity may meet. . . . Remember there is a way that seemeth right to a man, but the end thereof is death . . . such activities bring destruction.
>
> (3704-1)

The problems and opportunities within the bounds of marriage are almost numberless. Each requires personal attention and individual choice, but none can be solved creatively unless

106

the Life Force which God gave each of us is called into play, directing our activities into new channels that move us in an upward direction. The lighted way means that each of us, whether in or out of marriage, has the opportunity to handle our relationships in a creative manner that recognizes the place of sex in one's life, sees the importance of meditation as part of one's soul growth, places one's action in accord with spiritual rules, and emphasizes the benefits that come from any sort of constructive artistic endeavor.

Cayce said it this way:

> Then let each—in thy daily activities—think not on that which satisfies thyself alone, nor yet that which be indulgence of the other; but rather as to how ye may each become the greater, the better channel for the glory of *Life*, of God, of His gifts, of His promises, of His peace, of His harmonies—that they may manifest in thy cooperation one with another.
>
> (1523-6)

OTHER RELEVANT READINGS

Q. 6: Is my attitude toward sex the right one?

A. 6: This must be answered in self, as to whether it is that which is ideal in the light of that known by self respecting such relationships. This would not be answered from here; for, as has been given, there must first be the desire for a change before there might even be given that which would be helpful to make such change. (912-1)

Q. 5: Are the present intimate girl friends the right influence?

A. 5: Some are, some are not. Be governed by that one and those who have trained, who have counselled well with the entity as respecting these. Then weigh same in the balance of the ideal held by self, and make decision for self—for out of *little* things do *great* conditions and associations and relations grow. Harbor not that in *any manner* that would eventually bring to self even discontent, and—most of all—the discouragement of self's abilities. Do not lose faith in self, but not *pampered*—but tutored in that way as is known in self is towards the *ideal* as set by Him, in that—"Though He were the Father,

107

yet in the Son came that relationship with man and woman that exalted, honored, *glorified, womanhood!*

(1738-1)

Q. 3: Would the practice of continence be advised, to obtain better health?

A. 3: As this is a natural effect of an active system, it is advised that this occasionally be a portion of the activities of the body; where it adds in the *draining,* or in producing that within the system which allows for activities that become dormant, stale, inactive, inertia, that make for distressing effects at times in a body.

(642-2)

Q. 10: Should men or women who do not have the opportunity to marry have sex relationships outside of marriage?

A. 10: This again is a matter of principle within the individual. The sex organs, the sex demands of every individual, must be gratified in *some* manner as a portion of the biological urge within the individual. These *begin* in the present with curiosity. For it is as natural for there to be sexual relations between man and woman, when drawn together in their regular relations or activities, as it is for the flowers to bloom in the spring, or for the snows to come in the winter, when the atmospheric conditions are conducive or inducive to such conditions.

When a man or woman has chosen (for it must be choice, and it is only by choice that one remains out of relationships with the opposite sex in marriage)—if it has chosen to not be in such relationships, then be true to the choice; or else it is to self a sin! For that which one would pretend to be and isn't is indeed sin!

(826-6)

Q. 9: Is continence in marriage advisable except when mating to produce offspring?

A. 9: This should be, and is, as we have indicated in the matter of education, the *outcome* of the *universal* sources of supply of the individuals. For some, yes; in other cases it would be *very* bad on the part of each, while in others it would be bad on one or the other, see?

There should be, then, rather the educating as to the *purposes,* and *how—how* that the force, the vitality, that goes for the gratifying of emotions may be centralized in creating—in the lives of others about the body in all its various phases—spiritual blessings.

(826-6)

Q. 4: When one partner in a marriage loses desire for sexual relation and to the other it is still necessary, how may this problem be met?

A. 4: Only in a united effort on the part of each to fill that which *is* the need of each.

(2035-1)

Q. 7: Since my husband has been impotent these many years, would sexual relationship with some trusted friend (a bachelor) help me so I can function positively and rhythmically in carrying on the normal business of home life and work? Please advise me in regard to such.

A. 7: Such questions as these can only be answered in what is thy ideal. Do not have an ideal and not attempt to reach same. There is no condemnation in those who *do* such for helpful forces, but if for personal selfish gratification, it is sin.

(2329-1)

As the records were kept, these bring to the entity's experience the abilities to write, to compose, to wind men around her own purposes. Use it, don't abuse it, and you'll have most anything you wish materially in this experience.

(5040-1)

Elements have their attraction and detraction, or those of *animosity* and those of gathering together. This we see throughout all of the kingdoms, as may be termed, whether we speak of the heavenly hosts or of those of the stars, or of the planets, or of the various forces within any or all of same, they have their attraction or detraction. The attraction increases that as gives an impulse, that that becomes the aid, the *stimuli*, for an *impulse* to create. Hence, as may be seen—or may be brought to man's own—that of attraction one for another gives that stimuli, that impulse to the criterion of, or the gratification of, those in the experience of individuals or entities. To smother same oft becomes deteriorations for each other, as may come about in any form, way or manner. Accidents happen in creation, as well as in individuals' lives! Peculiar statement here, but true!

(364-6)

109

8

BIRTH CONTROL AND ABORTION

Those then that besmirch same by
overindulgence besmirch that which
is best within themselves. And that
should be the key to birth control
or sex relations, or every phase of
the relationships between the sons
and the daughters of men—that
would become the sons and daughters of God.

(826-6)

In the midst of one of our trips to the Midwest, Bill and I had lunch with a delightful woman. She was then in her fifties, and because she knew of our love for the unusual ways and manners that children get into an earth experience, she had been waiting for several years to tell us about her experiences.

It seemed that she had always been psychic to an extent—she could see auras, had precognitive dreams, and often was aware of other people's problems when she "tuned in." She had taught school part-time on occasion, and her husband worked for the postal service. They didn't really want any more children, feeling they couldn't afford more than the three who had already come.

One night while she was taking a shower, however, out of the corner of her eye, she saw a blue light appear near the top of the shower curtain. She looked, and it went away. Then it reappeared. Then she realized that it was a light most of us would not see, representing a soul wanting to come into her family. "Go away," she said—and she meant it. It did leave, but it came back again and again. This went on for two years. Finally she gave in and said, "All right, all right," and she became pregnant. The blue light disappeared.

110

They had their baby, which she knew intuitively would be a boy, but that wasn't the last of the blue light phenomenon. Three years after that, it reappeared. Both she and her husband declined vigorously this time, and both used contraceptives. But the woman, who was now the mother of four little ones, was not sure this protection was really adequate, and, sure enough, one day the blue light disappeared again—less than a month later, she realized she was pregnant once more. The resentments had worn off by the time a little girl was born; the new addition to the family was welcomed, and our lunch partner told us how this little infant grew into a lovely young lady who is now in college.

In spite of our best precautions, then, birth control is not always effective.

Late in the spring, after he had returned from Hawaii, where he goes every year on business, one of our patients had a dream which shook him up a bit. In the dream, he was in Hawaii on a business trip, having taken his wife and their two children with him. While the family was in a hotel, a man dressed in a white robe approached our patient, smiled gently at him, told him that his wife was pregnant again, and handed him an intrauterine device (IUD). Then the man disappeared, and the dream was over.

Since their two children were ten and twelve years of age, and since his wife had been wearing this contraceptive device for six years, the idea of pregnancy was disturbing. His wife felt the same way, so they dismissed the dream. Then, since nothing happened, they relaxed.

The next spring, his work became too involved, and he decided not to take his family to Hawaii. When morning sickness appeared, and his wife's periods stopped their regularity, our patient suspected that something had happened—and it had, while he was home instead of in Hawaii.

His wife had a normal pregnancy, and when she went into labor, I delivered the IUD *before* I could bring the child into the world. I handed it to the father, who was in the delivery room, smiled at him gently, and said, "Your wife's pregnant!" He just

111

grinned. Both the husband and wife knew this one was meant to be here, and they intended to give this entity a royal welcome.

The whole problem of birth control may be presently more confused than we think. It may be negative to begin our thinking in how we should *limit* the size of our family. There is always a positive way to approach a subject, and as we understand our purpose in life and as we visualize what we think our experiences should be, perhaps we should plan on how many children we *should* have.

Several years ago I received a phone call from a student at Arizona State University. He had apparently seen my name in the phone book as a woman physician, or else he had found out from some other source that I give talks occasionally. He wanted me to give a talk to the Planned Parenthood Group at the university.

I told him I'd be happy to give a lecture, but that I would prefer an afternoon date, since I like to spend my evenings with my husband and children as much as possible.

"Oh, you have children?"

"Yes," I answered.

A short pause, then—"How many?"

"Six," I replied.

Silence this time, prolonged. I waited. Finally—"Well, perhaps we could ask you to speak some other time. Thanks."

In our own particular situation, my husband and I had planned our family, but we had planned on how many we would *have*, rather than how many we could *prevent* ourselves from having. We planned six, and we had six. We don't think that is particularly our success—rather, we think God has a hand in most events that happen, and we attribute our numerical accomplishments to His hand in our affairs.

It may be more in line with eternal reality, from the standpoint of being souls on a journey in this world, if we were to move in this direction of positive solutions. Some couples choose to be childless in their marriage. If this is what they feel deeply should be their path through the marriage experience, then they deserve help in achieving that goal.

112

Choice is a positive factor, then, but not when one chooses for other people or another person. The choice must come from the individual for it to be a growing awareness within him, and that growth, that expansion of awareness and consciousness, is what we are here for.

If two people choose to have a limited family, then this is the solution for those two. Whether for reasons of finance, lack of educational qualifications, emotional problems, fears, or whatever, the choice is the proper determining factor.

Education concerning the real purpose in becoming a father or a mother is perhaps the primary need in establishing real birth control. But education is hard to come by, and if God does have a purpose for man, then any teaching that leaves out all mention of what God may desire is of no avail.

Bill and I think of all individuals in this world as being on the side of a mountain. The top of the mountain is where one finds the total awareness of God's purpose and man's relationship to himself and to the Creator. But none of us is at the top. We must orient ourselves at the level where we find ourselves. Yet, if we don't know which direction we must go in order to get to the top, we are lost to begin with.

Each level on the mountain is a type of awareness of things as they are. Every person looks about him and sees something just a bit differently than does his friend, who may be very close. But his friend doesn't see that tree around the corner of the rock, so his understanding of the mountain, his awareness of the world and God's plan, is just a bit different, just *that much* different than that of his friend.

Birth control, of course, fits into this pattern of thinking. There are many reasons why it is necessary—all of these depending upon the people who find themselves at various spots on the mountain. If one were to view things from the *top* however, he would undoubtedly see that birth control of all kinds is not really necessary in the total scheme of things. Like many of the foibles we human beings conceive of as large problems crying for solution, birth control and its application grows out of a need we ourselves have created.

113

We need birth control because of what and where we are in consciousness in this world of ours; therefore it is necessary and we should have it. I will never forget what Cayce said once to a questioner who wanted to know if he should take castor oil. Cayce replied (perhaps with tongue in cheek): "If you have a castor oil consciousness, take castor oil."

Such a principle applies here. Mankind has created a situation. In the world today, as we know it, birth control is proper if utilized in a creative, constructive manner.

We will never forget the time when our youngest son, David, who was then eight years old, came home from school after a discussion on the population explosion.

"My teacher told us in class today that families shouldn't have more than 2½ kids in them—that what she said was right! And I think our family is too large!"

With almost one voice, his brothers and sisters jumped on his remark: "All right, David, if we start to eliminate people in this family, who do you think will go first?"

David got the point. He was rather quiet the rest of the meal, and he hasn't brought the subject up since.

Cayce had some fascinating things to say about this subject and brings to mind a point that should never be forgotten. When we talk about birth control, we talk about *birth*—and without that spark that comes from the source of life, there would be no need for birth control.

> Q. 5: Is the broadcasting of birth control information advantageous in improving the race?
>
> A. 5: It is like shooting feathers at an eagle: It's a move in the right direction, but that's about as much as might be said. This should be rather the *training* of those that are in the positions of *being* the mothers and fathers *of* the nation, of the peoples!
>
> What are the factors in the lives of those that broadcast such? Look into those and ye may easily find the answer to your question. Not all, but *most* are prompted by something that is lacking in their own makeup.

Where an opportunity has been missed, a problem arises. So

it was with an attractive but distraught woman in her mid-thirties who not long ago came to seek help in our office.

Her husband had been in Vietnam for eighteen months; she was the mother of five children, the youngest being seven; and examination proved that she was pregnant. This, she said between tears, was a one-time mistake; and if her husband and children were to find out about it, what would it do to the entire family?

What is the answer to such a situation? The lonely wife had an opportunity to be true to her husband, but she missed it. Thus, the problem arose. Yet, if no abortion were to be performed, a whole family might come apart at the seams.

This type of dilemma is almost commonplace in a doctor's office. And it brings up in legal and medical circles certain questions which perhaps should be redefined before they are answered.

When, from the moment of conception, does human life begin in the fetus? At what biological point does an abortion constitute the taking of a human life—or is destruction of a human fetus within the uterus always different from the destruction of a human body after a human being is born? Does an unborn infant have rights, and what are they?

These questions have been approached both by those who oppose abortion in any manner and the proponents of abortion-on-demand. So there has been no lack of opinion on abortion and the problems it raises in human conscience and consciousness. Because this subject is so close to my everyday living and strikes so deeply into the nature of what I believe about life itself, I have read extensively on both sides of the problem. Nowhere, it seems to me, have I seen discussion of what life *is!* Unless we define this word in some manner, we have not sought a proper answer. Unless we know something about the origin of life, we cannot understand very logically where it goes when it is snuffed out.

Throughout this book we have relied on concepts evident in the Edgar Cayce readings. These concepts, in turn, most frequently relied on biblical truths as they were evident to Cayce's unconscious mind, and drew on what he called the Universal Sources of information. Our own conclusions, then, have grown out of our study of life itself, of the Bible and its story of man's travels through the earth, and of the material in the Cayce readings.

Cayce had very little to say about abortion directly, but he had a lot to say about life and what brings it about in the human form. Abortion is the taking of life in one of its manifestations—the growing fetus, living, developing, and expanding in the uterus. Life is probably most poignantly described by Cayce when he was talking about conception. He said, "[Ovulation] is the law of nature. Conception is a law of God." If this is a factual statement, when we interfere with the products of conception we rather abruptly find ourselves dealing with something God has created.

Perhaps we are in the same boat as two people when they get married. For they promise "in the presence of God and these witnesses" that "whatsoever God has joined together, let not man put asunder." But man *has* put asunder millions of these divine unions, and we don't look at it as too bad, because some of the situations were horrible and needed an end. It may be much like that in the case of abortion. Maybe what has been created is much too terrible to continue.

But this is because, as we discussed just a short while ago, we are still somewhere on the side of the mountain of consciousness, and we just don't see the real picture. Perhaps God is trying to at least *show* us the whole picture, so we can strive *toward* it, if nothing else.

Man has always shied away from his true destiny. He does this today in the medical and legal field. He never mentions God or how man truly comes into creation, while he tries—often so ludicrously—to solve problems that must remain unsolved until God, the I Am That I Am, the Creative Energy, is considered in context with the problem.

In the days of the Old Testament, God was the guide for the children of Israel. When they needed Him, they called on Him, and he was their King. But then they lost sight of what this meant in their lives. Time glossed over the reality, and in their blindness they insisted on an earthly king. Because He loved

116

them, God allowed them to have a king, but He warned them that this would cause them trouble, and it did. They had trouble from then on, in a variety of ways, until they no longer had kings. If we continue to develop spiritual cataracts in our consciousness, if we still refuse to recognize where life comes from, we will build even more distance between ourselves and the solution to our own problems.

Contraception differs from abortion in that abortion must come *after* the beginning of new life, conception *before*. Cayce always, however, saw the promise of life itself to be of utmost importance:

> ... [that] there be visioned rather that hope, that promise which has been ever in the hearts of men since it has been given, "Be ye fruitful, multiply, establish thyself in the earth. . . ."
>
> (1238-1)

But when, from the moment of conception, does life begin in the fetus? We have already suggested that a divine creation occurs when conception takes place. This might cause us to draw premature conclusions. But such divine spark is at work in every living creature, since God created all things. And the biblical injunction is that *all* of creation was for man's benefit and spiritual growth. Where does that leave us?

Cayce moves us further along when he brings in the placement of the human soul. For man is different from the animals in that his soul is unique, created in the image of God, and unlike anything else in all of creation.

When the fetus starts its growth, the soul has not yet joined it. The soul hovers over and around the mother during the gestation period, until the first breath is taken. It is *then* that man becomes a living soul. Of course, under certain circumstances, the soul may enter the body not at birth but several hours later, or several hours before, as Cayce described in several readings:

> Q. 1: How long a period between the physical and spiritual birth?

117

A. 1: Some four and a half hours.

(566-1)

In entering the present experience we find there is a difference between the physical and the soul birth of the entity. Those experiences and conditions surrounding this are a bit unusual.

(790-1)

Between three and four o'clock. You see, in many instances the physical birth and the soul birth are somewhat different. With this entity we find very little variation in time of the soul birth or spiritual entering and the physical birth. And the physical birth, as we find, was three thirty-one (3:31).

(816-6)

Such a concept gives us loopholes, then. From the top of the mountain of consciousness it is always a challenge for man to be in accord with that which God has created. He wants us to be creative in the same manner. We see the sanctity of the human soul in its experiences, and we would not want to disturb it once it has taken its place in the human body that the mother has been forming in her own womb.

But we are not at the top. According to where we stand, we see things differently. Before the infant takes its first breath, we see reason enter the picture; it is at this point that laws will be established to regulate what might be done. A soul cannot make a choice until it is in the body—this is an obvious truism.

But, we have a sneaking suspicion that there is also great importance in not disturbing the fetus, which we called God's law in action. Where we are on the mountainside is the present, the focal point in this time-space relation that we call *now*. All of us would agree that if a fetus can draw a breath when it is born, prematurely or not, it is a proper vehicle for a soul to experience the earth. So our problem in abortion lies in that period between conception and viability.

My husband and I have drawn certain conclusions which perhaps are obvious. We feel acutely the reality of God's creation when the moment of conception comes about, and we would not disturb it, for it is part of the eternal plan. But we realize that too many times God's plans and man's are at variance. And this is perhaps proper, since God created man in His own image, giving him the power of choice, even to rebel against the power that created him.

So once again abortion becomes a question to be handled by the individual. Those who decide actively, one way or the other, will grow through the decision. In the meantime, in the workings of those institutions where laws are made and reshaped, mankind will establish legal boundaries representing where we are today as a nation and as a people, as we attempt to climb the mountain of our aspiration.

OTHER RELEVANT READINGS

Q. 1: Is it right to bring a child into being in a world such as we have today, even though it may never know a normal life but only one of war and killing and anger and hate?

A. 1: The doubt as created in the self, from the very asking of such a question, may be answered best in considering the attitude, the conditions which existed in those people's minds and activities at the period given as an example. If that does not answer, then to this entity it cannot be answered.

(457-10)

As each soul enters in the earth, there are purposes other than that which may be arising from desire of those that are physically responsible for such an advent.

For, the soul seeks from the realm of spirituality to give expression of that it as an entity or soul may do with its experiences in the mental realm, as well as about that it *has* done in a physical realm.

(541-1)

... physical development, and much respecting those things or conditions that surrounded the body during those periods of conception and development. The whole condition as a period has had to do with some tendencies that exist in this developing body at the present time, the manner and care of the body during presentation and during those first hours that there was the determining of the physical and soul or spiritual births; for these varied in this body.

(459-1)

119

9

PREPARING FOR PARENTHOOD

> [Ovulation] is a law of nature. Con-
> ception is a law of God.
>
> (457-11)

After our son Carl was born, and while Bill was intern-
ing, we asked a college student to babysit for us one night.
She was a very capable young girl who said she loved children. When we got home late that evening, she was greatly
upset. She had thought that our baby was a girl and when on
changing his diapers she found out he was a boy, she was
shocked to the core. She had babysat only for little girls up
to that time, and for some deep, unknown reason, she just
didn't want to take care of boy babies. She even stated that
when she herself had children, she certainly hoped they
wouldn't be boys.

As time passed, she came to love Carl and completely forgot
the statement she had made. She was married some time after
that, and we followed the progress of her family as it grew in
the northern-most forests of Maine. Her first child was a boy.
Then she had another boy, and another. Then, finally, she had a
girl, who lived just one year.

Who knows what past life activities brought this entire karmic pattern into expression? But once built, it was deeply set
within her and was manifested years later, where that which she

rejected came into being. We build with our minds and emotions—and neither can be left out of the picture.

George is a confirmed bachelor. For fifty-seven years he has been avoiding the entanglements that might come with marriage. He often visited our home before our little ones grew up. The first time we handed him one of the babies and said, "Here, George, hold him for a minute," you would have thought he had been given an atomic bomb which could wipe out half of Arizona.

But George held Johnny for a minute, and he survived. The next time he visited he got John for five minutes. His continued education with a little child was a beautiful thing to watch, and it grew into a genuine liking for little people. On rare occasions George would even offer to babysit, and he talked with the children as they grew older.

George won't have the occasion to be a father in this lifetime—the experience of Abraham and Sarah is not for him. But he has started himself in the direction of being a father during his next lifetime. Some of the fears, the holding back, the mental patterns he had built up—perhaps over the span of four or five incarnations—are breaking down into a loving concern for youngsters. And love of children of any size is a great asset for any parent, because children are children far into their adult years.

One important but seldom answered question is: "Why do you want children, anyway?" It's too often evident that we *do* want children, and we bypass the "why" of the situation. Some think children will fulfill some longing or that they are manifestations of love that two people have for each other. Other reasons include: we need someone to love and care for, and without a child, we do not feel complete; or we want to have our names carried; or we find in children a possibility of success that we ourselves could not achieve.

One unusual answer to this question is suggested in the reading Cayce gave to a couple who had been putting off having a family while they pursued a secure financial position. Again, a law is involved:

Q. 3: Has there been much lost in spiritual development in these past years of absorption in material existence, or was this experience a necessary foundation for that yet to come?

A. 3: It can be made such, as an experience needed. If it is used as an excuse, if it is used as something to shield self and companion, then it is lost. If it is used as the opportunity now, for fulfilling the purpose, it is gain. For, what is the first command by the Creator to man? "Be thou fruitful and multiply." Yet this sets a natural law, a mental law, a spiritual law in motion, according to whether such activity is for the gratification of the flesh, of the mental self, of a complete relationship to the Creative Forces.

(457-10)

"Be thou fruitful and multiply." Just what does such a statement really mean? What is it that we should multiply? Perhaps it is not just the bodies of other human beings that are involved, but also the love or the hate, the good or the bad, the selflessness or the self-centeredness, the faith or the fear, the light or the darkness, the life or the death. If we want loving children, we had best be loving ourselves, for this is what may be multiplied on the earth.

For many generations, our Western world has been looking for more information about this physical earth and its contents, more secrets about the mind and its workings. We have been fruitful with our minds, tickling our fancies with new bits of data and satisfying our desires to know more. Now our fund of knowledge has multiplied to the point where we are unbalanced in our living and know relatively little about our spiritual nature.

We need to be fruitful in multiplying the love, the selflessness, the light in the world—in this way we may in reality be fulfilling a "complete relationship to the Creative Forces." This may be one of the most often hidden reasons "why" any of us really want children in our lives.

As Bill and I came to know each other better in those courtship days in Ohio and Arkansas, we found we had both grown up with a deep desire to be parents. Even in those early days we planned to have six children. Now our family is just that size, and we are continually amazed at how the mind creates what it conceptualizes as a firmly set pattern.

It wasn't until just before our last two children were conceived, however, that we understood that there is more to preparing for parenthood than just aiming in that direction with a wish in one's heart. Even before we were married, of course, we were planning to some extent what kind of children we would have—this is obvious from the genetic heritage we brought to the union of marriage. But through our introduction to the Edgar Cayce readings and through our participation in the study-group program that grew out of Cayce's life and work, we began to do some of the other things we now believe should also be part of the heritage of every child born into the world.

We realized that we already had some of the necessities. The first step, of course, is choosing the right partner. Another important building stone is for two people to enter marriage in full agreement about how many children they desire.

To make his point about this type of preparation, Cayce reached not only into the unconscious storehouse of knowledge, but into biblical history and some of the famous stories of the patriarchs. He implied in all of his readings that it is highly important for parents to prepare themselves in specific ways and manners. Cleansing of both the mind and the body influenced the type of entity that would be drawn into the family. The attitude of the future mother and father both become strong guides. When they are considering the conception of a child, parents are dealing with the Source of Life itself:

> Those, then, that would make of themselves channels, their bodies, their minds, should practice those purifications for the periods when there may be those activities—as bodies with bodies—that may bring that awareness of that to which they have been and are building themselves for its expression.
>
> (541-6-1)

> Too oft individuals are prone to look upon conception or childbirth as purely a physical condition; rather should it be

123

considered as it has been from the beginning, that life—sources of life—is or are from the One Source.

Remember, how Hannah prepared herself, and as to how others as Mary—prepared themselves. There are many recorded and there are many others of which nothing is heard, and yet, there was long preparation.

(2977-2)

How exactly *does* one prepare for conception? Physically, we keep our bodies clean. That means, not just taking baths, of course, but eating a health-producing diet that gives the body what it needs, not pampering it in its wants only, and balancing body activities and energies through proper rest and sleep, work and recreation.

The mind is being fed constantly by what we hear, see, and read. We add to the mind by what we think; spiritually, we build through what we choose to think, by what we read that inspires and uplifts, by our habits of prayer and meditation, and by acting toward others in the spirit of love.

A question was given to Mr. Cayce by a member of a study group asked:

Q. 4: Should I read any books for my spiritual development besides *A Search For God?*

A. 4: Read the Book of all books—especially Deuteronomy 30, and Samuel—considering especially the attitude of Hannah, the conditions, the circumstances which existed not only as to its relationship to its husband and to other companions, but as to the needs for spiritual awakening in that experience—which exist in the world and the earth today.

If the entity can and will so place self, and then studying John 14, 15, 16 and 17—can ye make yourself as one with Him? These, as combined with the study of the preparation physically, may give the understanding; not as duty but an opportunity to be a handmaid of the Lord.

(457-10)

Cayce's story of how a child is conceived and how a soul is brought into the world is fascinating. It does not agree with the known scientific laws of the twentieth century, but then, when has spiritual law *ever* wholly agreed with man's built-up concepts? Man has not yet proved God's existence, although every truly great scientist has probably admitted that he knows so very little about the real truths of the universe that there has to be a Creative Force in this whole scheme of things.

Spiritual knowledge has always been ahead of material knowledge in the same manner that God's prophets were always showing the way to kings and priests. It is proper that God's knowledge is greater than man's, but it is sometimes humorous, sometimes terribly tragic, that man considers himself God, or else creates God in his own image. Cayce paints a picture of conception as a law of God, ovulation as a law of nature. This is perhaps the point that bears the closest inspection. In the animal kingdom, ovulation occurs regularly in the female of the species, and, of course, the male is continuously generating sperm.

But, when the ovum has been released and is then surrounded by the sperm, the actual process of conception becomes an act of creation. A new individual is being formed out of two separate cells, which, by themselves, have a consistent destiny of degeneration and death. An act of creation—a law that was set in the beginning to insure reproduction of species on the earth. Perhaps this was what Cayce meant when speaking about the human destiny. He said that there was an attraction which came from those two people in the physical world calling to the sources of generation deep in the fleshly bodies and to the sources of creation in the realms of the spirit. When two people are having intercourse at the time of ovulation, an attraction is created round about these two people, much like a radio station. A soul, seeking a period of expression, an incarnation into the world, is attracted to it, is drawn there, *if* there is that likeness between the soul and "that about the bodies, when there is the period of presentation."

Conception is a special event, which brings into it the creative elements of the spiritual realms.

A woman who was having trouble getting pregnant asked

for a reading, and her information fits well into our present material:

> Conception is a gift of God; it should ever be considered such.
>
> Q. 1: Why has conception not taken place?
>
> A. 1: Ask self! For, in the light of such as we have just indicated, only in self may the answer come. Has God seen fit to give thee that thou seekest? Hast thou prepared thyself as a worthy channel of His consideration? Only self may answer.
>
> Q. 2: Was there not enough time allowed before the menstruation?
>
> A. 2: This is not a matter of purely a physical act. Do not consider same from that angle alone; else it will be to thine own undoing.
>
> (457-11)

Preparation is not solely the mother's chore, of course. With singleness of purpose and a desire to work toward that common goal, a couple can provide what might best be described as a vibrational field that attracts an incoming soul to it. "Like attracts like" has always been a law, and what we create as an aura, an energy field, a mental-spiritual-physical atmosphere, formulates the type of being who will be coming into our homes as a child. One parent is as much responsible as the other, and they should hold a cooperative attitude not only when preparing for the conception of the child, but throughout the pregnancy. This helps formulate the actual mind-attitudes of the child:

> Q. 6: Also the attitude, is it important at moment of conception or rather the daily and continuous attitude of both parents?
>
> A. 6: Attitude is as necessary as the act itself.
>
> (457-11)

As they prepare, then, prospective parents are setting the stage for the individual who chooses to be in this family. Another reading discusses this in detail:

126

Hence the law is ever present; like attracts like; like begets like. Hence there is the attraction as from the desires of those in the physical calling to the sources of generation in the flesh, to the sources of creation or of spirit in the spiritual realm.

Hence there is often a real purpose in the soul ... seeking a period of expression of self; and finding it in that about the bodies when there is the period of presentation. For, while the physical begins at conception, the spiritual and mental is as the first breath taken into the physical—that becomes then a living soul, with a physical organism for manifestation during the sojourn in that particular experience.

(541-1)

My husband and I gave our second course on home and marriage at the A.R.E. Headquarters in Virginia Beach in 1962. Rev. Floyd Barnes, a minister from Canada, was one of the attendees. He had studied extensively in the Cayce readings, and one morning he gave our class the basics of what we now call five types of conception. (I'd like to discuss these briefly, but would suggest that the reader do his own personal research in the A.R.E. publication entitled *The Revelation,* a compilation of readings and study group commentaries on the Revelation of St. John in the 281 series of readings—and especially 281-48.)

In the course of our daily lives we see around us the results of at least four of these manners of conception, but people don't have neon signs on them to identify in what manner they were brought into the world. But as Jesus told us, "By their fruits ye shall know them" (Matt. 7:20).

The five types of conception are: (1) carnal, (2) mental, (3) unity of purpose, (4) ideal, and (5) immaculate conception. Cayce had something to say that I think is helpful:

... warning of those conditions, that there be not a departing from the way in which self has brought self to an understanding, in its present concept of true mental and spiritual relationships; for, as has been given, Michael is the lord of the Way—and in the *ways* of understanding, of conception, of bringing about those things that make for the changes in the attitudes in physical, mental or material relationships, is the *guide* through such spiritual relations; for the spiritual is the

127

life, the light, the mental is the builder, the material and physical are the results of those activities as applied in the material, carnal or physical plane.

(585-1)

With such ideas as a background, let's consider these methods of conception not as strict rules or even as definite realities in themselves, but rather as ways through which we can better understand the entire process.

When two people have no thought of mental or spiritual implications, when they are concerned only with the gratification of sexual intercourse, this is what we call *carnal* conception. It is a purely physical act based on physical desire, and conception takes place without any preparation, most likely without any thought about pregnancy or parenthood. (Probably there would be more thought revolving around the hope that there will *not* be a pregnancy.)

We are visited in our office by a multitude of young girls who have extended a lively party into a sexual relationship. So here they are, unmarried, pregnant, not in love with the other partner involved in the situation, confused, and often looking for some way out. Such a pregnancy would be typically (although not always, of course) a carnal conception.

This type of conception also occurs within the marriage relationship, when marriage partners have little more than physical attraction to hold them together. Here again there is no conscious or subconscious preparation to bring into their lives a soul whose purposes might be met in a union of desire and direction.

Children drawn into such a family pattern are often afraid and confused; their condition largely depends on just what attitudes dominate in the parents. Of course, there are souls who need this type of an entrance into the earth experience, but carnal conception does create many problems that are difficult to solve.

A *mental* conception is different, of course. Here the husband, the wife, or perhaps both create a strong mental image of

128

what is wanted in an offspring and hold that image as a clear, strongly-defined thought form. This, according to Cayce, is what happened in the instance of Ishmael:

> When Abraham and Sarah were given the promise of an heir through which the nations of the earth would be blessed, there were many years of preparation of these individuals, of the physical, mental, and spiritual natures. Again and again it is indicated as to how they each in their material concept (watch the words here, please, if you would understand) attempted to offer a plan or way, through which this material blessing from a spiritual source might be made manifest.
>
> Hence we find as to how the material or mental self— misunderstanding, misconstruing the spiritual promises— offered or *effected* channels through which quite a different individual entity was made manifest and through same brought confusion, distress, disturbance one to another in the material manifestations.
>
> (281-48)

Here we see the result of Abraham and Sarah's impatience, not waiting to see what would be the outcome of God's promise to them, but rather forcing His hand. Abraham had a son by Sarah's handmaid, Hagar, who of course had different ideas than Abraham. There was probably no real love between the two, so it became a mental conception.

From the Bible and Cayce's words, comes a second illustration of such a conception:

> Then we have that illustration in the sons of Isaac, when there were those periods in which there was to be the fulfilling of the promise to Isaac and Rebekah. We find that their *minds* differed as to the nature or character or channel through which there would come this promise; when, as we understand, there must be the cooperation spiritually, mentally, in order for the physical result to be the same. *Here* we find a different situation taking place at the time of conception, for *both* attitudes found expression. Hence twins were found to be the result of this long preparation, and yet two minds, two opinions, two ideas, two ideals. Hence we find that *here* it became necessary that even the *Divine* indicate to the mother

that channel which was to be the ruler, or that one upon whom would be bestowed the rightful heritage through which the greater blessings were to be indicated to the world, to humanity, to mankind as a whole.

(281-48)

In our own study group we heard the following story which deals with the idea of a mental conception.

The mother was a beautiful singer, while the father had no interest in his own voice. Both parents had followed a commitment to service that probably was established before they were born. But before their first two children were born, this couple had little concept of how they might influence what type of entity they might draw into their family. Conception was just a thing that happened. The mother was much more interested in having children that were attractive, intelligent, and well-motivated than she was in producing great singers. The father felt much the same way, but admitted he didn't think anything at all about vocal ability. The two children born in this framework developed into what their mother (and father) both wanted—what might be called a conception in a unity of purpose. But they had not built a mental desire for a good singing voice; and these two children had trouble locating a musical note, even when aided by a piano and their parents.

Before the third child came, however, the parents had become aware of purposes, ideals, and the manners of preparation for conception. Their last child manifested that same deep commitment to service innate in both parents, but since the parents' desires were in harmony and their mental images clarified, the mother's love of music resulted in a child gifted with her mother's beautiful voice.

We see in this story not only the mental conception but also the third of these five types—the *unity-of-purpose* conception. The two partners in this marriage had made their goals clear, so they really had unity as far as their children's ideals were concerned. But had they both had a unity of purpose regarding the last child's ability to sing, then, rather than just having a beautiful voice, she would have been a great singer.

130

When there is a long line of doctors in a family, this is likely due to a unity of purpose in the parents, continued down the line from one generation to another. Both parents, in each instance, have such a regard for healing that they share that great desire to have children who will deal with those who are less fortunate in regard to health. Perhaps the Mayo family is a good example of this type of conception. My own family has a good start in this direction, since both of my parents are doctors, I followed the same pattern, and our eldest son Carl is a physician. We saw the development of such a unity of purpose in Carl as a little boy. At times we called him "Little Doc." He could locate and identify his umbilicus, his proboscis, and his olecranon before he even knew that most people call them the belly-button, the nose, and the elbow.

In the picture that gradually emerges from the Cayce readings, the *ideal* conception is the one most of us would choose to adopt if we had the opportunity or the strength of will and purpose. In this instance both parents have an ideal and are working toward it. They have not built a mental image of the type of child they want, but have instead opened themselves to God's will. They are willing to be channels through which divinity may manifest into materiality. These parents can find strength in the reading Cayce gave to a woman desiring motherhood:

> Remember, there is an example of such in the Scripture that the entity would do well to study, to analyze; not merely as a historical fact but the attitude not only of Hannah but of those about the entity who doubted the purpose.
>
> Then, in that same attitude as that entity may this entity in that way bring those activities as may best endow self, as well as the offspring, to be a messenger, a channel to the glory of God and to the honor of self.
>
> (457-10)

How would one bring an ideal conception into being? Cayce's point of view and our own concepts of ideals leading toward this goal might help one to understand. The full answer, however, can only be discerned by one's inner vision, if we can call it that. In other words, it is not within our capacity to know if

131

another person is really bringing an ideal conception into existence, simply because spiritual ideals, direction, prayers, and meditation all relate to the mind of God; only He knows what is in another's heart. It takes deep devotion and dedication to bring such into being, and when it does happen, as the mother and father watch the development of the child together, they "treasure in their hearts" the things that they see.

There is another story, of Isaac and his coming into the world, which is well told in the reading 281-48:

> Yet, when the last promise was given, that even in their old age there would be given an heir, we find that when Sarah thus conceived there was the development of a body physically, mentally and spiritually so well balanced as to be almost etheric in his relationships to the world about him, when the material manifestation had grown to maturity.
>
> Here we find, then, that mind and matter are coordinated into bringing a channel for spiritual activity that is not exceeded in any of the characters depicted in Holy Writ.
>
> What, then, were the characteristics, the activity of the glandular system as related to that individual entity? We find that there was a perfect coordination in and through the whole period of gestation, and the fulfilling of the time according to the law set in motion by the divine influence that was the directing force of both parents through the period.
>
> We find also that throughout the period of gestation the activities about the entity, the mother, were such as to *influence* the entity yet unborn, in patience to a degree not manifested in any other of the patriarchs. While the physical conditions made manifest in the body during the growth into manhood were affected by *material* laws, there was not the changing or deviating whatsoever from the spiritual through the mental.
>
> Hence we have that illustration of what may be termed the individual ideally conceived, ideally cherished and nourished through the periods of gestation.

The fifth type of conception is called the immaculate conception. Jesus came of such a conception, where the ovum is stirred into new life by the spark of the Divine. This is, of course, no new concept. In both the stories and legends of the Catholic

Church, and in Cayce readings, not only was Jesus born of a virgin, but so was Mary, his mother. This fifth manner of conception does not bear on our subject of preparation for parenthood, but it points out one idea that runs as a golden thread through all these types of conception—that bringing a child into being in this material world is an occasion where the material and the Divine worlds come together.

When conception finally does come about, one of the questions rarely solved until the birth of the baby is, "Will it be a boy or girl?" Prospective parents sometimes build up a list of possible names. On occasion, a couple will have a feeling or a dream, and both the gender and the name are revealed. Sometimes the child is born and won't have a name for days.

There is, however, a proper answer to the determination of the sex as the fetus develops inside the mother's womb. The answer lies somewhere in the physiological and spiritual development of a newly conceived infant. Scientific study has proposed that sex is determined by the sperm and ovum which unite to begin the process. Attitudes of mind, emotional patterns, and other factors have been hypothesized as affecting the mobility of the so-called male-carrying or the female-carrying sperm cells.

Cayce suggests possibilities that again are not in strict accord with present-day science. His comments imply that a dominance of mental desire on the part of the mother brings into being a boy; while that of the father brings a girl. He states that sometimes the sex is determined much later, not at conception.

> The sex of the child depends upon the attitudes of the individuals, and especially those held by the mother. As to whether it is the male or female oft may depend upon the discharge of the opposite sex. That of the mother brings the son, that of the father brings the daughter.
>
> Q. 10: Is the sex of child determined at conception or developed later?
>
> A. 10: It may be determined at least six to ten years after birth in some instances. Hence it is not at conception, but dependent upon the growth or the cycle of that vibration set about that produces the conception.
>
> (457-11)

133

So, clearly, Cayce places himself on the side of those who would state that male or female is not produced by the sperm with its specific chromosome present or lacking, but rather by an energy pattern set into a specific cycle by those same forces that brought about the conception itself.

Parenthood, then, is many things, yet it centers around a love for God manifested in all things that one does. If Cayce's suggestions are valid, the bringing of a child into the world takes hold on forces from the spiritual realm and sets many laws into motion. The relationship of a man to a woman probably holds the prime position in this preparation. How those two act, think, feel, pray, and meditate; their attitudes toward their fellow man and toward God—all these factors help design what type of conception they may experience.

Perhaps our last thoughts on this subject could be those that Cayce gave in a reading to a wife who wanted so much to be a mother:

> Do not then justify self by condemning one another! Justify self rather by living, being that which will be a constructive experience in the life of one another. . . .
>
> For, have ye either of you analyzed what real love is?
>
> It vaunteth not itself; it thinketh no evil; it endureth *all* things!
>
> And this is the purpose, this is the basis for that attraction, one to another.
>
> Rather, make thy bodies channels through which a soul may manifest! And in thy purposes, in thy desires, in thy love of life, ye may show—in that union— that as would bind thee closer yet to Him. . . .
>
> Then let each—in thy daily activities—think not on that which satisfies thyself alone, nor yet that which would be indulgence of the other; but rather as to how ye may each become the greater, the better channel for the glory of *life*, of God, of His gifts, of His promises, of His peace, of His harmonies—that they may manifest in thy cooperation one with another.
>
> (1523-6)

134

OTHER RELEVANT READINGS

Hence, we have found throughout the ages, so oft the time when conception of truth became rampant with free love, with the desecration of those things that brought to these in the beginning that of the *knowledge* of their existence, as to that that may be termed—and betimes became—the *moral,* or morality of a peoples. Yet this same feeling, this same exultation that comes from association of kindred bodies—that have their lives consecrated in a purposefulness, that makes for the ability retaining those of the essence of creation in every virile body— can be made to become the fires that light truth, love, hope, patience, peace, harmony; for they are *ever* the keys to those influences that fire the imaginations of those that are gifted in *any* form of depicting the high emotions of human experience, whether it be in the one or the other fields, and hence is judged by those that may not be able, or through desire submit themselves—as did Amelius and I—to those *elements,* through the forces in the life as about them.

(364-6)

Those, then, that would make of themselves channels, their bodies, their minds, should practice those purifications for the periods when there may be those activities—as bodies with bodies—that may bring that awareness of that to which they have been and are building themselves for its expression.

(541-1)

But ye each have an ideal—not ideas alone, but an ideal.

Study then, to show thyself approved unto that ideal. Not merely because of what others may think, or because it is law, or because of that which may be said or thought, but because self desires to meet the problems—here—now!

And these will bring harmony, these will bring understanding; if there is the determination on the part of each to give and take.

It is not that either shall demand this or that of the other, but *demand of self that ye measure up to that the other would have you be—in the Christ!*

(263-18)

Then, know the attitude of mind of self, of the companion, in creating the opportunity; for it depends upon the state of attitude as to the nature, the character that may be brought into material experience.

(457-10)

135

Let each study those things that have been indicated as being problems from the associations and activities in the varied spheres of experience, that are to be met; endeavoring, trying to be the best *possible* channel for each to fulfill that ideal chosen by each in a cooperative way and manner.

With this study would be the prayer which also may be cooperative; that each be privileged to meet those requirements necessary in the activities, in the mind of Creative Forces.

Then in the same way and manner make your bodies the better channel; that there may be that expression as He—in His mercy, in His love, in His care—may give into your keeping; a soul that may manifest best through the body created by your physical activities.

Pray together, openly, verbally. . . .

As has been prayed, or the prayer of each—let this be together, verbally, openly. *Declare* the purposes! It makes a lot of difference in attempting to put the desires into words, even in the presence of one another. . .

Q. 12: Would the continuing of castor oil packs for dissolving adhesions interfere with pregnancy—or tend to eliminate impregnation? Advise.

A. 12: Rather it would be advisable to use same, that when there is pregnancy it would prevent a great deal of distress and anxiety.

Oft analyze self *to* self. But let each say little of detrimental nature to the other. Remember: you are to be a helpmeet one for the other; to encourage, not discourage.

(1523-12)

10

PREGNANCY

Let the body know, let the body
comprehend that it is being chosen
as a channel for the expression of
divinity into materiality!

(480-28)

Although Sarah was ninety years of age when she conceived Isaac, she had to go through the full nine months of pregnancy. Between the joys and the expectations, the fears and the trepidations, every would-be mother probably often thinks that that period of waiting is really ninety years!

This time, however, should be the most beautiful in a woman's life—those long hours and days when she and her baby and the Creator of All Things can dwell together in silent, constant communion. During those nine months a host of things happen. The development of fertilized ovum into a squalling and kicking infant is affected by every conceivable influence.

It is in such times that the mother can impress the little life, soon coming into manifestation, with all the hopes and high purposes she holds for its future. Environment, both internal and external, lends its support or acts as a detriment. The mother's diet is important to the health of a growing fetus, providing the foundation for the proper development of the rapidly dividing cells within the mother's uterus.

It is during these months that the mind wonders what should be done to make the pregnancy better and more creative. What

137

thoughts should be held in mind; what attitudes are most constructive in forming the life just coming into being? What experiences should be avoided? What sort of people should the mother surround herself with?

Throughout my medical years it has seemed only reasonable to me that external environmental factors which disturb the senses and the natural balance of the body become likewise harmful to the pregnancy. I was puzzled that mothers paid no attention to these things and really mystified that most other doctors placed these ideas in the category of fiction.

It is interesting that these same people are finally beginning to think otherwise now that appropriate medical studies have been performed and the results published. But the problems have been there all along, whether we believe or not. (Perhaps that is the nature of man, who has not yet awakened.)

Auditory stresses, such as supersonic booms and high noise levels, have been found to shape the development of the fetus adversely, starting at the time of conception.[6] Chronic alcoholics bear infants who fail to develop normally.[7] A variety of hormones often given to the pregnant woman have been found to create problems in the unborn child, some lasting a lifetime. A whole host of drugs, from aspirin to LSD have been demonstrated to cause physical difficulties to the infant, ranging from brain damage to flaws in the chromosomes.[8] The effect on the unborn child from the variety of polluted environments is still another hazard.

The question of whether a pregnant woman should engage in sexual intercourse has been debated throughout the history of mankind. Recent opinions in the Western world, at least, have been lenient on this score. However, there are those who quote scores of reasons why a woman should not engage in coitus during pregnancy. I myself have advised against it for my patients beyond the seventh month of pregnancy. However, I recently

---

[6]"Supersonic Boom May Affect Fetus," *OB-GYN News,* February 15, 1970.
[7]"Alcoholic Mothers' Babies Fail to Thrive," *JAMA 213:9,* p. 1429, August 31, 1970.
[8]"Prenatal Hormones, Diet, Drugs Can Harm Neonate," *OB-GYN News.* June 15, 1970.

found a rather explicit statement on this subject in the Cayce readings:

Q. 40: Does intercourse while carrying child interfere with the physical or spiritual development of the child?

A. 40: After three months, yes.

(457-9)

From this point onward, my advice will be to refrain from intercourse after the third month of pregnancy. But for those who won't accept this counsel, I'll offer an alternative choice of seven months. Even though they are pregnant, mothers must choose in many ways, and each choice helps to shape the infant they carry.

In his advice to pregnant women, Cayce always seemed to hit the central core of things and arrange everything else around the edges. He said much to Mrs. 457 in a number of readings, but the following is appropriate here:

While as an individual entity, (457) presents the fact of a body, a mind, a soul—it has been given as a promise, as an opportunity to man through coition, to furnish, to create a channel through' which the Creator, God, may give to individuals the opportunity of seeing, experiencing His handiwork.

Then, know the attitude of mind, of self, of the companion, in creating the opportunity; for it depends upon the state of attitude as to the nature, the character that may be brought into material experience.

Leave then the spiritual aspects to God. Prepare the mental and the physical body, according to the nature, the character of that soul being sought.

(457-10)

But sometimes it is very difficult to keep one's mind on constructive things when one has to keep house and pick up after two or three children. One of our study-group friends back East was in this category. Joan was pregnant with her third child at six months along, and she was weary. At that point, she may have been resenting the pregnancy a bit, in spite of what she knew to be right. To make things more difficult, several of her friends told her of their dreams about how she would have a very difficult time during pregnancy, which made her even more despondent.

139

At that time her husband, Greg, was asked to give a summer-school course at Virginia Beach, where Bill and I were scheduled to speak, so the four of us met and we were able to catch up on events. That night Joan had a dream in which she saw an old man approaching. He was tall, gray, walking with a firm step, and had a smile on his face. He came up to her, greeted her gently, and said, "Read the twenty-second chapter of Genesis." Then he disappeared, and the dream was over.

Greg had to give a class the next morning, so he didn't meet with Joan until lunch. In teaching his class, Greg got sidetracked and, to illustrate a point, he started to read the long 281-48 reading that dealt with Abraham and Sarah. He didn't really know why, but he read it through to the end. In the meantime, I was telling my class about the importance of attitudes during pregnancy. I also got out the 281-48 reading and read it through to the end.

We met at lunch, and Joan related the dream. In almost the same breath Greg and I said, "But that's the story of Abraham and Sarah—and I read that to my class this morning." We were all quite impressed, for if one is looking for guidance and help in life's journey, every happening is likely for a purpose.

This seemed to be a real turning point in Joan's pregnancy. It was almost as if they had received a direct message from the spiritual realms which said that, if they would keep their purposes and ideals straight and wait patiently until the baby was born, everything would be all right. The baby was very normal, bursting with health, vitality, and energy, and has been a delight in their lives ever since. We hear from Joan and Greg frequently, and they consider that dream to have marked a new awareness in their lives.

If we look at the essence of the Cayce readings, attitudes become of prime importance during pregnancy. Continuing the constructive, creative, and helpful attitudes that have been developed during the period of preparation and conception is strongly recommended. Three readings deal primarily with the attitudes one should hold during pregnancy:

> Remember, the attitude is the main purpose—and the willingness to be the channel; not merely for the gratification

of self—or that there may be offspring, but *wholly* to the glory of the Father through the Christ.

(457-8)

... proper attitude mentally and physically ... is as much dependent upon the father as the mother....

Q. 2: [What attitude should the] ... husband take?

A. 2: That of the same relationships as brought about that projection of life, in love, affection, and not pampering—but in that of the attitude that brings contentment in not gratification of desire alone, but of a well-balanced condition wherein each are considered in whatever is undertaken or done.

(903-6)

Know that Life is God; Life in self, then, is God. Then the use of God in its relationships to others is to do to others what you would have others do to you, or have your *God* do to you! For as ye do it unto others ye are doing it to the God in *yourself!* Thus you are by example as well as precept making for the true relationships to Creative Forces that may aid thee from without to the influence or force of God *within* self...

Who is thy father, who is thy mother? They that do the things necessary in thy experience that ye may learn, that ye may know, thy *heavenly* Father the better.

(1436-3)

Too often we tend to minimize the thoughts, emotions, and problems that a husband allows himself to dwell on during his wife's period of gestation. They affect both mother and baby. One story that remains vividly in my memory has to do with a mother and father who were having real financial problems.

Joe was a salesman, and a good one. When Jean conceived her third child, they were really hard pressed and didn't know whether they would be able to afford another baby. Joe had his percentage on several large sales tied up in a business which was threatening to go bankrupt, and his deep depression and emotional upset continued throughout the length of his wife's pregnancy. Jean had been depressed at times, but she was in to see me often and seemed to be sailing through the pregnancy in good shape.

141

Joe's problem grew worse toward the end of the nine months—he spent some time under direct psychiatric care and wasn't in good shape when the time came for the child to be born. The delivery was normal in all respects, but one thing was wrong—the baby did not respond normally. It was as if we couldn't get her going. After three difficult days of working with her, she died from causes that were not obvious. An autopsy revealed the reasons—seven deep stomach ulcers. Joe's problem was also the infant's difficulty, and that was too much for her.

Perhaps the real chain of events included a decision by the entity itself not to come into such a situation. If one can choose which home he is going to be born into, I suppose he can also choose to change his mind, if the situation just looks too dismal for him and his needs.

Cayce had an answer that probed this problem for one woman:

Q. 10: Do emotions such as fright, excitement, etc., have any effect on the child?

A. 10: Depends upon how much of this goes beyond the real purpose of the individual entity caring for, or carrying, the child.

(457-10)

Then, in seeking to do what is constructive during pregnancy, we need to consider the emotional stresses that we come under. It is easy to take for granted that one does not eat too much salt on her food; that plenty of protein is added to the diet; that a patient does not gain too much weight and doesn't take too many fluids. But it is easy to forget that the mind must be fed all the time, and properly, or the results will be damaging. The right books should be read, the right thoughts should be encouraged; the mind as well as the body should enjoy a constructive, balanced diet.

Meditation feeds the mind in one sense, but, as we have seen, its real purpose is a movement of energy through the body to bring about a change in the individual awareness. During pregnancy, meditation becomes of even greater importance because of its implications to the infant. Steps should be taken to join with one's mate in regular daily meditations, making them a part of the daily life. Prayer and meditation during pregnancy strengthen not only the mother but also the offspring. Repeated efforts soon become a habit, and habit then becomes second nature.

Of course, one must learn to meditate just as one learns to do other things:

> ... there must be a conscious contact with that which is a part of thy body-physical, thy body-mental, to thy soul-body or thy superconsciousness. ...
>
> Then, purify thy mind if ye would meditate. How? Depending on what is thy concept of purification! Does it mean to thee a mixing up with a lot of other things, or a setting aside of self, a washing with water, a cleansing or purifying by fire or what not?
>
> Whatever thy concept is, be *true* to thine inner self. *Live* that choice ye make—*do it*! not merely say it but *do it*!
>
> Purify thy body. Shut thyself away from the cares of the world. Sanctify thy body, as the laws were given of old, for tomorrow the Lord would speak—as a father speaketh to his children. Has God changed? Have ye wandered so far away? Know ye not that as He has given, "If ye will be my children, I will be thy God." and "though ye wander far away, if ye will but call, I will hear?" And He will speak, for His purpose has been, "When ye call, I will hear, and will answer speedily." He is not far from thee. He is closer than thy right hand. He standeth at the door of thy heart! Will ye bid Him enter? Or will ye turn Him away?
>
> (281-41)

In creating the proper environment for the developing infant, it is always necessary for individuals to follow through on their choices. Both in the Bible and in the Cayce readings we find the injunction that it is sin if one knows what to do and does not do it. "Live that choice you make—*do it*! Not merely say it, but *do it*!" This is what Cayce meant, I think, in the reading quoted above. Being true to the inner self, then, is a partner to the choices one makes.

143

Choices may be based on a slight bit of ignorance—we all have that capacity and exercise it only too often. Then we have two options—to ride out our choice, which may lead us to varying degrees of karmic difficulty, or to seek guidance on the correctness of our decision. This brings us back to the subject of dreams.

Dreams that are not interpreted are like letters that are not opened. I've been told that this concept arises from the Talmud, but it is a valid and instructive statement whatever its source. Every mother would find a world of guidance in her dreams if she were to study them over a long period of time.

Having taken a direction, one can then ask for guidance, in prayer, before going to sleep. Dreams will often indicate whether one is moving in the right direction or not. This takes a bit of doing, but it frequently works. Many years ago, when we were in the market for a house, we found one that we liked and were about to make a down payment. We didn't even ask for guidance, but that night we got it anyway! Bill dreamed that he saw a house take off from the ground like an airplane. It went up several hundred feet, flew over a hill, and started to lose altitude as it approached the city. Then it went into a steep dive and crashed into the city hall. The city hall itself was not injured, but the house was destroyed.

On the basis of that dream we looked up some of the legal details concerned in the agreement and found enough information that made us give up the idea of buying the house—and we can be thankful that Bill had the dream.

During pregnancy, dreams of reassurance and dreams that aid in understanding the nature of the incoming child come to the mother. Past incarnation dreams are frequent, if they will be looked for. If the psychic quality of the dream state is probed regularly, relationships may become clearer. Sometimes highly symbolic dreams will come to a young mother illustrating the beauty and wonder of the creation of a new manifestation of God. Whether they give instruction, inspiration, guidance, or information, dreams are always a means of contacting the higher self within one's own being, and should be

144

sought as such, for their aid is a mark of the new age we are living in.

One of my obstetrics patients, Elizabeth, had been a nun. She left this calling because she just couldn't fit it into her concept of how her life should be lived. She came out West, and it was here that she met her husband, who had been in study-group work for a long time. They fell in love with each other and were married less than a year when she became pregnant. Deep in her heart Elizabeth wondered if the vow that she had taken would affect her pregnancy, and she and her husband both prayed about it. As a matter of fact, she did have a difficult time of it—going into labor and then out again—whereupon she found out that the baby was a posterior presentation. She knew that meant trouble, and she was afraid. We worked with her, however, and she relaxed. She probably gained considerable insight from this dream she had recorded earlier in her pregnancy.

> I was standing in a large open field with my husband. It was beautiful, with a clear blue, cloudless sky above, and the sun was shining down on us. I looked up into the sky, and to my amazement, saw two stars in another part of the sky, bright and shining in spite of the sun. The stars were side by side, a short distance apart, and as I watched, two shafts of intense light shown down on the field where we were standing. Greatly excited, I pointed all this out to Bob, but he just didn't see it.
>
> Next thing I knew, we were still in the field, and I felt a few drops of water fall on me, as if it had just started to rain. I looked up where the stars were—they were still bright and shining like at first—but now the shafts of light had given way and streams of water were coming out of the very center of the stars, as if they were really fountains and the water was really gushing out.
>
> Then, between the two stars, I suddenly saw appearing a point of light—a small dot that

145

gradually enlarged. As it grew larger, it started to
descend from the stars and the sky down toward
me, and I woke up, afraid.

Inspiration, beauty, promise, and reassurance come from
symbols that have had meaning since man first appeared on the
earth.

Bearing a child is a mixture of joy and pain, of love and
fear—no emotion is by itself in the pageant of life. Perhaps most
of the symbols in this dream speak for themselves, but Elizabeth knew within her heart that her love for her husband and
for the unborn child was a blessing from God that might be
likened to the vows that she took when she married her loved
one—her love is like the pure rain that falls from an unblemished sky to fructify and bless the field of divine life.

She had the baby in fine style. Her child is now a beautiful
little girl with a tremendous sparkle in her eyes and a wonderful
curiosity toward life.

Dreams in a sense are subconscious thought patterns, and like
conscious thoughts, they, too, have an effect on the unborn
child. Cayce said it like this:

> Q. 9: While carrying the child, do thoughts and impressions
> have any effect on the child?
>
> A. 9: To be sure. Thus, if surrounded with beauty, the more
> beauty there may be. Has thou not read how that when
> Mary spoke to Elizabeth, the child leaped within the
> womb?
>
> (457-10)

One of the most unusual stories relating to dreams and pregnancy involved an entire family. The children's maternal grandfather died on a January day several years ago. Within two
months of his death, the mother in the family became pregnant.

She has always had vivid dreams, and her pregnancy was no
exception. During the early months, she dreamt that she saw
her father—not sick, but rather hale and hearty—lying in the
same bed that he had used before he died. He looked rested and

peaceful, and on his lap was a little baby boy. The baby had the exact same expression on his face as Grandpa did—its face, in fact, a miniature image of his. This meant to her that her father was coming back into the family as her own son.

One of the daughters, who was then thirteen years old, knew nothing about dreams particularly, but one night she too had a very vivid dream which she related to her mother the next morning: "I dreamt that I went to Grandpa's funeral, and there were several of us there from the family. I knew he wasn't there, but everyone else said that he was. He looked at me and shook his head, and I knew he wasn't there. Then he became like a baby doll, and I put him in a paper sack and brought him home with me on my bicycle, and I knew he would be staying with us."

The baby was born on December 7 at 4:10 P.M. Grandpa had died January 7, the same year, at 4:10 A.M. But the coincidences did not end there. As the child grew, he developed strange dietary habits. He just loved a bit of coffee in his milk. Grandpa was a coffee-lover too. The old man had died of a heart condition, and because he was holding so much fluid in his body, they had restricted fluids rather severely during the last days of his life. Practically the last thing he said was, "I want a drink." Now, the mother tells me, they just can't fill up the latest addition to the family with enough water. He's thirsty!

Experiences and dreams like these certainly make life more interesting—and they give one a deeper perspective on just what life is all about. The child who is growing within the mother's womb has a destiny. We may not ourselves live to see the end of that destiny on this material plane, but we need to give it a good start and make the path as straight as we can.

OTHER RELEVANT READINGS

... there must be the keeping of the mental attitudes in a constructive manner.

(480-46)

147

Q. 25: How can the mental attitudes of the child be assisted now to make the child's future development be unusual, mentally and physically?

A. 25: That of the *proper* attitude of those responsible for the moral, physical, and spiritual development. The perfect cooperation, coordination, between the minds, brings the proper development in such conditions. One is as much responsible as the other.

(903-8)

Q. 5: Do thoughts of future mother have any direct effect or influence on soul attracted to be her child?

A. 5: This should be, as ever, left in the hands of the Creator. Prepare the self mentally and physically, and leave that to the Lord; not merely passively but actively, knowing that in the same measure ye mete to others ye mete to thy maker. Then, what manner of soul are ye attracting?

(457-10)

Let the body know, let the body comprehend, that it is being chosen as a channel for the expression of *divinity* into materiality.

(480-28)

[Let yourself be] willing that those influences of an All-Wise, All-Merciful, an All Just Creator may use the body of self as a channel for showing forth the love of a merciful *Father* to the children of men!

(480-30)

11

A CHILD IS BORN

No soul enters [this world] by
chance, but [in order] that it may
fill that it has sought and does seek
as its ideal.

(3051-2)

One pregnant woman was mildly concerned when she found that I would be out of town for two weeks, since she was due to deliver two days before we were scheduled to return. But when I saw her just before I left she told me, "Don't worry about me—I'll wait until you get back."

Well, patients are always telling me that, and then they have their babies when they have them, but this girl wasn't kidding. We returned to town on a late evening flight and got home at 11:00 P.M. Our patient had kept track of our schedules and came over to the house at about 11:15. I think she wanted to see me with her own eyes. She said, "All right. Now I can go ahead, huh?"

"Sure—it's time," I said, and then I went to bed. At 1:00 A.M., she called me. She was in labor. Into the hospital she went, and I followed. Within two hours, she had a boy.

Usually, when that baby's head comes out, we aspirate the mucus with a rubber syringe. Well, this young one opened his eyes, looked at me as if to say, "Oh, no, you don't"—and spit that mucus out as if he had been doing it all his life. Here he was, saying, in effect, "Here I am, world. I'm ready for you—are you ready for me?"

When a child is born, the world suddenly becomes different for the father, or the brothers and sisters, if any; and for the doctor, too, for suddenly he has two patients instead of one.

Mother, however, finds her world opening up into new horizons because another soul has chosen to be born, and into the world come all the hopes, aspirations, and ideals of another human being. The child may end up as king or pauper, but here he is, and he must be cared for as a baby, nurtured until he is grown, and from that point on, dealt with as another adult influence.

At this time, parents dream about their child and what his future may be. Some dreams come true, but an individual's path through life is a maze seldom perceived before it is traveled. And youngsters being born into the world today are not like they were thirty, forty, or fifty years ago. One of my patients came to me one day midway in her pregnancy with the story that several months before, when she was not even sure that she was pregnant, her deceased grandmother had appeared to her in a dream to tell her that she *was* pregnant and that she would have a boy on July 31.

I had her record the entire dream, and we waited for corroboration. On July 31, she went into labor, and after thirty-six hours she delivered a boy—but by then it was August 1. Only a strong-willed child of the new age would have stubbornly delayed his arrival like that!

These *are* children of the new age. They know what they're doing and where they're going. We don't need to acknowledge their abilities too soon, because intelligence and commitment without guidance is like love without law. Love and Law are One. So it is proper that we give guidance, direction, and control to the children placed within our care.

Today, in the hospitals where I practice, husbands are allowed to be with their wives in the delivery room. This is as it should be, for their place is beside their wives at such times. Hospitals have had rules to the contrary until recently, however. Once I was in the delivery room, helping a woman with her second child, while her husband had been directed off until the child was born and the mother returned to her room. The husband loved Bible stories, so it was this book he chose when he sat down in the waiting room.

He had just opened up his Bible at random and started to read when the nurse told him the baby was born and that it was a boy. Moments later, when he was allowed to come back and visit his wife, he came rushing down the hall, all excited, waving his Bible in his hand. He insisted we all wait there in the hall, his wife lying on her cot with the baby in her arms, while he read us the passage he had turned to while the baby was actually being born:

> *Behold, my servant, whom I uphold, my chosen,*
>   *in whom my soul delights;*
> *I have put my Spirit upon him,*
>   *he will bring forth justice to the nations.*
> *He will not cry or lift up his voice,*
>   *or make it heard in the street;*
> *A bruised reed he will not break,*
>   *and a dimly burning wick he will not quench;*
> *He will faithfully bring forth justice,*
> *He will not fail or be discouraged till he has*
>   *established justice in the earth;*
> *And the coastlands wait for his law.*
>
> *Thus says God, the Lord, who created the heavens*
>   *and stretched them out,*
> *Who spread forth the earth and what comes from it,*
> *Who gives breath to the people upon it and spirit to those*
>   *who walk in it;*
> *"I am the Lord, I have called you in righteousness,*
> *I have taken you by the hand and kept you;*
> *I have given you as a covenant to the people, a light to*
>   *the nations, to open the eyes that are blind, to bring*
>   *out the prisoners from the dungeon, from the prison*
>   *those who sit in darkness."*

We couldn't move until he had finished reading us this selection from the first seven verses of chapter 42 of Isaiah. And that baby lay there in his mother's arms and listened to the whole

151

thing, not uttering a sound the whole time. He looked as if he understood what his father was saying.

When a child is born under such a promise as that—the prophecy of the coming of the Christ—one has certain insights into what his mother and father have been doing during those days of pregnancy and preparation. Perhaps this is what is meant by starting the baby off with the right kind of an orientation, the straight kind of a path, the lighted way. From the way this child of promise lay there listening to his daddy read that passage, I knew that his soul had entered his body. My patients often ask, "When *does* the soul enter the body? At conception? At birth? When?" I answer them all differently, mostly because I think the mystery is solved only by each individual as he is born.

Cayce answered the same question:

Q. 6: Does the soul enter the child at conception or birth or in between?

A. 6: It may at the first moment of breath; it may some hours before birth; it may many hours after birth. This depends upon that condition, that environ surrounding the circumstance.

(457-10)

I remember one young girl in particular. She was barely seventeen years old, unmarried, and really having a time deciding whether she would adopt the baby out. Finally, just before her due date, she decided that she would keep it. The delivery was not difficult, and the baby turned out to be a beautiful little girl, but when I went home, I told Bill, "You know, that soul isn't *in* that baby yet. It's just a baby—it's not a real she, not a real person."

When I went back the next day, I asked the mother, "How is she?"

"Oh, it's fine."

The baby was still an *it*. I did not think the soul was there yet. In a week when I had the mother return for a checkup on the baby, her answer was still the same. Finally, six *weeks* after the birth of the child, when I checked them for the sixth time,

152

the mother reported that "She is really growing, and I think she's darling."

It took that soul six weeks to decide that she was going to get into the body. Perhaps one might say that it took that long a time for the mother to really accept the child. But the baby really wasn't *all* there during those weeks. Cayce agreed with such a concept and gave it even greater depth:

> Q.: In former reading for this entity, what is meant by "Soul and spirit took possession of this entity late in the evening," as the body was born at eight o'clock [actually 7:58 A.M.] in the morning?
>
> A.: As the entity *found* in that body in life, so the spirit and soul entered in the evening—three, four, in evening. Life is a portion of the whole *cosmic* world, and *of* the *Creative* Energy. Entities, or spirits, or soul—with its spirit, with its portion of the cosmic influence—takes *possession* as it *seemeth* that influence *it* would have. That environ it would have; for all that a soul *may* experience is *visioned* as it enters that environ for its experience. Its faith, its hope in individuals as personalities, oft is shattered!
>
> (538-30)

Sometimes a newborn baby just doesn't look like anything at all. One of our new fathers took a picture of his son immediately after he was born, and the baby was mostly just a blob. But then when he was twenty-four hours old, the boy had his second sitting. This time, he was the apple of his father's eye, and he looked like it.

At a practical level, how can one tell when the soul enters the body? We don't have psychics around most of the time to give us a lead, but when the soul is there, it seems to me that there is a light in the child's eye. When you look in a dog's eye, for instance, you know he's a dog, but when you look closely in a baby's eyes, there's a different light there, an awareness, a comprehension. You know he's a person. But until the soul and the spirit join the body, the light is missing. If you look closely, you can tell. You are psychic, too, you know. You'll see that something of his spirit manifesting in his face.

153

When the spirit-soul complex joins the body imperfectly, it's much like a hand not yet fully fitted into a glove. The ends of the glove wiggle—they are not really formed. It's not a fulfillment. Sometimes this type of partial joining remains for a lifetime, as in the case of mentally retarded or brain-injured children. This is in direct contradistinction to the children whose souls plop into their bodies and who are 100 percent in control from the word go.

Some years ago, when we joined with a group of A.R.E. people touring the world to visit famous psychics and unusual people, we heard a lecture by England's Ronald Beasley. He drew on the blackboard the various colored auras he saw around people. For the most part these lines and areas of color were harmonious—where they weren't, they represented past or future problems.

One illustration caught my particular attention because it had to do with an irregular lining up of auras that just didn't come together at the top. This, Beasley said, was a "birth defect" caused by the fact that "the soul, when the baby was born, was not properly tucked into the body." His theory is that if there is a great deal of trauma or rejection in the atmosphere, the soul senses this, and there is a real disturbance in that soul's manifestation as it is being "tucked in" during the birth process.

Perhaps we should do everything we can to assure that the soul does get tucked in as the body is born. We can bless the baby and welcome it. Some mothers have told me they can make many of their daily household chores into a prayer, simply by holding the right attitude of mind as they work. This, they say, makes even washing dishes a happy thing, because the chore puts them in communication with the Creator. These women tell me also that they are praying in that same manner when they have their babies.

The delivery room, then, is a place where God is active in the lives of many. The newborn infant deserves to be welcomed into the world with more than just a spank on the bottom. That makes him cry, of course, and expands his lungs. But if the delivery is a natural one where medications and sedatives are not used, the child is often born crying and doesn't need assistance to take that first breath.

As the first one to greet this newcomer, I've taken the position that I should offer him the best that I have. So, when he sneezes or coughs or takes his breath, I say, "God bless you."

In ancient times a place of healing was a sacred place, so I believe there is no reason why the delivery room should not have the markings of a temple, for isn't there something going on there that is directly dealing with God and His Kingdom?

Perhaps, as the mother holds the baby immediately after birth, this aids in bringing soul and body into proper alignment. This may be part of what Cayce was talking about in that last reading (538-30).

In that reading, too, Cayce's assertion that "all that a soul may experience is visioned as it enters" its new environment and opens an interesting door for consideration. We wonder what that new one saw before it was born. What were its experiences, in past lives and between lifetimes? And why did it choose a particular family in which to experience another lifetime of relationships, disappointments, and fulfillments?

There is an old parable—I believe it comes from China, but my husband claims it for a variety of cultures—that illustrates how a little child may choose a particular group for his present experiences.

A group of pilgrims were climbing a steep hill and finding the going extremely difficult. All had heavy bundles on their backs, and as the day lengthened the weight of their packs seemed heavier and heavier. One grumbled a bit here, and another complained of the heat and the heaviness of his burden. As their backs ached and their feet became sore and tired, they complained the more—and each began to look at the backpacks of his companions, thinking those were much lighter than his own.

Among the pilgrims was a very wise old man who had made this pilgrimage many times. He knew the way was difficult, and he had heard the grumbling and the complaining before. After a while, as the sun came to its zenith, the group reached a resting place, and the old man called a halt to the climb.

155

The old man told the pilgrims to place their packs in a pile against the side of the mountain. Then they were to refresh themselves, eat a light lunch, stretch themselves, and take a short rest. Then they would be prepared to go on.

As the rest time drew to a close, the old man gathered the pilgrims to him and told them, "Now, I want you each to go to the side of the mountain where you have placed your bundles and choose the one which is most attractive to you." He started with the youngest and let them, one by one, choose the burdens they would be carrying. When he finally stepped up to take his pack at the very last, the old man found that it was his own. For all the pilgrims had chosen the same pack that they had, in the midst of their grumbling, placed on the ground.

It may be that the child, when he is born, sees the large selection of backpacks on the ground there, waiting for him to make his choice. And he chooses the one that is really his—the one that he had in the beginning, before he came to this resting place.

Later on in life, if he grumbles enough about what he has chosen to carry, that wise old man who dwells within each of us may allow him to divest himself of the pack long enough to rest up. But when he continues his climb, he will again choose what is his, because that is what he needs, what he really wants.

We would assume, then, that a child comes into our family for a purpose, needing that experience to find a fulfillment in his life, to meet the problems which he needs to face so that he can grow, become more aware in his relationship to God, and climb that mountain.

Somtimes in the course of a pregnancy, there is a miscarriage or a stillbirth. The mother sometimes desperately wants a child, but it is not to be. What happens in such an instance, and why—on the basis of soul decision—does the pregnancy not go to term? In his own cryptic manner Cayce discusses this problem.

God breathes into man the breath of life, and he becomes the *living* soul.

Then, with the first breath of the infant there comes into

being in the flesh a soul that has been attracted, that has been called for, by all the influences and activities that have gone to make up the process throughout the period of gestation.

Many souls are seeking to enter, but not all are attracted. Some may be repelled. Some are attracted and then suddenly repelled, so that the life in the earth is only a few days. . . . But those mental and physical forces that *are* builded *are* those influences needed *for* that soul which does enter!

(281-53)

A few years ago, a young patient, about two months pregnant and unmarried came into my office. She had gone to three other doctors who had all suggested that she have an abortion. But she could not bring herself to have this done. In her heart Joyce believed that she needed to carry this pregnancy to term and already felt a great deal of love for the baby.

She had decided not to marry the baby's father—she did not want him to feel that obligation. Later on, if they decided to get married, that would be another situation. But now she was accepting her role as mother, with all the hardships that go with it, knowing full well all the challenges and difficulties she would go through in raising a child by herself. With this sort of an attitude, she left the office.

Three weeks later she miscarried. She was especially disturbed, feeling that she may have caused it by her former attitude. But the very acceptance of her life the way it was, and her willingness to take the consequences of her action—these were signs of real maturity and growth. At that point the law of karma was set at rest, and she came under the law of grace. Her higher self knew that she no longer needed to go through raising a child by herself—she had learned the lesson that she needed to learn, and she miscarried then without any difficulty.

There is no question but that there are physical causes why a pregnancy doesn't go to term. It is not unusual, for instance, for a young married couple to experience a miscarriage with the pregnancy. Medically, this is often due to an immature uterus which cannot carry a pregnancy; the next baby will be carried to term. But it is, I think, the same problem of a soul that

157

chooses to enter at one point in time, reconsiders, and then leaves this earth plane. Sometimes I think it is more than just the uterus that is immature. The couple themselves have not grown to the point where they are ready to become parents.

Therefore, miscarriage is something that happens for a purpose too, because those involved have lessons to learn. Sometimes it is just the mother who needs to be taught; sometimes it is the entering soul that needs to experience the first stirrings of life and then rejection.

With a pregnancy which was not completed, the soul might have been attracted but never truly joined with the body, being "suddenly repelled."

But what about the child that is to be adopted out to other parents? Does he actually choose that course in life? Is that his load to carry, or have circumstances fouled him up?

The child who is adopted out usually has an unwed mother. As we saw earlier, the question of keeping the baby is often a very difficult problem for a girl to solve properly. The battle wages back and forth inside her, sometimes bringing grief and sorrow to her and others at a much later date.

Family attitudes play a large role in this situation. In the final analysis, of course, the decision must lie in the hands of the mother, however young, for she chose all her relationships in the first place, and she grows by choosing at this point. Sometimes the choice is taken out of her hands, but again, that harkens back to the time when she chose her pack like the other pilgrims: She chose these parents as part of that particular load that looked fitting and proper for her.

This rather extensive bit of advice might be helpful to anyone who finds himself or herself involved in such a situation. All parties have a challenge, apparently.

> There should be the completion of the preparation in the mental body of the young mother for the general aptitudes, the physical preparations of mind and body, for the vicissitudes of life; or, at least one more session or season in study and associations.
>
> While, unless there is every love and precaution put about

158

the body, the mother desire will not allow such a change to come about—but this, as we find, would be the better for the body.

Then, with one that may choose to give his love, his protection, his every effort in bringing about the body the proper surroundings, proper relations (that exist deep in the make-up of a *friend;* yea, more than the friend!), the baby may be taken—as by the outward aspects of the penal law—as one with, one among, those of the household.

Then do not, under *any* circumstances, put the child in such a place that it may not *some* day know the true mother love, the true mother affection that may be its—and is *every* soul's—birthright!

Make, then, some arrangements whereby—for the one year— it may be cared for, in an institution; whereby there is given every care, every protection. But with the stipulation that at the end of the period the *mother* will claim same, under the law, as her own . . . . But let it be *definitely* settled (for this child that has suffered so in every manner) that it, the baby, *will* be her very own. Let it be embued from day to day in the mind, in the heart, that it is a living duty, a living obligation; and that the child has that right as of a soul dependent upon the activities of the body itself who brought same into being.

For, a soul is *here*—that may go *far*, in bringing much to many. *Dedicate* this precious life to a service of the Creative Forces, to God, through Him who suffered little children to come unto Him; for "of such is the Kingdom."

Else we will find it will be as a canker in the heart and mind of everyone concerned, and will *eat*—and *eat*—and rust. . . . For, face the issue! Face the circumstance, and so give the body—(4926)—that insight into the forgiveness of the Father, that she may even be able to forgive slights spoken here and there. . . . There must be thrown about the body the atmosphere that it is the *duty,* it is the obligation, for everyone who has loved and cared for her, to act in that same manner as did Him towards such relations; that they show that love in reality. As given, not condoning—but *never* condemning, in act, in word, in heart. Be the real *friend—everyone,* as ye seek for the Christ to be *your* Friend.

For, he that aideth not one who in a moment has been weak—how can he expect forgiveness and love from Him who *is* Love, and Mercy, *and Life.*

(4926-1)

159

If an entity can visualize all that he will face, then certainly we can foresee adoption as well. The people he will be living with may be the real ones he needs to be associated with. It happens with uncanny frequency that such children are the spitting image of their adoptive parents. One family we know has two adopted boys who look more like the parents than their own flesh-and-blood daughter.

Cayce gave several readings for adopted children. Two are of special interest because both these children were adopted by the same parents, and it is fascinating to see the overlapping of the lives after such a wide variation in the points of origin.

Q. 1: Has the entity in previous incarnations been related by blood or marriage to his adoptive parents, (2998) and (3107); if so, what was the relationship, giving the names of the parties and the date?

A. 1: These should be paralleled by comparisons, and we will find that they have been closely associated. The entity depends upon him from the Egyptian as well as the Persian experience. So, set him aright.

Q. 3: In the present incarnation, did the entity know that his physical parents would do no more for him than furnish his physical vehicle, and did he know that he would become the adopted son of (2998) and (3107)?

A. 3: Not as individuals. As a condition in the love of fellow man, yes.

(3340-1)

Q. 1: Has the entity in previous incarnations been related by blood or marriage to his adoptive parents (2998) and (3107); if so, what was the relationship, giving the names of the parties and the date?

A. 1: As we find very close in the Persian experience as well as in Egypt. Though its activity required much personal sacrifice, these came closer and closer together. Hence, though the entity is shy where his brother is bold, we find that these may be combined to bring the better forces in the present experience.

(3346-1)

The Bible tells how John the Baptist received his name.

160

Zechariah was a priest in the temple in Judea. Both he and his wife, Elizabeth, were advanced in age, but they both had wanted a son. While Zechariah was conducting his priestly duties beside the altar of incense, the Angel Gabriel appeared to him and told him that his wife would conceive and bear a son and that the child should be called John, and he would be great among men in the eyes of God. Zechariah knew his wife was old, so he said, "How shall I know this?" Gabriel told him that because he had not believed, he would be struck dumb until the day the prophecy should be fulfilled.

When Elizabeth did conceive and the baby was finally born, the relatives wanted to name him something other than John because none of the family bore that name. But Zechariah, who asked for something to write on, wrote down that the boy's name *would* be John, from that time on he was able to speak again.

The Bible places much stress on names—perhaps this derives from Jewish tradition, since in Hebrew, most names mean something specific.

Jesus' name was given to Mary in a vision—when Gabriel also appeared to her. The child's name had to be Jesus, "For he shall save his people" from their sins. The angel told Mary that Jesus "will be great; he will bear the title 'Son of The Most High'; the Lord God will give him the throne of his ancestor, David, and he will be king over Israel forever; his reign shall never end."

The meaning and beauty of the stories, the manner in which the instruction came about, all point to the importance of a name when one has been given an important mission in life. A fascinating study might be gained by searching out the meaning of the names of the various characters of the Bible as they act out their parts in this symbolic-historical story.

In our correspondence we hear many similar and meaningful stories. One woman wrote us that some four months before her baby was born, she dreamed that a man in white robes appeared to her. He was impressed with her devotion to her unborn child, and he was there to tell her that she should name the child Clark. This name, he said, was derived from the name *Clerk*

161

which, several hundred years ago, was used to designate a judge, priest, or learned man. Her baby was a boy, and he was named Clark.

What did Cayce have to say about naming a child? Certainly he was steeped in the stories of the Bible, having read it through every year of his adult life. His readings would be expected to reflect the attitudes found there, but he always seems to give the information in a different light.

One person wanted to change his name to a more harmonious one, hoping he might find his work in the psychic field progressing better as a result. Cayce told him: "Pray three consecutive days, or nights. On the fourth day, there will be given thee that ye shall use." (2733-2)

But perhaps his most comprehensive comment was this:

> Names, to be sure, have their meaning, but as given by the poet, a rose by any other name would be just as beautiful or just as sweet. So may such be said of these. Yet, as given by Him, names have their meaning, and these depend upon the purposes when such are bestowed upon an individual entity entering the earth's plane.
>
> Have ye not understood how that in various experiences individuals, as their purposes or attitudes or desires were indicated, had their names henceforth called a complete or full name meaning or indicating the purpose to which the individual entity or soul had been called? So, all of these have their part. They are not *all* as indicated. For *all* is one. One is all, but each individual is impressed by the various phases of man's consciousness in materiality. These, as we find, have varying degrees of effect upon the consciousness or the awareness of individuals.
>
> For, remember, the soul that is brought into the earth is only lent to thee by the Lord. And the impressions, and that purpose that ye build into that, is that ye send back to thy Maker in the end.
>
> (457-10)

OTHER RELEVANT READINGS

> Here we have a variation in the physical birth and the soul birth, of some hours.
>
> (826-2)

162

We find the soul and spirit took possession of this late in the evening. [Her mother later told her she was born at 8:00 A.M.]

(538-5)

Q. 2: What was the exact time of my soul birth?
A. 2: Almost at the same period. For the union of the activities in the bodily forces was purposeful.

(1336-1)

Only a few breaths after the physical birth. . . . And as the soul came then with a purposefulness, that "I—even I—may be able to show forth His love among those I meet day by day," there was no tarrying. For ye are learning, ye have gained, ye may apply, *"As ye sow, so shall ye reap."*

(987-4)

Names have their vibration. To be sure, names have their element of influence or force, by the very activity of the name.

(934) indicates *strength,* virility; and Tillie almost the opposite. [12/4/66: "I can see the point. Calling me Tillie always made me feel sort of cocky, and I'm not the cocky type."]

(934-7)

12

CHILDREN IN THE HOME

In these periods of unfoldment instill that of right and justice . . . the
child will grasp much from observation.

(2148-7)

Give of thy love, give of thy patience, give of thy long-suffering.
For that ye *give*, that ye possess!
That ye spend in arguments, in suggestions that are self-centered, ye
never possess, ye never retain.

(830-2)

A child has his own particular way of putting things together in his mind. One such five-year-old had just returned from Sunday school, lessons in hand, and his Sunday clothes still moderately clean. Helping him change into his play clothes, his mother asked what he had learned this morning.

"Oh, all about how God created the stars and the moon and the sun, and how He made all of us from dust and how he made the oceans and the mountains and *everything*." Then his face took on a puzzled look. "But, Mommy, I don't see how He did all that with His left hand!"

"Whatever gave you that idea?"

"Well, my teacher told me Jesus was sitting on His right hand."

I'm fairly certain that most children don't think of God as having only a left hand free, but the workings of a child's mind are intricate, and we might find a great deal of guidance toward creating a better home environment if we understood that mind a little better.

In the light of reincarnation, we look at adults as having had many past life experiences, but often we think of the children in our home as being just children. They are more than that, certainly, and we need to look at their developing life pattern. Most often, those past lives show through in the emotions, reactions, likes, and dislikes. But while we think of children as other individuals on a journey, we must also remember that it is our responsibility to care for them in the most comprehensive way we know until, gradually, they take over the reins of decisions and life-shaping activities. So we have a duality to work with—a little child who is obviously dependent upon us, and a loved entity who will someday act much like a brother or a sister. And, at any time, out of the child's mouth may come a bit of wisdom.

One story that comes to mind occurred just after we had settled down in Phoenix. Our furniture had arrived, our routines were being established, and the children were finding beautiful hiding places in the oleanders and first-rate mudholes in the backyard. Our four-year-old Bobby had been out back by himself, blissfully covered with mud up to his elbows and knees, and I had been cooking something in the kitchen. I heard the door slam and looked up. Bobby was standing there with a look on his face that was distant and happy at the same time.

"Mommy," he said, "I know somethin'."

"What do you know, Bobby?"

"Well," he said, "I know that if I make a friend, and then he makes a friend, and then he makes a friend, and then he makes a friend, it will go a-l-l the way around the world and come back to me."

The love that Bobby was talking about is the same quality of truth and law and God that we wrote about earlier. It is called the Cycle of Truth, and it makes these laws of living and the love of our fellow man one and the same thing. It points up the necessity for a parent to observe in his own life the rightness of living, and the justice and control that are all part of the same picture.

Much has been written about whether environment or

165

heredity is the strongest factor in shaping a person's life. Those who argue these points never mention the effect of past lives—probably because they need to be "scientific," and no one has proved that past lives actually occur. But allowing such a law of continuity of life, one might realize that there is much more to heredity than the genetic pattern that one gains from his parents. It would seem more likely that Bobby, for instance, spoke his four-year-old bit of inspiration from the riches of a past life, rather than from what genes we had to offer, since Bill and I had never conceived of friendship in such a manner.

As we taught our children to use their dreams, we also began to see evidences of past incarnations in some of the symbols they described. Every child, encouraged along these lines, tells me his dreams as he comes walking out of the bedroom with the sandman still in his eyes. That's how it happened that one of ours said, "Last time, when I was a baby, I was a black baby." And our Beth, who is aiming her life toward a career in the field of medicine, told me, "Last time, when I was a doctor, I was a daddy doctor, not a mommy doctor."

There are many aids we can utilize to understand our children better. Astrologically, my husband is a water sign, and with me being a fire sign, one would expect a lot of sizzling and crackling, as there has been on many occasions. As we came to understand some of these implications better, we both found how to utilize the better parts of those tendencies we brought with us and let go the not-so-helpful portions. One can't boil an egg without hot water, and that takes fire and water in the proper proportions.

We looked at the astrological signs of our boys and girls as they grew up, and we began to notice something else. Perhaps we shouldn't have thought it strange after that incident of the seven palm trees in our front yard, but our children came in symbolic order according to the raising of the life energy through the glands. First came an earth sign, then a water, fire, and air—in that order. We waited a few years and started all over again with earth and water. We *had* to stop somewhere, but knowing these things, we do know our children better.

166

But with all the possible strengths and weaknesses from past life experiences, astrological influences, and family inheritances, there is still much that can be instilled in a child between birth and twelve years of age. And these constructive or destructive patterns of living probably have more effect than all the other influences.

Cayce suggests that the story of the Chosen People in the Bible is the story of our lives. If we would know our weaknesses and strengths better, we would do well to study these characters in the Bible, identifying with them as we try to solve some of the specific problems which face us. When we are in need of faith, for instance, we could learn from a study of Abraham's experiences from the time he was instructed to leave his home in the land of Ur.

In the Bible there is a steady upward progress for the children of Israel. They moved from lawlessness to a state of order. Then they found the word of God coming to them from the prophets, telling them that there was a greater awakening for them. The advent of Jesus was the birth of the full meaning of love into the consciousness of the world. So it is with each individual, even in one lifetime, in the proper environment. Love, as manifested through parents, can change anything; that is the nature of love. Since parents know the relationship between truth, law, and love, they can set boundaries for their children, teaching them justice, rightness, faith, and understanding by living them consistently in their own lives.

From the influence of past lifetimes a child may be born as a lawless individual, or as a lawabiding infant who knows the true meaning of love and will recognize the importance of regulations in the home. He has already learned obedience and the benefits of freedom that come from it. He will abide by whatever laws are established in the home simply because one never comes to the awareness of love until he—like the Christ—fulfills the law. But the lawless one *needs* those rules to abide by.

Parents cannot expect such responses from children unless they make certain commitments themselves and measure up to whatever laws they establish in the home. One of Cayce's statements to parents is specific on this point:

> For this is the problem, that ye keep the law and present same as holy to those who seek. Who seeks? *Every* child born into the earth, from the age of two and a half to three years. . . . But ye who set yourselves as examples . . . hold rather than to anything else to that Love which is unsexed!
>
> (5747-3)

Thus, the home that parents create is either a reflection of harmony, law, and love; or one of confusion. And a child, no matter what his past life experience, can be led upward or astray by what his parents are doing. It's a challenge, isn't it?

Every person can look back on his life and see where certain decisions, seemingly minor at the time, actually gave new direction to the course of his life. In the position of guiding other individuals as they grow in the world, we parents become increasingly aware of how difficult it is to teach in any practical way except through principles of action. What are persons, anyway, except a creation of God—here to gain in awareness and move toward the Source from which we came? Thus, each little decision based on such an awareness guides one in the direction he should go.

Perhaps the safest course for parents is to teach their children to follow the laws which God has set out for mankind. The young ones may understand them better than their mother or father! Then there comes the crunch on both child and parent for good cooperation, and the real opportunity to try out what they know is right.

It is probably a universal truth that if parents try to do their best, and if they continue to learn, they will be steering a constructive and creative course for their children. For the children that come into their lives apparently have had a good preview of what they are going to have to deal with as the years go by.

One of the procedures familiar to most people who work with the Cayce material is the making up a list of ideals—physical, mental, and spiritual. Bob, at the age of ten, created such a list, and among the things he suggested as his own personal ideals were "no enimies, good health, read a page in fifteen seconds, and house with secret passages."

While he hasn't yet achieved the house, Bob did take a course in speed reading some five years later and reads more than a page in fifteen seconds. He has certainly experienced good health. But it's interesting to follow up his expression of friendship at age four which brought through an ideal of "no enimies" at age ten. When Bob was eighteen, he graduated from high school and was asked to give the benediction on the night his class received their diplomas. I happened to confiscate the copy of his prayer and save it. Part of it expands Bob's early expression into a desire that the world sorely needs at the present time:

> ... And so, O Lord, I ask that we might become more aware of, and *awake* to both our friends and our enemies, seeing in them that beautiful spirit of love and kindness we so often miss. Give us the *courage to love*—and to love everyone, both Communists and Capitalists, both North Vietnamese and South Vietnamese, both Biafran and Nigerian, both black and white. Give us the *courage to face up to ourselves* and to find peace there, and finally the courage to let that peace be part of our lives.

Bob's prayer reflects the growth of understanding one might expect from a four-year-old who knew something so important about friendship. It also puts an exclamation mark on the reading which Cayce gave about the same subject:

> Let that rather be thy watchword: "I am my brother's keeper." Who is thy brother? Whoever, wherever he is, that bears the imprint of the Maker in the earth, be he black, white, gray or grizzled, be he young, be he Hottentot, on the throne or in the president's chair. All that are in the earth today are thy brothers.
>
> (2780-3)

So understanding of children grows as one searches for it and begins to understand himself. A closer relationship develops which makes living together a joy and a breathless, exciting adventure. And as the adventure progresses, I'm sure every mother finds the increasing value of faith. Believing that "all things work together for good to those that are called according to His purpose," both parents instill ideals and purposes in their children and can wait to see their faith bear fruit.

As a child grows he needs advice and counsel, but there is always a point where a growing child's developing ability to choose must be allowed to exercise itself. Where we must call a halt to our advice, we must exercise faith. It was at this point that a mother giving her twenty-year-old son too much advice was given attention in a reading:

> While the desire of the mother to aid is natural, is right, there must be the realization that the individual has his own life to live—and that even the great desire to aid may at times become a stumbling block to another individual.
>
> Then the greater aid is to counsel as respecting his purpose, his ideal.
>
> For each soul enters the material plane for the manifesting of its individual application of an ideal in respect to the Creative Forces or Energies.
>
> Each soul is then endowed by its Maker with that of choice, with that birthright.
>
> And to live another's life, and to direct or counsel even—other than that which is in accord with that of choice, is to become rather a hindrance than an aid.
>
> Hence the prayers of self, the counsel of self as respecting those things that are ideal in relationships to Creative Forces.
>
> For there are no shortcuts to knowledge, to wisdom, to understanding—these must be lived, must be experienced by each and every soul.
>
> In counsel then, let thy yeas be yea and thy nays be nay. . . .
>
> And though our physical relationships may oft have the experiences or appearances of the desires for a *material* advantage, for a material success—unless the soul and the real desire is founded in patience, long-suffering, gentleness, kindness—and most of all *sincerity*—we become stumbling blocks to others.
>
> (830-2)

The simple rules that can help a parent guide children in the home might also keep a nation stable while it's in rough water.

Deal in commitments, not promises. A *commitment* is a promise that has certain foregone actions attached. A commitment is the sort of thing that one goes through with; you can't back out of it or forget it. It's something like having a child—when you are a father, you can never *not* be a father. You are committed, whether you like it or not.

A better example of going all the way is when a woman gets pregnant and decides to go through with it. That's a commitment. When you tell your children you're going to do something and follow through on it every time, you are working with commitments, not promises.

We heard two young boys throwing a baseball back and forth. The older one kept throwing the ball past the little fellow, and he always apologized for it. Finally, I heard his younger brother say in exasperation, "You always say you're sorry. It's not enough to say you're sorry. You need to throw the ball straight."

When children are promised anything, it needs to be done. If there is the possibility that a promise might not be kept, they need a prior explanation. We have tried always to tell our own children that we are in the practice of medicine, and, if an emergency comes up, that takes precedence over what we have promised to do. They need that sort of understanding, for commitments breed security and constancy, while empty promises bring frustration and rebellion.

Consistency is a second cousin to commitment. However, it is regular in action. If I clean the kitchen and wash dishes every night, the consistency with which I do this is a lesson for the children. If I tell them they must do a certain job or suffer the consequences, they will learn more by suffering the consequences should the job not be done. This also is consistency. Words and action should go together.

When you tell your children that it is good for them to have prayer and meditation as part of their lives, be certain that it has already been established as part of yours, or your words and actions are at odds with each other.

171

Teach your children to choose. Choice is a gift to man from God, and it should be dealt with as such. The child needs to know that he has this ability, and as he grows and becomes more aware, he needs that opportunity to make his own choices—but not until you have chosen yourselves—wisely, you hope—shown him how, and then taught him how.

Many young people are never given this instruction, and they move away from their parents, leaving hurt and confusion behind them. One girl of eighteen, the daughter of a sincere but confused school teacher, told her mother that she didn't believe in the type of God her mother thought existed. Often young people like this are rebelling against what they find in society. Many are idealists who are crying out to understand a God of compassion and love, but they just haven't seen this in the world around them. They reject the hypocrisy of so many who make up society as it is today. They are exercising their power to choose, but not really understanding what choice is based upon or even where they got that ability in the first place.

If there are to be sides chosen, or if a battle line is to be drawn, don't allow yourself to be on one side taking pot-shots at your children. Be a buffer, be a guide, stay on their side. If there are to be battles, let those battles bring you closer to the other members of your family whom you are trying to aid and assist—don't let them bring sorrow and grief to all. Nothing but good can come from the parent choosing rightly in this instance.

We often don't think of it as such, but when one corrects a child, he is placing himself on one side and pointing the finger at the other. This brings its own rewards, and they are usually not good. Cayce talked about this, and his advice is not easy to follow:

> Quit the correcting, but *demonstrate* in rather the pointing to others but not holding it a fault in the body; but pointing to those whom the body considers as examples, or those it would like to be like! But do *not* continue to call attention to the fault! This creates in the *mind* of the body resentments, and will build conditions that will be hard to overcome.
>
> (608-10)

172

Stimulate your child's creativity. When our daughters grew old enough, we encouraged them to play with their doll houses and dolls. We know how much this helps in stimulating the urge to experience a healthy and fulfilling motherhood. Let the little boys play in tree-houses and build castles in the sand, let them look at the stars at night and dream their dreams. Urge them to build bridges, houses, and machines with their toy sets. Imagination is part of the building of the mind.

Above all, teach God through nature. Let them see how wonderful it is for a mother robin to tend her nest. Let them see the beauty of a plant that grows from a seed that they have planted in the earth.

We have two Samoyeds. Khushi, the male, was three years old when Fluffy was introduced into the family. All of our children were excited when Fluffy became pregnant. We even let them stay home from school for the big event. And when seven puppies were born, one after the other, all of our children were there, helping out, taking care of the new ones, their eyes wide with excitement. After I trained our two oldest boys in the intricacies of delivering puppies, and after I had missed a staff meeting and was half an hour late for appointments at the office, I left things in the hands of our children. Such wonders in a simple event!

Perhaps we have become too blasé in our society today. Because conception and birth happen so often, we have forgotten what a miracle it is for a mother to have a child. Watching these puppies coming into the world, and then seeing them develop into full maturity, has brought back some of the wonder that makes living such an adventure; some of the sense of God's purpose in giving us children to care for and to love.

In working with the children in our home, most of the things that need to be considered are based on principles and laws which have existed since the beginning of creation itself.

That which we have called the lighted way, however, always assumes a most important and powerful role, for we are building a world as we help children to grow to maturity. Cayce put it into a capsule when he gave this advice:

Train ye the child when he is young, and when he is old he will not depart from the Lord. Train *him*, train *her*, train *them* rather in the sacredness of that which has come to them as a privilege, which has come to them as a heritage; from a falling away, to be sure, but through the purifying of the body in thought, in act, in certainty, it may make for a peoples, a state, a nation that may indeed herald the coming of the Lord.

(5747-3)

OTHER RELEVANT READINGS

Q. 1: Can I nurse the baby? Are there any precautions or preparations to assure this possibility?

A. 1: To be sure, this—the nursing of the baby—would be the ideal way and manner. As to what may be done, much might be indicated in these directions; that is, in having and in keeping the body physically fit, with the well balanced chemical reactions through the body during the period of pregnancy.

Q. 2: Does this depend on physical characteristics of the body or the condition, which can be affected by proper food and exercises?

A. 2: The attitude, so far as the mental is concerned, must be builded within the body. And with that attitude there will be the desire and purpose, *and* the preparation by the keeping of the correct balance for same, as has been indicated.

(457-9)

Q. 13: In what way can I create a more harmonious attitude in guiding my older son, David?

A. 13: In these respects there can be the best direction by counseling with, though never forcing: though there is the necessity here of being quite positive. This is the better manner of creating harmony. But counsel with, not argue with.

Q. 14: What should be my attitude when David shows an argumentative or closed mind on certain subjects?

A. 14: Counsel with, and leave it there—but be positive that self is right and keep in that attitude.

(903-33)

... It would be well that each ... not attempt to find their differences but rather that upon which each *can* agree. There *are* agreements in some directions. There are differences in many; yet . . . it is *not* by chance that there is this union of activities in the present; but if each will accept same it is an opportunity through which each may be the gainer in the soul, mental, as well as material development.

If they each reject the opportunity . . . it becomes sin, and *must* eventually be met.

Then, there is *every* reason for the *attempt*, at least, for each to meet these differences and so little—save self, and selfishness—that prevents the attempt to at least meet the problems in the present.

(263-18)

. . . All of the God ye may know lies within thyself. Do teach the entity that, and to communicate oft with such. For thy body is indeed the temple of the living God and there He may meet thee. Do train the entity in these directions.

(4081-1)

Areas for Working with Children as Suggested in the Edgar Cayce Readings

(1) *Reason with the child; don't break the will.*
   . . . If there is the proper manner used for the activities with the entity, coercion or the breaking of the will or demands will not be made. For we find that cooperation may be had with the entity if there is love, and the practical answering as to *why* do this, *why* do that. . . . *Do not* answer the entity, especially in the early teen years, by saying "Because I said so," or "Because it is right," but explaining *why* you said so, and *why* it is right.

(1401-1)

(2) *Teach by precept and example.*
   In the periods of unfoldment instill that of right and justice. . . . And in the precepts given, live them in thine own experience . . . for the entity will grasp much from observation.

(2148-7)

(3) *Teach them the beauty of sex.*
   . . . Train ye the child when he is young, and when he is old he will not depart from the Lord. Train *him*, train *her*, train *them* rather in the sacredness of that which has come to them as a privilege, which has come to them as a heritage; from a falling away, to be sure, but through the

175

purifying of the body in thought, in act, in certainty, it may make for a peoples, a state, a nation that may indeed herald the coming of the Lord.

(5747-3)

(4) *Segregate the children who are spiritually inclined from those who are materially inclined.*

... If, or rather has the stress been laid upon the material or the objective lessons of life that are presented to them, then the necessity of segregation is in order ... these—to be sure—present in themselves many conditions that make for combativeness; yet these would be well to be kept in their own respective spheres of development.

(5747-1)

(5) *Bring out the creative and the imaginative.*

... develop its imaginative forces rather than the material or objective forces.

(5747-1)

... various types of dolls that may appeal to the developing in childhood towards motherhood. Few have considered as to the helpfulness dolls have been towards motherhood in any land.

(1436-4)

(6) *Use the power of prayer.*

He that would know the way must be oft in prayer. ...

(281-12)

(7) *Teach God through nature.*

Q. 3: How is the best way to explain God to a child under twelve years of age?

A. 3: In nature.

(5747-1)

(8) *Use the power of attitude and the power of suggestion.*

... Keep a spiritual atmosphere, not as of rote but as of promptings within would be well.

... [There should not be] an imposing of the personalities one upon another, but rather as of a guiding hand in those things as they unfold ... in its every phase of its life.

(1177-1)

(9) *Do not always question too closely the source of the child's information.*

176

And little may be told the entity of the stories of the Scripture that it cannot tell you more than you will tell the entity! ... *Do not question* the entity as to the sources of his information. *Do not correct* the entity as to that given, but keep a detailed record of what is given.

(2547-1)

(10) *We should be careful not to treat children as inferiors in certain ways, bearing in mind that as souls they have had as much experience as we.*

... the soul is as the Holy Spirit. For it is eternal. It has ever been and ever will be.

(5246-1)

(11) *Make spiritual laws practical.*

Training in the way of an *ideal,* and the purposes of the ideal—as it may enfold and unfold in the life of an individual—is to give such an one that basis upon which they will build their lives, as life in its many phases unfolds as daily experiences of the entity.

(276-2)

13

PARENTHOOD

We would minimize the faults, we
would magnify the virtues. For we
have many of each. And the greater
injunction may be: don't think
more highly of yourself than you
ought to think. . . . Think well on
these things.

(3640-1)

We have a big, rambling, white adobe home in Phoenix, surrounded by a lot of green grassy lawn. Over the years the lawn has been an opportunity for our boys to learn self-discipline, work habits, and how to be helpful around the home.

From the time Carl, the eldest of our six, was very little, he had a knack for losing tools—especially his dad's tools. It once got to the point where Bill gave Carl all the tools he had left—so that if any more tools were to be lost, they would be Carl's, and not his. Perhaps this lesson did help, but when Bill got a few tools that he really needed, he hid them in his clothes closet so that no one could find them.

One day when he was just fourteen or fifteen years old, Carl was out mowing the lawn. Having finished one section, he wanted to take a break, so he left the rotary lawn mower out where he had stopped it, which happened to be near the street. The television interfered with his intent to return at once, and it was afternoon before he went out to resume his chores.

I heard the rest of the story about four o'clock when I came home from the office. "Mom, you'll never believe it, but I lost the lawn mower!"

178

"You what?" I asked, hardly believing my ears.

"Well, I left the lawn mower out in the yard this morning and forgot about it until this afternoon, and now it's gone. Maybe someone stole it. What'll we do?"

I told Carl I didn't know, but we'd have to tell his father about it when he got home.

I met Bill at the door, took him into our bedroom so we would not be disturbed, and said, "Carl *really* pulled a boner this time." We sat there, discussing just what is right in such a situation. Should we punish Carl by grounding him? Should we require him to work enough extra time to pay for a new mower?

Finally, Bill said, "You know, if the home is supposed to be a shadow of the heavenly home, as Cayce says it is; and if the father is in a sense a real earthly symbol of the Heavenly Father, then really I should try to do what God would do. If God has forgiven me for all the horrible things I've done in this lifetime, then certainly the least I can do is to forgive Carl for losing something that can always be replaced."

This solution fit our philosophy, and we agreed that this should be our course of action. So we went out to the dining room, and supper was put on the table.

Carl was sitting next to his Dad. He had lost his appetite and was just sort of fiddling with his food. Finally he said, "Dad, did Mom tell you what happened?"

"Yes."

"Uh-I lost the lawn mower—"

"Yes, I know. Your mother told me."

Carl was sitting there, trying to eat, but he couldn't. Finally, he asked, "Dad, what are you going to do about it?"

"Your mother and I have talked about it, Carl, and we've decided that I should forgive you."

Carl was visibly shaken. He didn't know quite how to handle this.

"What do you mean, you're going to forgive me?"

"Well, it's this way, Carl. I'm a human being as well as a father, and I've pulled some pretty big boners in my own life.

179

God, as my Heavenly Father, has always forgiven me, no matter what I've done. I figure that the least I can do, as your father, is to forgive you for losing a lawn mower. So, I forgive you."

By this time, all our other children were talking about something else—it hadn't affected them much. But Carl just sat there. He couldn't finish his dinner and finally excused himself. As I passed by the living-room phone stand, I heard him talking to his friend, Doug, on the telephone. "Man, I'd rather he'd beat me—I don't know what to do. There he sits, and he says he forgives me, and he means it." There were tears in Carl's eyes.

Well, the years have passed, and Carl has grown up, of course. He perhaps now looks at this event from the other side of the family situation, as a dusty page in time's history book. But it was a growing experience for him, as it was for his mother and father.

In approaching the idea of parenthood, it would be proper to deal with the role of the parents as a unit, for as Cayce so aptly pointed out, All is One. So the parents are one and should in all respects act as one. It is because we don't understand ourselves, or our goals, or our ideals in life that we too often act as two.

A clear goal is achieved if both parents direct their activities toward it. Unity of purpose not only brings more results as they act in the capacity of parents, but it also implants in their children's minds the concept of oneness which is always a constructive, coordinating factor. Creating this sort of a pattern allows each individual to act as an individual, yet with a relationship to others based on the true relationship of oneness.

In the unconscious mind of man, the male and the female represent the positive and the negative, the two aspects of the atom which make it a capable building block for the universe itself. The right and the left hand, the day and the night, the heavens and the earth are some of the aspects of duality which, when taken together, make for wholeness. One without the other lacks expression, as in the familiar image of one hand clapping.

We use or abuse this truth every day as we are teaching our children. If one parent tells his children always to be honest and

180

to tell the truth to their friends and school teachers, and the other parent instructs them when the doorbell rings to "Tell them I'm not here," then, indeed, there is no unity in expression, and the children are taught confusion, not oneness.

If the parental role is to be fulfilled, words and actions must go together like husband and wife. If a father were to tell his son that smoking is bad for him while he himself was lighting a cigarette, the actions would speak so loudly that the words would remain unheard. Teaching comes about through precept *and* example, and one is to some extent incomplete without the other.

Cayce always implied the workable principle that children are taught even better by example than by words. If one must make a choice, he should probably *live* what he wants to teach his children and keep his mouth shut.

Nevertheless, there are laws, rules, regulations, and suggestions for guiding people into a better life, and they take effect in the children's lives when parents clearly speak about them. It's like Thumper of the Disney movie *Bambi,* whose most famous saying was, "If you can't say somethin' nice, don't say nothin' at all!" That's another way of magnifying the virtues in another person and minimizing the faults, a rule that can well be used at the dinner table. By themselves, parents can practice the rule on each other. Magnified faults never help a relationship; they only build walls and barriers that so frequently bring dissolution to relationships, whether in a marriage relationship or between parents and child. But a constant recognition of the better points of another shows love in one of its aspects, creating happiness and, once again, a unity.

As parents find their relationship growing over the years, as their children develop from infants to mature adults, they find a unity undergirding all their activities which helps them act as one and be of service to many. One of Cayce's readings implied this state of affairs:

> For life and truth and understanding, and happiness, in its greater sense, are but a growth. For ye grow in grace,

in knowledge, in understanding. And knowledge without wisdom is indeed a dangerous thing!

Then . . . as ye have applied that ye have gained, so does the ability come to be of that help, that aid to those who are stumbling—some blindly, some gropingly, some discouraged, some overanxious, some overzealous of their own peculiar twist or turn; yet all seeking—seeking the light.

(1301-1)

Perhaps fifteen years ago, a father was under treatment in our office for ulcers of the stomach. He was an industrial chemist, and his wife was a full-time mother. Not only was his ulcer acting up, but his blood pressure was sky high, and he was as nervous as the proverbial cat on a hot tin roof.

His real problems came out in bits and pieces. His son was seriously dating a girl that neither parent could see as a potential bride for him. She was from an "inferior" family, did not have their son's education, and wasn't in the least attractive in their eyes. Actually, the father was much more adamant in his point of view than the mother, who was disturbed about the situation, but quiet in the discussion. (She also had no ulcer.)

For years, father and son had been having pitched battles about his interest in racing cars. While the boy was given enough money to build a racer from scratch, he was denied permission to race it. As the story evolved, it seemed that both parents were at home much of the time, but spent a great deal of that time in arguing and taking opposite sides in a variety of subjects.

My position as a working mother has made me very sensitive to the *quality* of parenthood. I didn't have enough time to give it as much *quantity* as these folks did.

When I grew up in India, my father was often away from home for two or three months at a stretch. But during those times we never felt that we were fatherless, for we knew that Dad loved us and that we were secure in that love. That has been the way Bill and I have felt: It doesn't really matter how much time we actually spend in the home. I've always believed that where your treasure is, there will your heart be also, so my heart—my love, my concern, my kindness, my forgiveness, my willingness to do for others—has always been in my home. For our home is where our treasure is, and our love resides there to make it a unit. And the children know it and feel the quality of the time spent there.

When our Johnny was just thirteen years old, he attended summer camp in Virginia Beach and filled out a questionnaire designed to bring out of the young people certain feelings and thoughts that might otherwise be hidden. For instance, question 6 was: "I wish my parents knew—" and a blank was left to be filled in. We read his answers with a bit of trepidation, because no matter how parents try, there are always failures here and there, and we just aren't anxious to see where we fall short. But we read it.

Some of his answers are revealing in terms of the idea of quality of time spent in the home as it compares with quantity.

Here are some of the questions and John's answers (which I've put in quotations):

> My brothers and sisters "are nice sometimes."
> When I read math "I feel sick."
> I don't know how "to do a lot of things."
> When I have to read, "I read."
> I like to read "the Bible."
> I wish I could "handle a situation my own way."
> On weekends I "read the Bible."
> I wish my parents knew "how I feel sometimes."
> I wish my mother "would be home when I go home from school."
> I wish my father "would help me more often."
> To be grown up "means to act right."
> I would like to be "at home right now."

His answers pulled at our heart-strings because no parent wants to fall short of what their children want of them. But the fact that he wanted to be "at home right now" gave us reassurance. No parent is perfect, no child is perfect, but the spirit of every individual recognizes when another soul is trying to move

183

things in the right direction, and home was where John wanted to be. That's where his treasure was.

The father in the earlier story, who was at odds with his son, made the mistake of building barriers during the time he spent at home. He gave the home a lot of time, but it was warfare, and warfare always kills something—this time, his relationship with his son. Choosing up sides for the daily fight produced the inevitable. The boy left home, left his inheritance, married the girl, and has lived these many years without contacting his father and mother. They are alone.

Parents whose time—no matter how little—is spent in quality relationships with their children and with each other—will be listening to one another, helping one another, magnifying the virtues and minimizing the faults.

Parents who have moved in this direction and established a viable unity discover that they are agreeing with their children in many ways, establishing inroads of communication and trust. They find that young people are trying out their wings most of the time anyhow and need the exercise in expressing their opinions, if only to find out whether they were wrong or right.

Rules are helpful in setting up routines, but in considering the problems or opportunities present in the family, principles, rather than rules, must often be the guide. This is especially true when teaching children about creative energy—sexual energy and its use.

When our eldest son Carl was twelve, he was home sick from school one day, suffering silently with his cold. Bill and I hadn't really had an opportunity to talk to him about sex except in the context of creative energy and meditation, and I thought this would be a good chance. So I brought home one of the booklets that we keep in our office for young people that tells about sex in a gentle, yet physiological way.

When I came home from the office the next day, Carl was up and about and back to his normal self. I went to his room and looked for the booklet, but I couldn't find it.

"Carl, what happened to that book I gave you?"

"Oh, you mean *that* book? I got rid of it. I don't think the

184

kids ought to be reading that stuff." Carl was exercising his position as leader of the pack. He knew this stuff, but the younger ones should not be exposed!

Nothing in the parent-child relationship is as difficult as the proper guidance and instruction about sex. We have tried to teach our own children through the example of the movement of energy in meditation; through seriously answering all question, no matter how foolish they may seem on the surface, when they arise; and through the lessons one learns in nature.

Through our experiences in the field of medicine, we have attempted to make the birth of a child appear to be a beautiful thing. We relate a child's secondary sexual changes at puberty to some of the internal physiological developments occurring at the same time. But we have never really believed in instructing our children about the detailed physical aspects of sexual intercourse, simply because we believe that most of this is instinctive in the first place. When two people are to be married, there are books that cover this subject well.

It is an interesting fact that sex, which probably has caused more problems and heartaches than any other emotion, is also given less honest study. It is almost universally agreed that we need to know more about it, but the big question is: "*What* do we need to know?"

As the child goes into the age of puberty, there is an awakening of the sexual glands and their activities. At the same time, according to the data in the Cayce material, a host of memories from past lives relating to the emotions of that particular glandular center enter into the individual's active subconscious mind. Each gland is a storehouse of memory and retains memories of emotional relationships associated with the influences of that particular gland.

So, at puberty, there really *is* an awakening! And, especially in these formative years, the child should receive instruction in the care of the body and its sexual functions and in the preservation of its relationship to the Creator of all things.

Perhaps the subject of homosexuality does not belong in a book dealing with the home, marriage, and children. However, like abortion and divorce, homosexuality *is* found there occasionally and should be considered—in other words, what do we do with it or about it?

We read much about this condition in our practice of medicine, but one prevalent thought is that homosexuality is the most common serious disturbance in sexual identity. It is considered a medical problem, and in our experience has always been a disturbing element within the individual presenting himself for our assistance.

If followed to the extreme, of course, homosexuality prevents the establishment of a home such as we have been talking about. The sexual desire of man for man or woman for woman can bring about sexual gratification, but offspring cannot come of such a union. In our created universe there is a duality which cannot be denied.

In· the story of creation, God created man and woman—again the duality, with testosterone dominant in one and estrogen in the other. Things tend to polarize or migrate, like iron shavings in a magnetic field. The duality of things is found in our concepts of how the world is put together—we have the north and south poles, the heavens and the earth, the yin and the yang of oriental thought, the right and the left, the positive and the negative electrical charge in the atom which permits the formation of the universe, and the male and the female, about which we must center our thoughts as we consider homosexuality.

As one searches the Bible for guidance, he is led very clearly to the idea that it was sexual deviation, principally homosexuality, that brought Sodom and Gomorrah to be utterly destroyed by fire and brimstone. But every soul has come into the world for a purpose. Each individual has within the dusty memories of his being a need which must either be fulfilled now or put off until later. But eventually, the soul must face that need.

All our experiences as practicing physicians, our religious studies, those relationships that have occurred in our home, and extensive information available in the Edgar Cayce readings suggest that there is an equality of all souls, having been created in

186

the beginning by an All-Wise Creator. But we have entered the earth, and we have each creatively designed our own experiences. In the process, we have fashioned the life, body, awareness, and desires that we are experiencing at the present time. This, we believe, is true for all of us. Thus, such a consideration must be granted these people whom we label homosexual. What they are experiencing in the present they have created through desire and activity.

Those who have studied reincarnation extensively find a reason why one would come into the present life with these desires—abnormal, in that their expression is not constructive in the movement of creative energy. When one lives a lifetime as a female, perhaps a number of such lifetimes, and then is born as a male, he has a possibility of retaining a lot of female characteristics. This would make him more feminine than most of his friends and would give him the innate attraction to the male of the species—another type of holdover from the past.

Such an explanation leaves a lot of questions unanswered. Doesn't it put the blame outside the individual, on those forces which caused him to be born as a male this time? It leaves aside our premise that man is a creation of God, given the ability to choose. And nothing in creation is stronger than the will of man. If God had created man with a will that could be completely manipulated, even by Him, man could not have had the opportunity to *choose* to be a companion to God. He would have been a puppet; and thus, assuming that God has free will, he would *not* have been created in God's image.

It is perhaps on this basis of free will that homosexuality can be understood and dealt with. For then this problem must be laid at an individual's own doorstep—it becomes his own to work with, his own problem to solve. And it assumes the nature of a problem since it keeps him from experiencing the relationship with his Creator which was intended in the beginning.

The Cayce material gives a unique insight into people's lives. From the standpoint of Cayce's unconscious mind, every entity was just as precious as another, and to those who asked him questions he always had encouragement, advice, and understanding.

The Cayce readings suggest that the individual who follows homosexual tendencies has lost his way, has established practices and desires which lead only to turmoil, confusion, and despair. But the person afflicted with confusion about sexual urges was no different to Cayce than the husband erring in not caring properly for his family or the elderly woman suffering with cancer of the uterus. All were in need of assistance, and Cayce did his best to help. His readings searched out what he called the *records* of these people, and the information was almost always highly meaningful.

There are only four people indexed in the files at Virginia Beach who requested help for homosexuality. Two were men in their forties. Both, interestingly, were given suggestion to have treatments involving the use of low electrical energy, but only *after* the mind was clarified as to the direction they would be taking.

The first was told to seek a psychiatrist who could offer him strong suggestive therapy leading him away from contact with other homosexuals; then he should have the other treatments. The second was told to study spiritual truths; to learn Matthew 5 by heart; and study and then live the ideas found in John 14 and Romans 12.

A young man in his early twenties was told:

> There is nothing impossible for the entity to attain in fame or fortune or in its spiritual unfoldment and yet these will *not* be easy until the entity has conquered self.
>
> (5056-1)

This "conquering of self" apparently means that he needed to put his physical emotions in their proper place, under the control of the higher self within, so that the mental and spiritual emotions would take their place. Case 5056 was told that he should tie himself down to a specific job for a year, and save every penny that he made except what he needed for bare living expenses and music lessons. He should create physical hardships for himself—"Sleep on a hard, hard bed. Don't eat too much, don't indulge in things such as sweets or add to the body nor

188

engage it in those activities in which the movies (such as are shown today) are a part of the activity. Refrain from same. Oft go for days only on bread and water, but do it of thyself if ye would succeed, and ye may become even a greater pianist than Hoffman [Hauptmann?]." He was told *not* to get married before he was thirty-two and to study only the piano.

Where did such tendencies arise that required such difficult and stringent measures? It adds insight into this man to look at one of his previous incarnations:

> Then, as indicated, we have those unusual experiences in the earth by the entity and the definite urges which are at variance to the general activities in the sex relationships. For in the experience in the Atlantean land, the entity sought to be both and wasn't very successful at either.
>
> Before that we find the entity was in the Atlantean land and in those periods before Adam was in the earth. The entity was among those who were then "thought projections," and the physical being had the union of sex in the one body, and yet a real musician on pipes or reed instruments.
>
> (5056-1)

Balance within the body, then, became necessary for this person—bringing him more to the acceptance of his normal sexual male tendencies. Then, from the scant correspondence available, he did apparently overcome much as the years passed by and did become an accomplished pianist in the classical field.

The fourth man was nineteen years of age when he got his first of several readings. His problem was not an overt one apparently; and he was gifted with a psychic ability which was causing him some difficulty. Cayce felt close to this boy, having been associated with him in some capacity in a past life. In answer to one of his letters, Cayce answered in part—and this was the conscious man this time, giving of his thoughts and assistance:

> ... the real work, you will have to do yourself. Study the paper very closely on Meditation and apply it in your own way and manner, and you will get a real awakening and one that will help.

189

Sex, of course, is a great factor in everyone's life, it is the line between the great and the vagabond, the good and the bad; it is the expression of reactive forces in our very nature; allowed to run wild, to self-indulgence, becomes physical and mental derangement; turned into the real influence it should be in one's life, connects man closer with his God, and that is the use you should put it to. That the expression of same becomes *psychic* in its nature is true, and the visions the body experiences is that the mind holds as its ideal, its goal to attain. The call has always been to every man and woman: "If ye will be my people, I will be your God." We as individuals have to accept that challenge. We say we believe it, then the only thing to do is to act like it. We are all "Gods in the making" for we seek to be one with Him even as the Son, Jesus Christ, who has said and promised, "that ye do and ask in my name, that will ye do, for as I abide in the Father and ye in me, so may the Father be glorified in the earth." If we let our minds run to baser things, then we lose sight of His Power working in us, for man alone can and does defy God. His love is ours if we will use it, but in relying on self or depending alone on man-made things we lose sight of His promises, and thus lose our way in the maze of conflicting emotions that arise through the experiences that confront us. But if we hold fast to His love we grow in grace and knowledge and understanding, for the Godly life is a growth; not a cloak put on and taken off, but a growth.

That your experience has brought you manifestations that have at times, or often, expressed themselves in sex is not to be wondered at, when we realize that that is the expression of creative life in the earth. But if we lose sight that it is an expression of God and accredit it to something else, we deny the very promises He has made us all.

Study over the reading, (1089), read with it the 14th, 15th, 16th, and 17th chapters of St. John; then read Romans 12, and you will catch a vision of what has been promised and how it may be fulfilled in your own experience.

That you have been shown in vision, in many mysterious ways, is still proof of what has been said by the Psalmist: "He will give His angels charge concerning thee, lest at any time you dash your foot against a stone." But if we continue to deny the faith, well, He departs—or rather we accept some other way.

While he was awake, Cayce's view of the individual seeking his way in the earth was not different from what he expressed at a different level of consciousness.

190

Perhaps, again, it would be the choice of the individual as to whether he continues in a path that denies the nature of creative energy as we have gradually understood it—or whether he sees how he can choose the path which, ultimately, his own soul would choose.

Training in her early years may have been missing for Marian. She had trouble not only with her heterosexual desires, but with drugs. From the age of fifteen on, her activities created a great division between her parents and herself. She found in her friends what she apparently could not find at home, but her mother refused to condemn her—or in fact, to do anything except maintain that sooner or later the standard of beliefs that she and her husband had kept as parents would bring the girl back home. While their daughter was at the time highly unstable, the mother insisted that she and her husband had to maintain their stability. So the two of them loved Marian, tried hard to understand what she was saying by her actions, and waited. After a long two and a half years, Marian left the drug culture, came back home, found what she needed there, and is now in college, looking forward to a nursing career.

Training comes in setting the example, of course, as Marian's parents did. They never fought their daughter, never turned their back on her, never took sides between themselves on the question. They waited, with patience, for what they knew would happen. One of Cayce's readings must have been talking about Marian's parents:

> For it is a unison of desire that brings a seeking at any time for expression, and *not* in *combative* reactions at all! For when there is the combative self-assertion, egotism and selfishness rise to the forefront *as* that ordinarily known as self-protection —which is a first law.
>
> If the world will ever know its best, it must learn cooperation!
>
> For remember, the mind and the body is a growing thing. Grow with same!
>
> Unless that growth is apparent, then the parent becomes to the growing mind a "back number," and out of date. . . .

191

To deny or to build a barrier between one parent and another in its correction, then this again builds a barrier. And they (the children) cannot love two masters. They (the parents) must be one!

Well that the world would learn that given of old, "Know (O parents) O Israel, the Lord, thy God is one!"

(759-12)

It is probably a healthy course of action to think in terms of preventing problems rather than of solving them once they have occurred.

Cayce was giving a reading for a ten-year-old, the age group that he talked about as needing instruction for living. And if the next extract had been given to Marian when she was ten years old, perhaps her attempt to find her way would not have been necessary.

So think ye on these things, and begin where the light begins—and that is within thine own heart and mind, as ye read, as ye study, as ye talk with the Lord of thy heart. . . . He asks and entrusts to thee thy place to be fulfilled by thee to His glory, His honor, and then will there be peace, harmony, happiness into thy life experience throughout. . . .

Remember, He has given thee father, mother, home, opportunity. . . . And the meanest, the littlest man in the world is one who is unappreciative of what has been done, what is being done. That is why, when he forsakes God [he] feels so low, [he] becomes so little in his own sight.

(2780-3)

Unity between all members of a family lets barriers and walls be built elsewhere. When a real problem arises in the young life under their care, the parents become the first ones to be consulted. And their advice is valued because it comes from demonstrated love. Those ideas, confessions, and secrets brought to a parent are offered in the confidence that they will be treated with gentle understanding. Cayce said it like this:

This should be kept inviolate. But let rather this be answered from the Giver of those opportunities, these privileges that are in the experience of father and mother. For

192

those that may be lent them are of the Lord. Let such associations, let such desires be "Not my will but Thine, O Lord, be
done *in* and through me."

(939-1)

It might also be said that parents are given to children as a
gift from the Lord. One day, when our children were small, one
of them had heard some of his little friends calling their parents
by their first names, so he called his dad by the name I use all
the time—Bill. I stopped him right there. "My son, you have
only one person in this world whom you can call Dad or Father,
and there are literally billions whom you can call by their first
name. Hereafter, speak to him properly when you speak—he is
your father."

It is interesting what a father means to a child. If any father
were to take his two-year-old son across the busiest street in
downtown New York, holding him by the hand, the little boy
wouldn't be worried by the traffic—he goes anywhere, happily
trusting in his father for his safety. The nature of fatherhood
creates trust and faith in a child, and if one were to be the
perfect father, it should continue in that manner.

But there are no perfect fathers, so when children grow up,
they must find that their mother and dad are but other individual souls seeking to find the way, who are also fallible, and
thus that they must, like others, be forgiven when they err.

However, this ultimate growth in understanding has no
direct relationship to the manner in which a small child looks
at his father and mother. He sees in his father that which
symbolically might guide him through the difficult places in
life until he reaches the age of choosing for himself. In the
eyes of the child, the father is not just another friend—in the
first place, he's too old to be that—but he has that innate
symbolic relationship to the Heavenly Father that sets him
apart from others. (And it would be good for every father to
realize what his son sees in him, consciously and unconsciously.) In his mother, the child sees symbolically that from
which his very life arose. He cannot help but instinctively give
her love and obedience.

193

Naturally I feel very close to this subject, since I have given birth to six children. I've watched these little ones in my arms as they grow and respond and become like flowers answering the light and heat of the sunshine. As I've worked with my husband in trying to create a home that is in itself creative, I've wondered how a woman can best train herself to be an ideal mother and a cooperative wife so that a child can grow up in the best atmosphere.

My own answer to that is certainly set in ideals with a spiritual origin and destiny. Material and mental problems have their real solution in such a spiritual course of action. So perhaps if a mother keeps up prayer and meditation and holds to the ideal to which she can aspire, she is moving in the right direction. I like the ideals which are inherent in these two readings which Cayce gave on motherhood:

> Thy handmaid, O Lord! Use Thou me! Let my meditations, let my activities be that there may be manifested through this channel *that* Thou wouldst have in this experience.
>
> (480-28)

> For the duties of motherhood and the duties of a son are so akin that if the divine forces are kept in the mind of each, their proper relationships, their proper activities become not a duty, not an obligation, but rather a loving influence that is constructive ever in the experience of each.... Hence the advice, the counsel, is to *know self* and *what is thy ideal!* Not in *who* or in what ye believe, but in *Whom you believe!* And know *He* is able to keep that thou hast committed unto Him against any experience that may arise in thy associations with thy fellow man.
>
> (830-2)

OTHER RELEVANT READINGS

> Each experience, each meeting is a purposeful one. If any association is allowed to work upon the faults, upon the vanities, upon the material expressions, it is harmful. If it is used to *strengthen* the spiritual import of the life, it is turned to helpfulness!
>
> (1523-6)

194

In interpreting the records here for the entity, we would minimize the faults, we would magnify the virtues. There are many abilities in the entity. There are the abilities to attract others and to very easily set others in their place, as it were, by a look or a word.

Thus thy abilities may be used for weal or woe, just by thy conversation. (3285-2)

Q. 1: How is the best way for her mother to handle the conditions that arise in her life?

A. 1: As indicated, set by precept and—most—by example, that there is an ideal, and that the ideal must be in the spiritual life: that judgments in the moral, the commercial, that material, the mental world may all be judged by the *one* standard—which is set in Him who *blessed* Junie in that far land.

A. 5: *Do not* make so many corrections! Make it once and then let it pay the price for same! Not in punishments as in bodily punishments, but rather the denial of things that are liked!

(608)

As ye would be forgiven, so forgive the shortcomings in others that are oft reflected in self.

(2468-1)

Never then, be hardboiled, dictatorial—these get no one anywhere; but be patient, just. *Demand* of others justice in the same measure as ye *mete* it to others—no more, no less; but all of that!

(1537-1)

Q. 7: Should we tax him with his lessons at home?

A. 7: If you make a game of it, it's very well! If you make it a burden, it's not so good!

(1519-4)

Positive, loving counsel is worth more—much more—than the rod for this child, that he is to be not merely good but *good for something.* Show appreciation for that which is of a constructive nature, and *he will desire more to do such.*

(2889)

Be positive but don't break the will of the entity. Make the whole conversation to the body interesting to the body, and so that the body ever wants more. Do not so oft say "don't—don't—don't." More oft say "do—do—do!" Let it be something

195

the body likes to do. And this may be found better by instruction as to "Shall we do this, that or the other?" But always let it be constructive in every way. And you will find agreements that will be worthwhile. Do it.

(2752-3)

As has been indicated, the body is super-sensitive and *is made aware of self's short comings or self's virtues by a continual impressing* on same. Listen to the entity's arguments, always, never tell her to shut up or stop, but hear it out! Then *parallel same by counsel*, as respecting *what might be better*, if paralleled in that direction.

(1179)

... the condition that exists in the present as related to the relationships in sex—or the greater cause for the lack of judgment ... is from the lack of education in the young *before* their teen-age years!

For few there be who have the proper understanding ... of what the biological urge produces in the body! ...

But even in the *formative* years there should be the training in these directions, as a portion of the material things. Even as the child studies its letters, let a portion of the instructions be in the care of the body, and more and more the stress upon the care in relation to the sex of the body and in the preservation of that as to its relationships to its Creator.

For it is through such factors, through such bodies of activity, that there may become a manifestation of the spiritual forces such as to bring *into being* those of one's own flesh and blood. ...

Do not begin halfway. Do not begin after there has been already begun the practice of the conditions that make for destructive forces, or for the issue of the body to become as a burning within the very elements of the body itself—and to find expression in the gratifying of the emotions of the body!

For, to be sure, relationships in the sex are the exercising of the highest emotions in which a physical body may indulge. And *only* in man is there found that such are used as that of *destruction* to the body-offspring!

(826-6)

... those in every walk of life make for the adding to or taking from the energies, the powers, the motivative influences ... upon those that are susceptible to influence. Who, then, is susceptible? Those in their juvenile years. ... *All* have their

196

influence and create the environment that makes for the adding to or the taking from the delinquency of *any* individual in its associations through any particular experience. ... It is taken from when there is fault-finding, petty jealousies; the consideration of the aggrandizement of the exercising of the elements and influences in the body-forces, in sex, in taking what may add to its ability to satisfy the cravings of what has been builded by the entity.

Hence, those who would be helpful, know the problems in the soul! ... For the more oft the girls or boys in their teens, in their younger years, [are] misdirected when they are only attempting to give *soul*-expression of that which *moves* them! Those that are ground in their *own* subtle selves to *their* idea, without an ideal, *misconstrue* the individual child's intent and purpose.

(5747-2)

The conditions in the social life, in the marital life, in the experience of groups of various characters, confront the world, the country, the home, the individual today. When men and women reach the age of puberty, when there are those changes biologically taking place, they should be taught, trained, given to understand the sacredness of that function, that factor, in their experience; and that these organs are for the purpose and in the nature of Creation itself, and not for the gratifying of self-indulgence or self's desires. Rather should it be understood that such forces are for the propagation only of species in that given direction which the Creator gave as a law; that each thing, each creation, has within itself the ability to keep within itself its own re-creation, re-presentation, the resuscitation within those bodies of the bodies themselves.

(5747)

Next is the prevention of the manner in which there is the lauding or defaming of activities of men and women in their relationships one to another, through the press, through the literature, through verse or song, through movements of the body in the entertainments that may be depicting conditions in the experiences of peoples' lives and their assocations. When there is the lauding of activities that have been for self-indulgences or self-aggrandizements, it becomes sin. For what is the Law? Each produces within itself its own kind. and begets that of an exalted nature or otherwise.

You as individuals may present, in your relationships with

197

your fellow man, those very principles which if gradually set in motion may change the whole relationships in your social, marital and home life throughout this land! What is lacking? Education of the youth; not in their teens, but in their first nine to ten years! Teach them the beauty of their sex, not the indulgence of their sex! Teach them how they may contain or do contain within themselves that God-given power which was manifested in that Body who has gone before you, whom you worship as your Brother, as your Lord, who is the Mediator, who has shown so oft through the ages how that there may come in the body the beauty of the Lord.

(5747)

This [homosexuality] is ever, and will ever be a question, a problem, until there is the greater spiritual awakening within man's experience that this phase biologically, sociologically ... must be as a stepping stone for the greater awakening; and as the exercising of an influence in man's experience in the Creative Forces for the reproduction of species, rather than for the satisfying or gratifying of a biological urge within the individual that partakes or has partaken of the first causes of man's encasement in body in the earth.

(5747-3)

Ye have comprehended thy affection. This is not merely the satisfying of an emotion in sex or in thy relationships with the opposite sex. This ye feel, ye know—or have comprehended— but too often have neglected or forgotten what the first feeling was when thine own offspring caught hold of thy hand! This was not of sex—this was not of emotion only, but an answering of that which is the birthright of each soul to be made aware of the Love of the heavenly Father to His creatures!

(1901-1)

Then, the greater influence will, in the present earth plane, come in the training of the entity to the point of controlling self. While we have the artistic temperament, with love for weird music and of the weird conditions; hence the will's development in the line necessary to use rather than abuse the conditions these urges bring to the individual entity.

(4211-1)

... as to that injunction which would be given to every parent ... *Ponder* well the *expressions* that arise from the *emotions* of a developing child; for as has been forever given,

198

train them in the way they should go and when they are old they *will not depart* from the way!

(1521)

Where lives are chosen to be made as one, in a moral and penal manner, these should be allowed to work out their *own* salvation, with that counsel or advice *when* sought. Not that one is to dissassociate self with the interests of, nor the bonds of sympathy, of motherhood, or such—but these should be kept rather as of old, *"pondered* in the heart"; *holding* that mental attitude as will make for that seeking of association, counsel and advice, *when* needs be. Not by word, act, or deed, so separate such relations . . . from that already chosen *by* each—but holding such a mental attitude in the periods that the self enters into the quietude of self's own introspective moods, or when entering into those periods of concentration—so conduct self's own mind, holding only that of the best; knowing that that *is* is for the best for those who *love* the Lord. *Keeping* self, then, not aloof—but in oneness of mind, and in oneness of thought concerning such. . . .

. . . let body be sought, as has been indicated and not attempt to pigeonhole or set bounds about same through the advice unsought—for this must, of its very nature, build a barrier that must eventually either be broken down by conditions that would be brought about, or this must be builded as a *unity* purpose; so that the counsel, the advice, that ability as may be manifested *through* the self—in being able *to* advise *when* sought. *Seek,* would ye find—not go and demand, or tell beforehand. He that would seek God may find Him. He that would be able to counsel *with,* must often keep quiet. He that would have the ability must be able first to rule own self, own tongue, own activities.

(4113-1)

199

14

OPPORTUNITIES IN THE HOME

> Each experience, each meeting is a
> purposeful one. If any association is
> allowed to work upon the faults,
> upon the vanities, upon the mate-
> rial expressions, it is harmful. If it is
> used to *strengthen* the spiritual im-
> port *of* the life, it is turned to help-
> fulness!
>
> (1523-6)

In our thirty years of living together, Bill and I have
found our share of problems and opportunities. We won't go
into too much detail, but we maintain that there isn't a good
marriage on the face of the earth that has not been tried in the
heat of everyday living and strengthened by the test—*if* those
two people were each seeking to be a worthy helpmeet to the
other.

During most of our marriage I've had the vague suspicion that
my husband disapproved of my housekeeping abilities. In fact,
my suspicions were heightened by his frequent verbal statements to that effect. It was at first hard to believe that a husband could seriously be bugged by such a trivial matter. After
all, weren't *all* Sagittarians just a wee bit untidy? But look at
how happy they are. Couldn't my husband understand that?

But then the light began to dawn—he was a Scorpio, and they
say that fire and water don't mix. *That* was the reason ... or
was it?

Then, as the years passed, I began to realize that we could
solve the problem very simply. After all, I was actually trying to
be a good wife, and he was doing his level best to be a helpful

husband. And during a period of five to ten years, those comments simmered down and were no longer in verbal evidence.

When I looked deeply, I saw that there was no longer resentment on his part—none at all. And, like a ray of sunshine, there appeared an idea in both of us. I had to spend a lot of my time at the office practicing medicine, so why didn't we hire someone to do *all* the housecleaning for us? Presto, a problem was solved at the physical level, when on a spiritual plane the solution had been growing into reality over a long span of years.

If a husband or wife does not know that the soundness of a home rests on the cooperative solution of little problems as they arise, that home is destined for much trouble and turmoil. Small solutions pave the way for larger clarifications and a sounder basis on which to live a life together. One practices forgiveness in this manner, and in each home there comes that opportunity to forgive in a large way.

Did Bill and I consciously forgive the other as we went along? Since we had our eyes on an ideal for living, perhaps we missed understanding what happened in those little events. Far-off vision sometimes blinds us to what is going on in the present, but we can take comfort in the fact that when we have our eyes on that star, we never lose the way.

Cayce had so many things to say about relationships in the home that it is difficult to pick out the most significant. But the following chooses a worthwhile theme:

> ... know that, though the world may appear large, there is not sufficient room in same for strife among those who would serve properly those forces that are to build in the life of each, for in humbleness of heart, humbleness of purpose must each present himself as wholly to blame for every element that may bring the seed of strife, and there can be no perfect union of strength with strife existent.
>
> (257-22)

Such a simple matter as housekeeping is more complex when you consider its implications regarding the law of cause and effect. Paul told the Galatians: "Whatsoever a man soweth, that

201

shall he also reap." (Gal. 6:7) If this be true, everything that one is currently "reaping," he has at some time in the past "sowed."

Such an idea is somewhat of a shock. Perhaps my husband really deserved to be faced with a house that was not what he wanted. And perhaps I deserved words of criticism. But it is fortunate that forgiveness and love moves these things out of the way. Depending on the number and noise of the children as plotted against the nervous-tension capability of the mother, there occurs a syndrome which I have called "mother's battle fatigue," a real tension that can be expected in many homes.

Here, much depends upon the husband. If he chooses to come home from work at night, eat dinner when it is placed on the table in front of him, and then sit in an easy chair and read, snooze, or watch the television until bedtime, the syndrome has become active.

The battle fatigue grows more and more intense, ending in visits to the doctor or strained relations in the home or both. Principles of action to be taken here are obvious—but usually only to those who are not involved. Mother needs help of a constant, intuitive nature, plus a vacation from the children at times. Father needs to be aware of his wife's needs if the ideal of a home is to survive. One of the readings gave an adequate solution:

> ... love is giving; it is a growth. It may be cultivated or it may be seared. That of selflessness on the part of each is necessary. Remember, the union of body, mind, and spirit in such as marriage should ever be not for the desire of self but as *one*. Love grows; love endures; love forgiveth; love understands; love keeps those things rather as opportunities that to others would become hardships.
> Then, do not sit *still* and expect the other to do all the giving, nor all the forgiving; but make it rather as the unison and the purpose of each to be that which is a *complement* one to the other, ever.
>
> (939-1)

One of our good friends sought my husband's help in the office not long ago. On weekends, her husband would hardly move away from the living room TV until the last football whistle had blown late in the day and it was time to go to bed. No weekend activities with the children, no shows, no entertainment—nothing until the long, long football season was over. What to do?

Bill could have told her about the problems *some* people have, but he didn't. This one was serious to her; she needed some advice. He suggested that the whole family gather closely around the TV as if they were all very, very interested. Maybe that would turn him off.

"No, that would suit him great!"

"Well, maybe you could tell him that you need time together with him on the weekends," Bill suggested. "Tell him you love him and that you need his companionship.

"During football season, I don't think I could get his attention long enough," was her reply.

Bill told her the story about farmer Jones and a mule who, the mule trader insisted, would work willingly and steadily all day as long as he felt loved. Jones bought the mule, took him out to his farm, hitched him up to his plow, and waited for the mule to start out across the field. The mule just stood there.

"Mule," Jones said, "I love you. Let's go!" But he just continued to stand there. "Mule," Jones said again, "I told you I love you—come on, let's get moving." Again—nothing.

Finally, Jones got out, patted the mule on the nose, put his arm around him and loved him a bit; then got back behind the plow and said, "Now, let's get going." The mule just stood there.

The mule trader happened by at that moment, saw Jones' predicament, and came tramping across the field from his car. The exasperated farmer explained what had happened. "You said all I had to do was love him and he'd work. But he just stands there!"

The mule trader walked around the animal, lifted up the mule's head, and looked in his eyes. Then he turned around, seaching the ground for a few moments, and picked up a four-foot long two-by-four. He went up in front of the mile, turned

203

around, and suddenly whacked him over the head with the board.

The mule staggered for a moment, then started off for the other end of the field, dragging the plow and Jones behind him. Jones hung on and called out over his shoulder, "But you said all I needed to do was to love him!"

"That's right, Jones," the mule trader called out after him. "But first you have to get his attention!"

At the end of the story, the football widow had a faraway look in her eyes. Bill cautioned her not to use a two-by-four, and she assured him that she wouldn't. And although she never did tell us how she did it, a solution was reached. She did love her husband, and I suspect she was using one of those remarkable eternal principles of action based on love. And, after she got his attention, her husband knew she loved him.

A sense of humor has brought us through a great many difficulties in home and office. It is one of the spiritual qualities that can really take the edge out of any situation. We stop all serious arguments around our dinner table by making the participants all smile. The simple act of smiling takes away the capacity to be angry. It is sometimes like magic, especially with children. (With some adults, however, I suspect one would need a two-by-four.)

On the other side of the ledger is the energetic, active business leader, whose work keeps him busy night and day and whose energy never seems to sag. His wife may find in him the same problem in caring for the home—a lack of time and interest and an inability to stand still long enough to watch the children grow.

A psychiatrist friends of ours, William McGrath, sensitively described[9] such a man and his needs: "A chap across the street, a young executive, goes out every morning to jog for a mile or two. The exercise is good for him in itself, and there's a physical release of tension. Still, at some point, I wish he would halt. I wish he would tarry to look at the stars or to watch the slow

---

[9]McGrath, William B. "Anger," *Arizona Medicine*, vol. 26, no. 5, May, 1969.

setting of the moon. His pulse, his metabolism, all his body fluids, unchanged for millions of years, might settle back into harmony with nature for just a little while. Sometimes his vigilant mind, the sentinel, could look on a peaceful scene. . . ." And, Dr. McGrath might have added, he *might* take a small hand in his and wander through the changing fall colors of the woods, listening to the ants as they build their little houses, and following a leaf in its zigzag flight down to the floor of the forest. This retreat from frenzy would bring into his family's life more of the nature of God, as they seek in their own way to make their home a center of light.

For every home can grow into what might be called a point of light. Whenever people live together as a family and attempt to solve their problems with some aspect of what we call love, there comes from that home an influence that is best called "light." It is always an aid in meeting problems as they arise, not only at home but in outside situations.

In a sense, the disagreements, the factions that develop in a home, are born of emotional entanglements that are not really understood by the conscious mind. It is as if the higher, decision-making portions of a person hold the reins of life until an emotional challenge arises. Then the lower parts take over and direct activities. Not until those emotions are understood and used creatively does there come from that person a steady stream of light. The same, of course, holds true for a home.

The process of trying to use one's abilities in this manner builds a home that might be called "holy," as it is described in the following reading:

> Magnify the virtues of all, as ye would have thy God, thy Maker, magnify thy trying, thy attempts to be holy—not righteous; so few can ever attain that; none in the material world—they can only try. All can be *holy;* that is, dedicating body, mind, and purpose.
>
> (3621-L-1)

We can see some of the problems when one is left a widow with three children: It's an incomplete home. Yet a home is

205

where a person dwells—any person, or any group of persons. Anna is such a person, a Norwegian who lives in Louisiana. When she lived in another southern state, an A. R. E. group met regularly in her home. She has always tried to make of her dwelling a place where others would like to come and visit. Her three children enjoyed bringing friends home, and appreciated the fellowship of the study group members.

Some time after her group moved into a friend's home for its meetings, she decided to start a new group. But this one was different. She went to the state prison, which was close to her home at that time, and started a "Search for God" study group there, with the blessings of the prison warden. The members were all men, and it wasn't long before she realized that they would all shortly be getting out of prison. They wanted to continue the group after they got out, but since none of them was married they had no place to meet.

Anna was worried—with three children in her home, was it safe to have five ex-convicts there? She decided against it, and she rented a hall which, because of its extremely large size, didn't cost much.

Then, one night, Anna had a dream. It wasn't long, but it was clear and quite graphic in its detail.

In the dream, Anna was in the hall she had rented. She saw the five men in the hall, but they did not see her. Instead, they were hard at work putting together what looked like a human form. As it developed, she saw that it was a monster—a Frankenstein-type thing.

While she stood there, looking at it in disbelief, her deceased grandfather appeared suddenly beside her and asked what the men were doing. She told him that they were creating a Frankenstein monster. He watched them for a moment, shook his head rather kindly at her, and said, "You know, Anna, these men really shouldn't be here." That was the end of her dream.

When she awakened, she realized that she had been talking to these men in the prison about faith and love, understanding and forgiveness. And then as she rented the big, empty hall for their meetings, she found herself acting in fear instead of faith.

206

Because she wanted to protect herself and her children, she had decided not to have the group meet in her home. She was denying the words she had been speaking, not being willing to live out her beliefs where it was difficult.

If she really believed what she said, no harm could come to her—it was part of the promise. So she called the men and gave them her phone number and address. The group met at her home, and not once did she have trouble. It was with a degree of real sorrow that she was transferred with her job to another city. But Anna's study group had lasted well over a year and has been a real experience in her life—a growth in faith, in seeing how light can come when principles are applied.

As she decided to apply faith and trust at a time when it didn't seem emotionally as if she should have, she may have escaped developing a karmic situation. But that's where most karma resides, in the unpurified aspects of one's emotional self. Had she listened to her fears, she may have experienced the Frankenstein monster in her own life as these men found not the friendliness of a real home, but the thoughtforms that undoubtedly surround a large, empty hall.

Anna was aware of what Cayce had to say at one point about karma. She forgave these men for the actions they *might* have perpetrated, and thus the law of love came into being through forgiveness.

> Q.: What karma do I have to overcome in order to free myself mentally and spiritually?
> A.: Karma is rather the lack of living to that *known* to do. As ye would be forgiven, so forgive in others. *That* is the manner to meet karma!
>
> (2271-1)

Unlike Anna's, most homes have both husband and children, but this brings no less of a problem, certainly.

Problems in the home are as extensive and multifaceted as the creative abilities of the humans who inhabit it, so one could find endless opportunities for overcoming personal problems within the confines of that nebulous structure. For some brides,

mothers-in-law become a problem when the new husband compares his wife, after a time, unfavorably with his mother. The
problem husband, the hard-to-understand wife, the difficult
child—all make their mark as problems to be solved. But it is
important for us to remember that our husbands, wives, and
children have all been attracted to us for a purpose. Like
attracts like. Our soul growth comes about as we face what we
have in reality created. Then, if we live in a manner that we
know, deep within us, is constructive, loving, and helpful, this
brings the kind of solution we are searching for.

Biblical approaches to a puzzling emotional deadlock do not
appeal to most people, and many look at Paul's writings in the
Bible as prejudiced against marriage in the first place. This is not
really the case, however. Paul may have sounded like it on
occasion, but when he wrote to the Corinthians he had this
information straight:

> Let each man have his own wife and each woman her own
> husband. The husband must give the wife what is due her, and
> the wife equally must give the husband his due. The wife
> cannot claim her body as her own—it is her husband's.
> Equally, the husband cannot claim his body as his own—it is
> his wife's. Do not deny yourselves to one another except when
> you agree upon a temporary abstinence in order to devote
> yourselves to prayer. Afterwards you may come together
> again.
>
> (I Cor. 7:2-6)

Paul sounds much like Cayce in his adherence to the sanctity
of the marriage relationship. These next readings speak clearly
as to how each individual might act to bring light and understanding to any decision:

> In giving the interpretations of the records, there is much
> from which to choose. Here we would minimize the faults, for
> so will the Christ, if the body, mind, and soul will but take
> Him as a guide. Remember, as that one taken in what man
> called a fault and the law demanded the life by stoning, yet
> the Master forgave, so may ye be forgiven.
>
> We would then, as would He give: Magnify the abilities and,

208

as He said, keep those abilities in the home, in the efforts for beautiful homes, that love may reign in the homes of those who are about the entity. Thus may ye, even as Marie [Mary Magdalene?] of old, become a shining light because ye have known how to forgive, because ye have been forgiven.

(5231-1)

Those, then, who hold animosity, hold grudges are building for themselves that which they meet in confusion, in abuse of self, abuse of others, abuse of groups.

(2072-15)

But "vengeance is mine, saith the Lord." Hence those who attempt to "get even," or those who would stand for their rights irrespective of what may be brought about for others will find disturbing forces in their experience in the material sojourns.

(1539-2)

So, there are principles which should be understood, and basic rules that are necessary in a home as much as a physical body is needed for material existence. And guidelines for action in a home are important if decency and order are to exist.

Whether man's law or God's law, rules are a part of the law as much as principles are a part of love. In the material world, we have substance of things to work with; and man, dealing with material substance, establishes rules which become the law. But in the spiritual realm, it is the essence of things that becomes a principle of action, and this in turn is the manifestation of love in the world.

One finds karma active in the rules of living because it is the law, in a sense. Grace, however, comes into being as a part of that which we have known from the beginning as love, in its manifestation in the earth—and it manifested as the Christ.

I recognize that a mother's place in the home is different from that of the physician. At this point, I am not a doctor but a mother, and a mother has the right to be proud of her children—I'll maintain that to my dying day. Thus, I think my

209

opportunities in the home would not be complete without the following incident.

When David was eleven, he found out there was a "My Dad's the Greatest" essay contest at Los Arcos Mall in Scottsdale. Without our knowledge, he entered it. He didn't receive first prize or even honorable mention, but his heart was in it when he wrote his piece:

> My dad's the greatest because he helps people who are sick to get well and live a happy life. Besides he's the best father I ever had. He helps around the house and tells me not to do things. He helps me practis baseball and baskitball. He also helps Mom and *Loves* me and the family very, very much.

What can a mother say when she sees someting like that coming from her youngest son? I love that boy!

To bring the two realms together, to change the material world, karma must be changed to grace in action; and this happens when forgiveness is brought into the picture. The acceptance of the role of obedience in one's life brings about a recognition of love, and out of this grows the awareness that allows one to forgive. Using such principles, we might find great opportunities in every home for soul growth, for establishing an ideal home, for preventing the misery that comes from anger and discord, arguments and disharmony. This is what we call the Golden Rule. Cayce said it once in this manner:

> ... live right *self!* ... Let the moves and the discourteousness, the unkindness, all come from the other. Better to be abased [your] *self* and have the peace within! ... Act ever in the way ye would *like* to be acted toward. No matter *what* others say, or even *do.* Do as ye would be done by; and then the peace that has been promised is *indeed* thine own.
>
> (1183-3)

> For remember, "As ye would that others should do to you, do ye even so to them" is the beginning of wisdom.
>
> (1950-1)

210

OTHER RELEVANT READINGS

Q. 7: What are the reasons that the entity has not found happiness in his marriage?

A. 7: Ye are seeking the gratification of self. Suppose God, suppose Christ had done that same for Himself, where would you be?

(4083-1)

Happiness—a state of mind, not of being—for the mind and the being are of different elements; and happiness—as sought as happiness—fades, as does the secular beauties of life. Happiness from within lives. Seek that satisfaction of self being at an at-oneness with that beauty of the creative energies for the benefit of others, and *not* of self.

(2071-2)

Think not that there is any shortcut to peace or harmony, save in correct living. Ye *cannot* go against thine own conscience and be at peace with thyself, thy home, thy neighbor, thy God!

(1901-1)

... to find happiness is to find that the Spirit of Truth is *directing* thy footsteps; yes, thy activities; yes, the very thoughts day by day.

(1436-1)

And peace is the longing of the soul, and to be at-onement with Creative Forces alone may bring peace in the consciousness of any.

(622-4)

This ye know, ye will never find harmony by finding fault with what the other does. Neither will the other find harmony without considering what the other will think, or be, or care for.

(2811-3)

In the desire to create harmony—physically and mentally, and in relationships with those in the home, in the work, and in other environments, this, of course, the entity must understand and also comprehend: Harmony must first be within self.

So long as the activities of others are allowed to upset the body, this produces first inharmony within self.

211

This does not necessarily mean to become indifferent, but in the physical and in the mental and in the spiritual, there is required first the surety within self. Know not only what ye believe, but Who is the author of same. . . .

(303-39)

The entity oft tends to become a bit pessimistic and to blame someone else. This is not well. For every tub, yes every cup, must sit upon its own bottom, its own legs. For since the giving of the Son of God Himself that man might be reconciled to God, no man pays for the sins of others. It is all in self—in self.

(3440-1)

Q. 8: What knowledge of . . . and her personality does . . . require to aid him in understanding her?

A. 8: Study rather not the whims or fancies that may be gratified, but that which would bring out the best in each. As [939] would for . . . , as . . . would for [939]. Study each other; not to become critical, but as to become more and more the complement one for the other. . . .

In the associations let them, as it were, each have their own jobs; yet *all* in common.

(939-1)

Q. 3: What are . . .'s peculiarities and what are mine, so that we may adjust our lives harmoniously?

A. 3: These as indicated are to be studied in each other; and the peculiarities, the oddities, the errors are to be minimized, *not* dwelt upon and increased! *Minimize* rather than crystallize or magnify any faults in the other. *Know* that thy associations are to be on a fifty-fifty basis, not forty-sixty nor twenty-eighty but *fifty-fifty!* and that ye must adjust thyselves to each *other's* idiosyncrasies or peculiarities. For *out* of same ye should create that which is thine own in unison that may make thee a peculiar people, a channel through which the glory of God may be manifested.

If the choice, if the activity of each is given in such a way that you look to make of yourselves the ideal mate for the other. Not continually seeking or finding fault, either one with the other—but correcting the errors, the faults, the shortcomings in *self;* and ye will bring the best that is in self and make for the manifesting of the best that is in thy helpmate. . . .

212

There may be rules or regulations that have in thine own mental self been abused—or misconstrued—but if thy heart and purpose is right, then is this to keep each of you in that way in which each is serving the other and not the family. Remember, ye are marrying one man, *not* a family, *not* a church! Ye are to live in thy associations one with another the purposes, the desires to fill that place thy God, thy Savior would have thee fill!

(1722-1)

Study, as one, to show selves approved unto the God within, without; keeping self unspotted from contention, from strife; making for that as is the greater help in each; *presenting* self—in self's *own* mind—unquestioning the other.

(939-1)

The natural tendency of the entity . . . is to be the leader, the impelling influence. Do not let this, then, overshadow the abilities or the activities of the mate in *any* way or manner. This does not mean to become, from the mental or the material side, as subservient to his ideas; but let each give and take, knowing that this is to be a fifty-fifty proposition, with you each supplying that which is best within yourselves.

(480-20)

. . . when an individual has a friend that is lovely to him, to make other friendships does not lessen the love for the other. Should there enter jealousy, doubt, fear, as to the place in the individual's own heart or mind being supplanted, these are physical; these are selfishness in their manifestations.

(696-3)

Let love be without dissimulation—that is, without *possession*, but as in that manner as He gave, "Love one another, even as I have loved you"; willing to give the life, the self, for the purpose, for an ideal. Other than this, these become as that which will bring in the experience that in which each will hate self and blame the other.

(413-11)

In considering conditions that exist in the marital, physical, and material relationships, that there may be peace, harmony, and the fulfilling of the duties, obligations morally, mentally, spiritually, that there should exist in the home, all conditions should be taken into consideration; as to what the home and such relations are a manifestation of in relationship to the

213

home, the social surroundings, and the spiritual represen-
tations that should be manifest there.

In the attitudes of self, then, there should not be contention
in any manner, nor the producing or causing by word or act
that which brings contention of *any* nature. This does not
signify that one should countenance or give moral support by
not speaking when there are indications of those relations being
such as to not be in keeping with that the home and such relations signify; for when such relations do not produce that which
is constructive and creative of mental and spiritual relations, or
that which is constructive and creative of the higher or better or
good relations, then sin lieth at the door of someone.

The attitude should be rather in loving action and word that
the differences be pointed out, rather than by contention,
abuse, or any word or act that condemns anyone for their
activity that would bring detrimental forces to action in such
relations.

Then, there should also be the pointing out of the moral,
material and physical obligations that each should bear one
toward another, and when such has failed wholly on the part
of self or another there should be then the activity as in relation to the physical obligations; then when this has failed,
prepare self for what may ensue by the activities of others.
These as we find, though, carried forward in a manner that will
not produce contention, will bring peace, harmony, and an
understanding that will make for the better relationships in
every sense.

(585-1)

Q. 6: In what way can I handle the "mother-in-law situation"
so that our married life will be governed by ourselves?
A. 6: That's the trouble to oft in self, "to handle." But so live
rather thine own life that there are no question marks as
to thy purpose, as to thy intent toward her son—and no
questions a problem. Thus may the situations, the conditions that arise oft in such be that thy own conscience
does not condemn thee. Then ye are able to look every
man, every woman in the face and say, "The Lord forgive thee—the Lord bless thee . . ."

It is not then that there may be the satisfying of the mental
or material body, or mind. It is not to the indulgence of, nor
to the glory of self alone, but that—through the very activities
of the body and mind—the fruits of the spirit of truth may be
manifested in the material experience. . . .

214

This does not preclude that ye have joy, but that ye have joy and have life and have it more *abundantly*—and not in a manner that ye have or do become or may become subject to those things which would bind or hinder thee in thy thought, thy purpose, thy activity.

Let thy prayer, thy meditation then be—as ye choose this day whom ye will serve, whether the fleshpots of thine own carnal self or the duties, the joys, the harmonies of Him who has given, "Come unto me, ye that are disturbed or heavy laden—take my purpose, my yoke—learn of me, and ye shall find rest unto thy mental, thy material, thy spiritual self . . ."

By living the life to fill the married purpose in the experience one of the other. It cannot, it must not be a one-sided affair. Have the perfect understanding—what has been given by that as an ideal, who became the mother of the channel through which He came materially? "Thy God will be my God, thy people shall be my people!"

(1722-1)

. . . oft may the body ask self, "If the Creative Force or God is mindful of man, why does He allow me to suffer so?"

Know that though He were the Son, yet learned He obedience through the things suffered in body, in mind, in the material or earthly plane.

(1445-1)

There come periods in thine experience when doubts arise as to that which brings material success in your experience, and you seest about you those that disregard law, order, or even the rights of their fellow man—yet from the material angle they *appear* to succeed in gaining more of this world's goods. And they are apparently entrusted with the activities even among their fellow man that will have to do with the lives and activities of many souls. Then thou in thine ignorance, proclaim: "What is the use of trying to be good? What is the use of setting a high moral or mental or spiritual standard, when such /people/ succeed in entering into the joys of the earth?" They indeed, my son, have their reward in that single experience. But hast thou looked into their hearts and seen the trouble and doubt there. Hast thou looked into their lives, in their associations with themselves, and seen the fear, the doubt, the shame even, often that crouches there?

Rather . . . live each day, each hour, each association, in such a way and manner that thou canst *ever* look upon the

215

activities of that day and feel not ashamed to present them to thy Maker.

(531-3)

Q. 5: What should be my procedure to hasten my spiritual and mental development?

A. 5: Make haste here slowly. For this—the spiritual and mental—is as a growth. Ye *grow* in grace, in knowledge, in understanding. And as the application is made daily in thy relationships to others, so is the growth accomplished.

(510-2)

Put into practice day by day that as *is* known. Not some great deed or act, or speech, but line upon line, precept upon precept, here a little, there a little.

(257-78)

15

DIVORCE AND SEPARATION

The *law is, not* that ye may go one
this way and the other that, and
then your ideal and purposes be
one; but where the treasure is, there
may the heart be also, there may
the activity be united.

(263-18)

We had just finished an evening's lecture on Home and
Marriage, and we had been given written questions that we
might work on for a while. Somewhere in that audience was a
woman who had real troubles. This unknown person's problem
wasn't exactly typical, but it points up the heartache that can
come about when two pathways in life begin moving in different directions.

"Dr. McGarey, my husband has told me, without malice or
anger, that because our ideals and values are so divergent that he
will leave me when our children are raised. He says that when a
couple holds opposing sets of values such as we have, no other
choice is possible. Also, he says, his respect and regard for me
causes him to let me know now, so that I may plan for my life
without him.

"Can you help me to cope with my feelings of loss and pain?
How do I escape depression and fear while we complete our
time together? Our children are eleven, thirteen, and fifteen
years old. We have been married eighteen years.

"I do love my husband and want him to be happy and content within himself. I believe I can make a life for myself alone.

217

My problem is to retain balance in the interim." The note, of course, was unsigned.

We have no record of how we answered the woman's question, but I've thought since: By the very nature of how God created us, we are given the opportunity to choose either up or down. The up looks so difficult and the down so easy. And we are so prone to take the wide road, the pleasant path, the easiest way of doing things.

There is a problem in choosing this easy way—and that's what that woman's husband chose. The difficulty is that the path which looks the best invariably turns out to be littered with broken glass and boulders. The terrain, as one moves along, becomes dark and forbidding. We don't realize it, when we start on the path, of course, and only when it is too late do we find that we have lost our way in our journey back to that Source.

The husband in question respects his wife, has high regard for her, and doesn't actually want to hurt her or the children. He is not aware that these values spell love for the other person. It is the *attempt* to be kind, to be thoughtful of the other, to be considerate that is real love. Cayce once called to mind for a questioner the unsexed love that "you felt when first that little hand was placed in yours." So the husband really does love his wife. But like those who were climbing the symbolic mountain he just hasn't climbed far enough to be aware of it.

When he talks about divergent "ideals . . . and opposing sets of values," he has brought the discussion down from the levels of a real love to the level of everyday—emotional interplay and reactions. This commonplace reality rather has in it none of the soul purpose that each of us brings into this life—rather, it is centered around our wants, our appetites, and our material goals in life.

Where your treasure is, there will your heart be also. This husband's treasure was outside the home and the love to be found there. Indeed, his path had been divergent from hers for a long time—such actions are not formulated in a moment—and his heart was elsewhere. So, despite a true love for his wife and

218

his children inside himself, he was on the way to destroying the creation that they brought into being when he and his wife were married.

The question of divorce is remarkably like that of abortion. In the eyes of God, two people were made one—much as when, in conception, a law of God is brought into play. Once this oneness has grown into reality, should it ever be destroyed? Again, our analogy of those climbing the mountain gives us an understanding. There is action at every level of consciousness, so the appropriate counter-action must take place at that level. This does not take away the possibility that an individual might—at any moment—be lifted to the top of the mountain, see how things really are, and then, back in his old location again, follow through in a new manner.

After some of the Jews tested Jesus by asking him, "Is it lawful for a man to divorce his wife?," Jesus asked them, "What did Moses command you?" In answer, the questioners told him that Moses allowed them to divorce a wife by a note of dismissal. Jesus said to them: "It was because you were so unteachable that he made this rule for you; but in the beginning, at the creation, God made them male and female. For this reason a man shall leave his father and mother and be made one with his wife; and the two shall become one flesh. It follows that they are no longer two individuals: They are one flesh. What God has joined together, man must not separate."

When they were indoors again the disciples questioned him about this matter. He said to them, "Whoever divorces his wife and marries another commits adultery against her. So, too, if she divorces her husband and marries another, she commits adultery" (Mark 10:1-12).

Jesus is quoted in Matthew 5:31, 32 and 19:1-9 as sanctioning divorce in the case of infidelity, but otherwise He really didn't leave much room for the husband of our question-answer period. That which has become one must not be put asunder: this is the viewpoint from the top of the mountain.

Cayce gave a reading completely devoted to the problem of impending divorce or separation. This places before the

219

individual again that business of choice—it is always there, no matter at what point one finds himself.

> True, an individual, a soul, must become less and less of self—or thoughts of self; yet when those activities of others in *relationships* to the mental, the spiritual, the *soul* developments, are such that the own soul development and own soul expression become in jeopardy, then—as He hath given, "I came not to bring peace but a sword. I came to give peace, not as the world counts peace," but as that which makes for those experiences wherein the soul, the entity, is to *fulfill* those purposes, those activities, for which it—the soul-entity—came into being.
>
> And when those relationships about same have been and are such that those conditions arise wherein there is the lack of harmonious effects that are possible, then as He hath given, put at naught those experiences, those influences. Let them be rather as they were not. . . .
>
> But when there have been all of those experiences, all of those attempts, and there is still *naught,* then the jeopardy of self, of self-expression, of self-activity, as related with Creative Forces becomes as He hath given—a division.
>
> . . . "There is today set before thee good and evil, life and death—choose thou."
>
> These then are as conditions in all the relationships, in the home, in the associations, in the domestic relations, in the activities. Whatever thy choice is, let these be ever with an eye single to service to that living influence of being a better, a greater channel of blessing to someone.
>
> Not of self-choosing as easier way; not of self attempting to escape that as is necessary for thine own understanding, thine own soul development; but rather ever, "Thy will, O Lord, be done in and through me—Use me as Thou seest I have need of, that I may be a *living* example of thy love, of thy guidance in this material experience."
>
> (845-4)

It is a recurrent theme throughout the Cayce material that every day each entity finds himself facing those things which he has brought into being—this being the nature of karma. If he continues to act in his accustomed manner, he is still in the path of that karmic situation, and he will experience—as Cayce indicated in quoting Jesus—the sword, which helps one to fulfill his purposes on earth.

A marriage experience may be filled with all kinds of relationships which are distasteful and cause rebellion in each of the partners. But this does not mean that they *cannot* find peace and accord. If they don't, it is because they have *chosen* not to find it; that rebellion within will bring about the cause-and-effect response, the hardships, the easy path suddenly turned difficult.

Children have a way of growing older, so the time arrives in every mother's life when her children are grown and married. Often, trouble comes at this point in the marriage. It might be fair to state that there is at *some* time trouble in *every* marriage. But trouble is just a problem, an opportunity to grow spiritually, mentally, and physically.

One mother found her daughter in the midst of a marital problem and applied for a Cayce reading.

Q. 4: How may I help my daughter ... to solve her marital problem?

A. 4: ... Remember, if the spiritual is put first and foremost, if the purpose of an individual is the right direction, the material happenings will eventually come right. These may at times appear confusing and as being contradictory, but the law of the Lord is perfect. ...

Individuals do not meet by chance. They are necessary in the experiences of others, though they may not always use their opportunities in the spiritual way or manner.

Thus the injunction—study to show thyself approved unto thy ideal, which is thy God. If ye make thyself god, if ye make thy hopes, thy wants, thy purposes thy god, they become selfish, they become monsters, they become destroying influences. ...

And do not condemn anyone!

(2751-1)

Just as there is no condition where a forgiving attitude on the part of both parties won't make for a new and wonderful marriage experience, so also there is no condition, no matter how

221

bad, where a new start after divorce won't head one in the right direction—if he chooses an upward direction at that point. For we have not yet found ourselves understanding what Jesus said clearly enough to follow it as a guide in our living. We will have divorces and separations, because we need them in the realm of awareness in which we live.

To return to the woman whose husband is planning on leaving her when the children grow up—what *can* she do?

The laws of human relationship are formulated around man's nature as created by God and in his ability to choose in what direction he will move. Thus, it becomes the wife's place to choose her actions according to what she understands about right and wrong, life and death, good and evil. Having chosen right, she will find her life fulfilled, no matter what happens.

Her husband has the same choice. He may be living in a completely different consciousness than his wife, regardless of their eighteen years of marriage. Whether he is able to recognize the nature of life and love and the necessity of service to his helpmeet depends on his willingness to open his mind to the things that have been written for mankind for thousands of years. Perhaps we could say it depends on whether he is willing to be carried to the top of the mountain for a few moments and then act in accord with that he sees.

God never forces one person to love another. In the same manner we should never force two people to live together or apart. It should be their choice, and upon that choice—sincerely made—their soul growth depends.

Unquestionably, the most common situation that pits man against woman is infidelity. It is probable that divorce comes about most frequently when one or the other of the marriage partners becomes unfaithful. But divorce is not always the proper solution—more would often be gained by facing the situation creatively, by continuing to love, by forgiving, by application of those principles of action that bring peace and unity into a home. In this manner, heartache and resentment can be changed into a life together that exceeds one's deepest expectations.

222

A mother of two children came to see me because she had a nightmare. She found herself standing in a group of people, telling them about a trip she, her husband, and their daughter were going to take into the forest. In reality, her daughter was twelve, the older of their two children, but in the dream she was a baby and the mother was carrying her in her arms.

As the dream continued, the story she was telling became real, and they were actually in the forest. She went walking into a clearing in the forest and became separated from her husband. Then a great dangerous-looking bear came into the clearing toward her. She started to cry out for help and was frozen in her tracks. She felt the bear grasping her and snatching the baby out of her arms. She awoke as she heard her husband's voice calling her, and she realized that it was only a nightmare. Her husband had wakened her by first reaching for her, then by calling her name.

As we discussed the meaning of the different characters in the dream, it became apparent that her real reason for coming in was that her marriage was about to break up. Her husband had been spending nights and weekends with another woman, unknown to the wife until just recently.

Now he told her that he didn't really know why he had married her in the first place, because of his present interest, love for her was nonexistent. He wanted a divorce so he could move out and marry his girlfriend; and he didn't want the responsibility of the two children. They would be better off with their mother.

Dreams have different meanings for different people, of course. But for this mother, the baby girl was a symbol of their marriage being taken from her by ugly and dangerous forces. It was important, I pointed out to her, that the nightmare ended happily when her husband's voice awakened her. And, it was her husband's arms, too, that were translated into the grasp of the bear just before she awoke. So perhaps in her dream, her husband's lower nature (symbolized by the bear) was threatening to take the marriage from her, but his voice was what awakened her and ended the nightmare. The voice is a symbol

223

of the highest creative effort, for in the Bible it was by the Word that all things were created in the beginning. So the higher nature of her husband was bringing her out of this horrible situation that he had really created in the beginning.

With this as a foundation, I suggested to the distraught wife that her place in the scheme of events was to act in accordance with what was right in her eyes, for in the nightmare was a promise that everything would really work out right, that her husband would not be able to turn away from his true nature as a loving partner in the marriage.

A later visit revealed that she had chosen to act with understanding and forgiveness, not holding it against her husband for having gone to bed with the other woman. She refused to resent or dwell on the things he had said about not loving her or not wanting to be married to her any longer. Something in what she was doing had an effect, she told me, for he had asked for a transfer to Seattle so that for just a few months he could be away from both his wife and the third point of the triangle.

Some months later, a letter from the wife told me that she had joined him in Seattle with their two children. They have found a new joy in life, a new direction, and the kind of happiness she would not have believed possible. For a while she couldn't understand that he no longer remembered the nasty things he had done, but finally she realized that one can be blinded to his own ideas and activities when this is necessary for soul growth, and it was up to her to forget them too. Apparently she did, for the last I heard they have a good marriage.

The two people in this story never read what Cayce had to say about divorce and separation, but this extract speaks clearly for their marriage, and many like it:

> Put into practice day by day that as is known. Not some great deed or act, or speech, but line upon line, precept upon precept, here a little, there a little.
>
> (257-78)

If reincarnation is a fact, all life situations, of course, are influenced by past life experiences. This helps explain those

224

relationships where a marriage breaks up and both partners find another mate with whom they are happy and content for the rest of their lives. Perhaps they have learned lessons from the first marriage that make the second successful. On the other hand, the first experience may have involved very difficult choices, and neither party was able to find the inner strength to meet the challenges these choices implied. Then, after new partners were found, past life experiences made the second try much more compatible.

Certainly there are times when two people just cannot or will not find enough areas of agreement to continue the marriage. Cayce referred to this in the following reading:

> ... an air or attitude of indifference in one, under which the general tendency or trend is to rebel at duty or obligation; and in the other there is the inclination to hold that which is to the mental self as an expression of the mental attitudes. ... if they are *still* rebellious and do not desire to meet each other half way—there is no hope for a united effort on the part of the individuals as separate entities.
>
> *No one* may force such an issue upon another. It must of necessity be a free-will choice, and a desire of one preferring the other before self. And this must be the attitude upon which each may reach a conclusion in which there may be determined within the own conscience as to whether it is a desirable thing, condition or experience, for each to undertake to make the experience become a *development* for each.
>
> For, as we have indicated, they each have in the present a personal obligation one toward the other—of a mental, of a material—yea, (from the former experiences) of a spiritual nature also. Without meeting such, it will become sin to each.
>
> (852-16)

So, even where Cayce sees that there is little hope for the survival of this marriage, perhaps the failure to meet such obligations still becomes sin in the final analysis—a turning toward one's own desires instead of seeking a pathway toward God, toward service to others, to a loving attitude in all things.

In a sense, the mountain story still holds up, doesn't it?

225

There is no one at the top except the Christ, and all those wending their way along the side are sinning when they head down the slope or fall along the way. When they face in an upward direction and climb, they are growing in a manner that satisfies their souls.

We are all given the opportunity to climb, at every stage of life. All past events are history, just like all past lives. But as we move through events we make energy patterns of habit and reaction. And unless these patterns tend to move us upward along the side of the mountain, they need to be disrupted, and new ones adopted. This is the difficult part, because we look at all those tendencies and attitudes and beliefs as being *right*. That's because of where we are on the side of the mountain.

Divorce and separation will continue to take place. Some will reject their soul purpose this time as they have done before. Others just won't know the difference. But then, also, there are those on the verge of destroying a marriage relationship who will look at what is going on, search deeply within their hearts, and perhaps allow themselves to be lifted up to the top of the mountain. Then they will follow through on making a marriage what it should be: Two souls striving together toward that star that shines in the sky, toward the light that glistens in the distance, toward the top of the mountain.

These people will find guidance and direction in what Cayce said to a couple who were having troubles of this nature, but whom he did not think should separate yet:

> We won't separate here yet. . . . This relationship which is the experience of each, must be accepted by each as a responsibility of one for the other, as one to the other; not something about which to find fault with each.
>
> There has been a pattern indicated in the experience of man, to Whom each should go. These are not old women's tales. These are men's, these are women's souls.
>
> There should be, then, a seeking together; not finding fault with what has been done or what may be done, not spying on one or spying on the other. Each can think for self, but before God and man there was the promise taken "Until death do us part!" This is not idle; these were brought together because

226

there are those conditions wherein each can be a complement to the other. Are these to be denied?

These have not been fulfilled. These have not been completed. For there is the love, the hope, the desire that each be in harmony and peace. But the harmony and peace must be within *self* first, if it is to be between one another. This ye know, ye will never find harmony by finding fault with what the other does. Neither will the other find harmony without considering what the other will think, or be, or care for.

Know ye this, each of you: The law of the Lord is perfect, ye cannot get around it. Ye may for the moment submerge it, but thy conscience will smite thee. Try it! For a period of six months, never leave the home, either of you, without offering a prayer together: "Thy will, O God, be done in me this day." This is not sissy; this is not weak; this is strong. For God hath a purpose with thee, else ye would not be conscious of thyself as being a living human being this day.

Then quit yourselves like children of God, appreciating that privilege. Speak to Him as to thy Father; He will answer thee as thy Father who loves thee.

(2811-3)

OTHER RELEVANT READINGS

Just study that indicated. You are devoted, but your differences have been magnified rather than that wherein you agree!

(3135-1)

Here is an entity who would be lost without its companion. Hold fast to same. Cherish love and honor and you will find she will continue to be an inspiration to guide, to direct. Never carry on thy business or thy activities without taking her entirely into your confidence! The judgment of two is better than the judgment of one, and where the two agree and they ask believing it may come to pass ... do not ask for seifish things, lest they turn upon thee and destroy thy good purposes. Ask only as the Lord wills.

(5346-1)

The entity was a good workman and also a good arguer. It hasn't lost much of that ability to argue, if the opening is given as to principles. Does nature argue with itself or does it work with itself? Do the sunshine and the rain become as warriors or do they combine their efforts to present to you, as to the rest of mankind, that which works together for good, of that which would be an increase in the knowledge of the Creative Forces?

(5733-1)

If there arises in the experience of self that which would become continuous as those upon which the entity would look back, in which the entity would think and think and worry, then continue—for the end is not yet.

(845-4)

... before God and man there was the promise taken, "Until death do us part!" This is not idle; these were brought together because there are those conditions wherein each can be a complement to the other. Are these to be denied?

(2811-3)

Q.: Am I correct in my suspicions of the certain women involved?

A.: This we would not give; for this is already condemning— without there being other than suspicion.

(585-1)

Q.: My present [second] marriage lacks mental and spiritual qualities of companionship. Should I get a divorce? My husband recently suggested we get a divorce.

A.: Let this be according to the dictates of thy own conscience, rather than from any other source.

There have been those periods in which there have been turmoils in other experiences with thy present companion; as in the Egyptian. ...

(1551-2)

As to divorce ... any withdrawal entirely is the denial of obligations. Obligations are not set aside merely by denial. But thy usefulness one to another has passed.

Q. 4: What caused my marriage to fail?

A. 4: It had failed before you began. These are karmic conditions. The partner didn't measure up as well as thou hast.

(3179-1)

Q. 3: Should divorces be encouraged by making them easier to obtain?

A. 3: This depends upon first the education of the body. Once united, once understood that the relationships are to be as one, less and less is there the necessity of such

228

conditions. Man may learn a great deal from a study of the goose in this direction. Once it has mated, *never* is there a mating with any other—either the male or female, no matter how soon the destruction of the mate may occur unless *forced* by *man's* intervention.

This does not indicate that this is the *end*, and should *only* remain as such. For, as we have indicated, *this* is indicated by the name and the meaning of the name itself. For this is the *extreme*. Just as indicated in all of the animals—the fowl or those that have become the closer related to man, and man's intervention in their surroundings and their activities and their adaptabilities; in their *natural* state these are in the forms as their *names* indicate. And from these man may learn many lessons; which *was* attempted in the beginning. And yet, as we have indicated, in same he lost self in that he found he could satisfy those emotions or *gratify* what might be builded as emotions from experience to experience. Thus there were gradually brought on the various polygamous relationships that have existed throughout the ages in many periods. And, as indicated in the lives of groups and nations, these become the stumbling blocks that are ever kept within the background—but that have made for the destructive influence that arose within the activities of such groups and nations, in such relationships.

(826-6)

Then when ye are, either of thee, in turmoil—*not* one shall do *all* the praying, nor all the "cussing"; but *together ask!* and He will give—as He has promised—that assurance of peace, of harmony, that can *only* come from a coordinated, cooperative effort on the part of souls that seek to be the channels through which His love, His glory may be manifested in the earth!

Do not let aught separate thee! else it will be the destruction of thine own selves through *this* experience!

Rather make thy bodies *channels* through which a soul may manifest! and in thy purposes, in thy desires, in thy love of *life*, ye may *show—in* that union—that as would bind thee closer yet to Him. . . .

Let, then, thy yeas be yea, thy nays be nay. But keep the way open for thy better selves, for thy love, for thy respect, for thy faith, for thy confidence to expand.

Then let each—in thy daily activities—think not on that which satisfied thyself alone, nor yet that which would be indulgence of the other; but rather as to how ye may each become the greater, the better channel for the glory of *life*, of God, of His gifts, of His promises, of His peace, of His harmonies—that ye may manifest in thy cooperation one with another.

(1523-6)

16

THE IDEAL HOME

The home represents, then, that
which is as the haven, as the material representation of an abiding
place, a home, for the developing of
the mental, moral and spiritual relationships of those therein, as a
counterpart of that for which one
longs in the heavenly home or in
the spiritual kingdom.

(538-33)

In our home, one day, Bethie and David were rough-
housing it a bit. She was eight years old at that time, David five,
and Beth got her kneecap in front of David's foot. It wouldn't
have hurt if David's foot hadn't been moving rather vigorously
in a forward direction. We were unable to determine intent, but
Beth was holding her knee and tears came to her eyes.

"David," I said, as I rubbed Bethie's knee, "you didn't really
mean to kick your sister, did you?"

"No, Mommie, I really didn't."

"Then ask her to forgive you for hurting her."

"Would you forgive me, Beth?" David offered.

Beth didn't answer—her knee was hurting her, and she was
still a little angry with her brother. After a silence which was
long for a five-year-old, David couldn't stand it any longer, and
he burst out with: "Bethie, you've got to forgive me, because
forgivin' is part of livin'."

And, for David, in his living experience in the home, this was
an important thing. He needed to be forgiven—and, of course,
he was. His sister and he were friends once again, and another

of life's building opportunities was utilized by two growing souls.

The Cayce readings have literally dozens of things to say about what an ideal home is, and of course we had come across most of them while teaching classes on various aspects of home and marriage. But there seem to be lots of problems in establishing an ideal home. We have been trying for many, many years, but is it ideal when one of your youngsters kicks his sister in the knee? What about the tempers that flare over disagreement about where to hang your aunt's favorite portrait? Those tensions during the long months of waiting for a child to be born should not really be there but often they are. The father in the house may have to fix dinner for himself when he comes home from work. Then *he* is not happy. Literally hundreds of such things act to destroy the dream state that "The Ideal Home" implies.

When we had infants in our home, we traded off duties—I would get up at night with the children, and Bill would get up with the patients. This worked out pretty well, but not until our disagreements had waxed and waned on the subject. We were supposed to go fifty-fifty on changing diapers, but Bill wasn't exactly enchanted with the chore, and he would disappear at the most inappropriate times.

It would be impractical to believe that two or more people could live together without these stresses and problems that face us in our close human relationships. So, practically, how do we get at the real understanding of what an ideal home is? And if such a thing is possible, how can it be achieved?

We have some friends in Phoenix whom we've known—in this incarnation!—for at least ten or twelve years. Larry is a highly successful insurance representative. His wife, Sue, is at least as successful as he is, but her achievements have been in the home. And they started where nearly every husband and wife start, with the marriage relationship.

Sue was very interested in the subject of religion, but Larry had never paid any attention to it. When she started reading some of the books that had been published on Edgar Cayce's

232

life and philosophy, Sue realized that Larry couldn't care less about this information that to her was like life itself.

"Now, if I sit him down and tell him about all this stuff," she thought, "he'll think I'm crazy. Reincarnation? Auras? He'll just be turned off to the whole thing."

The alternative, as Sue saw it, was to use Larry's ability to sell things and to teach, which is what he did most of his waking hours. So she would find a particularly hard part of her book to understand and then take it to Larry.

"Larry, I just don't understand this," she would say. "Would you tell me what it means? It just doesn't make sense!"

Larry, of course, combining his ability with his male ego and his deep love for his gentle and loving wife, would take the book, read the section, and explain it to her.

It wasn't long before he became an expert on the subject, and he *could* teach her things about the whole fascinating field of study that she just didn't understand.

Now he knows what she did, but he loves her for it because he knows she did it because she loved him. It's that sort of music that makes home a wonderful place to be.

To those who were seeking, Cayce often suggested that the best way to promote relationships in the home is to "abase oneself"—to make one's self of lower esteem in one's own eyes, for that means holding the other in preference *first* in one's mind and action. The method Cayce suggests here is slightly different from that which Sue utilized, but both have the element of truth in them:

> Q. 1: Outline a specific method whereby I can get truth over to my husband.
> A. 1: This is better by the mode of example than by precept, and these combined will move *any* thinking body to the responsibility, obligation, moral fortitude and material relationships.
>
> (585-1)

Sue was willing to listen rather than to talk. She lived so as to

233

show her husband that not only did she have a greal deal of love for him, but also a high regard for what he could do and how well he could reason. So Sue triumphed in a major way to make her home more ideal.

Bill and I have tried consistently to build more toward an ideal home. When there is a particularly beautiful sunset—and in Arizona it happens often—we go outside, hold hands, look at it together, and drink in the glorious colors in the western sky.

We have a little pink-grapefruit tree in our side yard that we planted about two years ago. Every now and then we walk through our little grove of orange trees and inspect that little grapefruit tree out there by itself to make sure it is prospering. And we enjoy sitting across from each other at the dinner table, so that we might see things eye to eye and yet have our family around us. Little things. Cayce mentioned little things once:

> And in *love* show the *preference* for that *companionship*, in the *little things* that make the larger life the bigger and better! and *ever* keep this in the inmost recesses of the heart—that in love the world was saved and made; in hate and indifference the world may be destroyed.
>
> (903-3)

In trying to be a better wife or a more adequate husband, two people often are unconsciously working toward the establishment of a more ideal home. They may be just attempting to straighten out their own relationship, but somehow that is a necessity in achieving the home that would be the best to them.

There seems to be something in all of this that speaks of the same quality, the same essence—there is something that we are reaching for, striving for, aiming for. Most of the time we just don't have in mind the "ideal home" concept that we are trying to establish. It's a nebulous something that we call an ideal. Two readings were given, one for a husband, one for a wife, and both point the questioner to an ideal:

234

Q. 3: Wherein was I failing her, or failing my own soul and its progress?

A. 3: Doth God point out thy failings? The law is perfect. Study to show thyself approved unto an ideal. Have ye an ideal—spiritual, mental, material? Do ye keep the faith as ye profess in thy knowledge? Knowledge without works is sin. . . .

(815-7)

Q.: How can I be a better wife to (2528)?

A.: Who can tell a rose to be beautiful? Ye know within yourself thy ideal. Be as near that ideal as possible. Judgments—as ye will find—don't draw too quickly. Meet him, be ever that to him that makes him feel better of himself and of everyone else.

(2794-3)

Both partners in a marriage might catch the essence of an ideal home and put it into practice long before they think about its formation. For a home is where most of the real down-to-earth living takes place. And children make it even more so. One has trouble looking at a pile of dirty diapers and a sink full of dirty dishes and even thinking in terms of ideal *anything*, except, sometimes, more sleep or a dinner out with your husband. But we often miss what some philosophers have called the diamonds in our own back yard, especially when we fail to look closely at our children.

Our first impression of a child is, of course, that he's cute. Next, we think in terms of growth, because that's what he's doing, and then, instruction, clothing, feeding, aiding, guiding, and certainly paying for our child, who by now is well grown. We fail to see the diamond.

Each child, with all the things that the parent sees in him, is still something else. He is a teacher. If we love, if we are kind, gentle, and understanding, we learn easily from each child in the home, and it is a wonderful, happy experience. But if we sow seeds of disturbance in our approach to those same individuals and turn away from the fruits of the spirit in our associations, we still learn but without knowing we have learned, through sorrow and heartache and grief. But, even though it is a karmic experience, we still will have learned.

Our Carl has always been a teacher—maybe because he was first in line to enter our family. When he was just ten years old, he started asking his dad why he smoked cigarettes. Carl kept on and on and on. It took two or three years, but Bill quit smoking, and has never started again.

What is it, we wondered, that Carl is teaching us? We think of it as "Set standards for your living. Conquer self."

Over the years, as we listened to Johnny's thirty-minute recounting of his last night's dream, or as we waited for him to tie his shoes before we left in the VW bus for church, we have, in our minds, heard John speak to us, too. He was saying—and living—something we needed to hear: "Mom and Dad, you need to take time to do things. Be patient. Listen, listen, not only to me, but to the movement of life in the universe."

It was almost as if I were hearing one of the readings which Cayce gave many years ago:

> Then ye begin to sow the seeds of the Spirit in the mental attitudes and activities; which are first, Patience! For, "In patience possess ye your souls!" In patience you become aware that the body is but a temple, is but an outward appearance; that the mind and the soul are rather the furnishings, the fixings thereof, with which you dwell, with which you abide *constantly*.
>
> (1650-1)

Annie was our Leo—she was like mercury as she grew up. Her tears she often saved just for me. They could dry in the corners of her eyes as she changed from storm to sunshine. We heard her telling us, "Gain an understanding of the gentleness in every person by looking beyond the daily flurry of events—there is that quality there. In everyone." Again, as we heard these concepts in that unconscious communication between souls, we recalled a comment from one of the readings:

> For as you will find, as every other entity or soul will find,

> it is the little things, the gentleness, the patience, the smile,
> that bring goodness, the spirit of truth, to the hearts and
> minds of people, not the loud railings or determination. Only
> gentleness who is on the Lord's side. And who is your Lord?
>
> (5089-2)

Apparently we had a lot of lessons to learn for we had three other children. And they too were in the process of telling us something, of being teachers in their own right. We were indoctrinated into many concepts as we lived those years with the children. What were the others saying, in their own way of living and communicating?

Bob: "Obedience leads always to a true freedom. Be friendly to all. Love your fellow man."

Beth: "Never hesitate to choose, for in choosing, you grow strong."

And from David, the last of our half-dozen, we seem to be gaining still another lesson in a home experience—perhaps one more lesson to move us toward a more ideal home. David speaks to us from that unconscious relationship and tells us, if we will listen: "Love the world, Mommy and Daddy, and it'll love you back. The world is like that."

Apparently there are many ingredients that one should find in a home striving for the ideal. There are also many sources of learning just what those necessary factors are. Several years ago, while our family, in toto, was attending an open house at the desert residence of one of our friends, my husband became deeply engrossed in a conversation with one of the members of our church. It was apparently worthwhile, for they both seemed to find the session stimulating and enjoyable. They were even writing things down on paper, and I could hardly wait to get Bill aside and find out what in the world they were talking about.

The topic was a theological one, and at the same time it was symbolic—so we were fascinated. Bill's friend had told him that he understood man symbolically as one that had inside himself the ego and the Christ and that these were always at war with each other:

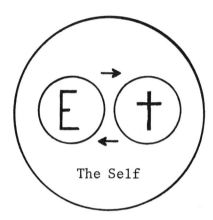

The Self

The resultant nature of the person depended, then, on which was victorious in the battle, but never would one win completely over the other.

Bill then showed his friend our concept. The difference was that we see man as the unit which is always in motion, choosing, acting, creating, moving in one of two directions, never still. Man is the complete individual, created in God's image, with the power to choose. The ego self (I) becomes gradually smaller as he chooses a direction toward God. The divine within (†) grows as man's will becomes one with God's will. One might choose selfishly—then one loses sight of his divine origin and he becomes lost in his preoccupation with his selfness.

As one moves and is active in taking a direction, he is in reality building an ideal, eventually becoming one with what or Whom he is choosing to serve:

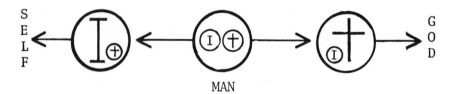

MAN

238

As we rode home we discussed these symbols that tell more than the words which are used to describe them. It seemed to us that an ideal in one's life was certainly important in creating a desirable home. But, practically speaking, how does one move in that direction? We can't just face east and be assured we are going the right way; eventually we'll come back to where we started. There had to be a better way than this. Then I remembered this reading:

> For, He that gives life—Him in whom we live and move and have our being—has set His moral codes, and they that err from same do so to their own undoing.
>
> Having chosen then whom ye shall serve—whether self, and the gratification of self's desires, or those obligations that have been assumed of self, those that have been given into thine keeping—let each, with that as is the answer—as in water the face answers to face—that which is known in self as the manner of *every* act, be guided accordingly.
>
> (903-17)

Just as we see our own face when we look down into the quiet pool, so we know within ourselves what we believe is proper. What did we see when we looked into the water? Forgive your husband; forgive your wife; forgive your debtor!

Maybe this was the key. Maybe, by using this concept of forgiveness, we could work out for ourselves some sort of symbolic Cycle of Creative Living—for that was what David was talking about, the one single factor in living which seemed paramount to us.

We have found, for instance, that when one accepts what life has to offer him he becomes obedient to life itself. You obey what you accept, whether it be a king, a president, a judge, or a simple rule. Obedience gives one a sense of peace, and he begins to recognize where his consciousness is. This recognition, then, gives birth to a new awareness. And when one is aware of a new level of being—a new height achieved on the mountain of his inspiration—he is more aware of God and better understands how to forgive. Forgiveness can be practiced before it is wholly understood, so it might be taken as an especially useful tool in the search for an ideal home.

Some years ago we set out to search for the difference between the material world and the spiritual. Perhaps we have not gained a high point of understanding about this particular problem, but several points have become clearer in our minds. A diagram helps:

SPIRITUAL ------ ESSENCE ------------ PRINCIPLES ------- LOVE ------- GRACE

MATERIAL ------ SUBSTANCE ------- RULES ---------------- LAW --------- KARMA

What does such a group of simple words mean? Well, we think that the material world, for instance, is a solid world of substance and form. In order to gain decency and order, there must be rules formulated, just to keep things in order. The rules are then gathered together by people appointed to do this, and it becomes the law. When men live by these material concepts alone, they fall under that which has been called karma, or the law of cause and effect.

This is the state of things when love is not brought into the picture. Fortunately, love is always available, if we *accept* it— and it can always be refused or turned away. If it is refused, we stay where we are, still under the law, living with "our" karma.

But, how do we accept love? There is that word, again— *accept!* When we accept, we become obedient. We begin to recognize new things; we gain a new awareness of our relationship to God. And presto, there is our ability to forgive.

Forgiveness, therefore, applied where the law is existent and active, changes things and lifts real action up to the level of spirit.

For the spiritual world, we found in our search, is the essence of things. It deals not with substance, but essence; not with rules, but with the principles involved. It deals with love, not law. And the end result which one experiences is not a karmic situation at all, but rather a matter of grace.

Cayce's comment that "the law of cause and effect is immutable by choice" becomes understandable. If one chooses to forgive at any point (having already accepted his lot in life), then the Christ Spirit, the Son, the Life itself, is active in bringing a new law in effect in one's life.

Cayce talked about it in these terms:

> Thy Lord, Thy Master—*thyself!* For He stands in thy stead, before that *willingness* of thy inner self, thy soul, to do good unto others; that willingness, that seeking is righteousness, if ye will but understand, if ye will but *see*—and *forget* the *Law* that killeth but remember the Spirit of Forgiveness that makes alive.
>
> (1436-3)

If these things are meaningful, we can place active principles into the relationship between the spiritual and the material as we have shown them. And depending on one's wishes, he can construct for himself a Cycle of Creative Living that can make his home a different experience in this incarnation. (The Golden Rule plays its unseen role in such a cycle, but it is there.)

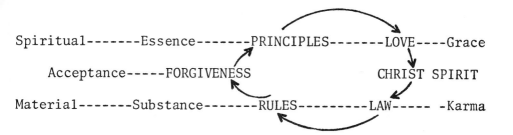

```
Spiritual-------Essence-------PRINCIPLES-------LOVE----Grace

   Acceptance-----FORGIVENESS              CHRIST SPIRIT

Material-------Substance-------RULES---------LAW----- -Karma
```

The key, then, may really be the forgiveness that one person can offer another. The essence of what is needed in any situation can be brought into play in one's understanding, and the important principles are there to be activated. Love can be manifested because the situation has been approached in a spiritual way—which is our heritage, since we are spiritual beings formed by a spiritual Creator, in His image.

Movement is required, isn't it? Movement toward an ideal set in the very life substance in our beings. If forgiveness is part of our ideal, then, as a little child told us, "Forgivin' is part of livin'. . . ." It's part of the moving process, and we find ourselves moving on the path of life, up that old mountain we've been talking about.

Then, is an ideal home in and of itself possible? Or rather, is the real crux of the question, "Is there an ideal *in* your home?"

In the course of his many readings dealing with the home and its possibilities Cayce suggested:

> Hence the greater of all the abilities of an entity is the ability to build an ideal in the home. Rather than so much the ideal home, the ideal in the home; that there may be the seed of the spirit of truth. . . .
>
> (1947-1)

Every home then, may be the ideal home by having the ideal *in* the home. We start where we are, with all our confusion, all our problems, all those material situations called for solution, and into that complex combination we instill an ideal chosen as we move not toward self, but toward God.

And then, the at-one-ment which grows out of this movement of the home as a unit will make of that home truly a shadow of the Heavenly Home. It is done with an ideal:

> Dare to do that that is right, and in accord with that ideal chosen as the standard for the home! Not what others will say, but—what is thine idea? What would ye have said of self? What would ye say in the same circumstance? What is thy ideal? So act, or so conduct self *irrespective* of what others may say or others may do. Be rather as he of old, "Others may do as they may, but as for me and my house, *we* will serve the Living God!"
>
> (903-17)

OTHER RELEVANT READINGS

Q. 4: How can I best help my family financially?

A. 4: There is much more important help to the family than the financial. If this is put first and foremost, you may lose the way. If the ideal is set first, the finances will follow.

(3653-1)

If the ideals, if the desires as to the purpose of activity in the material world are in accord, these then will bring harmonious material experiences. Though they offer oft times their own earthly hardships, if the purposes and the ideals of the individuals are in accord, then they may be very sure that the outcome of their oneness of purpose will bring a strength that will build constructive experiences in the sojourn of each in this experience. . . .

Hence be not overcome with the doubts and fears, but overcome them with the consciousness that He maketh not afraid.

(1173-9)

O that man would learn that lesson that good, or God, needs never be attempted to be justified, but glorified in the experience of any soul! Individuals need never attempt to justify themselves for their hope, their desire, if they know the Author of that desire—as to whether it is for self, self-indulgence, self-aggrandizement, or for the glory of God and the honor of self!

(2775-1)

If ye have builded such that hate, envy, malice, jealousy are the fruits of same, these can only bring dissension and strife and hardships. But if the seeds of truth and life are sown, then the fruition—as the life goes on together—will be in harmony. And He, the Father, being thy guide in all will bless thee, even as He has promised from the beginning. For in the fruit of thy bodies may many be blessed, if ye will but seek that *through* the union of thy purposes, of thy desires, with their import in things spiritual, such may come to pass.

Not that life is to be made long-faced, that no joy is to enter in! *Rather* be ye *joyous* in thy *living,* in thine association, in thy activities, ever. For joy and happiness *beget* joy and happiness; unless the import be of a *selfish* nature.

But when doubts and fears and troubles arise (as they must, as they will in the experience of all), come ye rather together

243

before the Throne of grace and mercy, as may be found in the meditation before the Lord. Take thine troubles to Him, not to thy fellow man! For *He* is merciful when *man* may be unkind, jealous, hard-hearted, set, determined. But let thy yeas be yea in the Lord; let thy nays be nay in the Lord. . . .

Q. 4: As my Life Reading gave that I might attain to the best in this experience thru music or the play, how may I coordinate same with marriage and express the highest in both?

A. 4: For in the home is the music of what? As indicated, it is an emblem of the heavenly home. And as these are made into the harmonious experiences that may come in the associations, they may bring indeed the music of the spheres in the activities as one with another, and those that must be contacted in the highest of man's achievement in the earth—the *home*!

(480-20)

The home is the nearest pattern in earth (where there is unity of purpose in the companionship) to man's relationship to his Maker

(3577-1)

The home—the highest of man's achievements in the earth. But let each give and take, knowing that this is to be a fifty-fifty proposition. . . . When the necessities require waiting and patience even, in those things that may at the time appear to be negligence on the part of one or the other, do not rail at such times or allow these things to become stumbling blocks; but always *reason* well together. . . . In *every* association, whether with one another . . . with thy own friends, or with strangers that enter, let thy activities be . . . more and more . . . directed to the spirit of hopefulness, helpfulness, in thy attitudes one to another. . . . And as these grow to the harvest in life, the *Lord* may give the increase.

(480-20)

Q. 4: If they marry, will they be happy and compatible?

A. 4: This, to be sure, is a state that is *made* so; not a thing that exists. For Life is living, and its changes that come must be met by each under such circumstances and conditions as to *make* the union, the associations, the activities, such as to be more and more worthwhile. Let each *ever* be dependent upon the other, yet so conducting self that the other may ever depend upon self. Thus will they find the associations, the mental forces, the spiritual activities that will bring peace and contentment in such a union. . . .

One for the other, ever; more and more selfless when it comes to associations. This does not mean *either giving up;* but they each should express themselves as a complement to the best that is in each.

(939-1)

. . . that even that (desire) of the flesh may be—with the proper concept, proper desire in all its purity—consecrated to the living forces as manifest by the ability in that body (Jesus) so brought into being, as to make a way of escabe for the erring man.

(364-6)

There is no greater channel, no greater place, than the home. For there it rightly should begin. For as has been said of old, "Train the child when he is young in the way he should go, and when he is old he will not depart therefrom."

Hence with the young, the unfortunate, those that have been taken by the wily influence of the world, may be the channels through which the activities of the entity may bring not only satisfaction but the greater peace and harmony and joy.

(1456-1)

Who is able to judge as to what is the right or the wrong, save that a home, a haven, a heaven, must present and produce peace, harmony, understanding! Then, let *each* conduct their lives in such a manner as befits that chosen as the ideal cooperation of each, as to their relationships to self, to each other, to home, and to their social surroundings.

(903-17)

Confusion is often caused, then, and is ever caused unless there is an ideal drawn or accepted by which all of these conditions, all of these experiences—whether physical, mental or spiritual—may be judged; or from which conclusions may be drawn.

Otherwise we are measuring ourselves *by* ourselves, and this becomes unwise. For it again leaves confusions as to what is another's standard. . . .

There then cannot be one measure for you and another for I, but rather is it of such a nature that it takes hold upon all that is, all that was, all that may ever be. For that consciousness is a part of same.

It is because the self has become enmeshed or entangled in the desires of the body, without full consideration of the mind and spirit that knows no *end*! and thus confuses the spiritual, the mental, the physical self.

Then the judgment, then the ideal, is that of the universal love, universal consciousness—that as was and is, and ever will be, manifest in Him, even the Christ—as was shown in the flesh in the *man* called Jesus! . . .

Then in Him, and in self, seek to know; using that thou hast—not unto the satisfying of any phase of thy own personality but to the glory of thy divinity, and to the *individuality* of thy Ideal! . . .

Walk and talk oft with thy Lord in thy own temple; and may there be done there that as will bring to thy mind, thy body, thy soul, *peace*—His peace I give you—His peace I would have thee seek! For only in that may ye know the joy of living.

(954-5)

For it will bring the greater blessings, the greater glories, the greater contentment, the greater satisfaction; the glorious harmony of adjusting thyself and thy relationships one with another in making same ever harmonious. Do not begin with: "We will do it tomorrow—we will begin next week—we will make for such next year." Let that thou sowest in thy relationships day by day be the seeds of truth, of hope, that as they grow to fruition in thy relationships, as the days and the months and the years that are to come go by, they will grow into that garden of beauty that makes indeed for the home.

In *every* association, whether one with another in thy relationships or with thy own friends, or with the strangers that enter, let thy activities be such that there may come more and more of that which is *directed* by the spirit of *hopefulness, helpfulness,* in thy attitudes one to another.

(480-20)

Thus ye will find peace as He has given, that peace not as the world knoweth peace, but that peace which comes from the awareness of the presence and of the promises of the Christ, that He has chosen thee as a messenger, as a light, as a haven for many—in the hour of stress, in the hours of disturbing forces; that ye may give that strength, that blessing to others in His name.

(2533-7)

246

And if each entity would so live in this material sojourn as if it were for an eternal home, much more beauty, much more joy, much more peace would be attained.

(1872-1)

Hence it behooves the entity to have before itself an ideal; not merely idealistic, but a judgment by which itself's activities may be drawn, to make for that in which there may come the experience—through the turmoils that arise in all the associations and experiences—of knowing what is the Right, the Ideal! not as for self.

For if ye would have life, ye must give it! As the laws are in the spiritual, so in the mental. For the mind *is* the builder. And if ye would have life, ye must give it. If ye would have love, ye must show thyself lovely. If ye would have friends, ye must show thyself friendly. If ye would have peace and harmony, forget self and make for harmony and peace in thy associations.

So oft is the ego so enrapt in self that it feels it will lose its importance, its place, its freedom. Yet to have freedom in self, give it. To have peace in self, *make* it—give it!

These are immutable laws!

And as the individual entity practices, works at, does something *about* such, so come into the experience those things that make the vision broader, the purposes worthwhile, the desires holy.

Then ye begin to sow the seeds of the Spirit in the mental attitudes and activities; which are first, Patience! For "In patience possess ye your souls!" In patience ye become aware that the body is but a temple, is but an outward appearance; that the mind and the soul are rather the furnishings, the fixings thereof, with which ye dwell, with which ye abide *constantly!*

(1650-1)

INDEX

PRINTED IN GREAT BRITAIN
AT THE UNIVERSITY PRESS, OXFORD
BY VIVIAN RIDLER
PRINTER TO THE UNIVERSITY